More praise for *1*

"Puhn offers a time-tested heal_____ ...es
that include diet, vitamins an_____ ies
and probiotics that will help ___, _____ ng,
healthy body and a sharp, confident mind. . . . [She] g___ ____ -by-
step, to becoming your own health detective so that you can discover the
solution to the mystery your body is trying to help you unravel."

—*Arizona Networking News*

"[A] practical program . . . She's especially good at explaining the links
between symptoms and underlying conditions, which guide readers
to becoming their own 'health detectives.' This well-organized, easy-to-
read reference explains the seemingly unrelated elements that can
keep you from operating at your best."

—*Belle* magazine

And acclaim for Adele Puhn's *New York Times* bestseller *The 5-Day Miracle Diet*

"*The 5-Day Miracle Diet* teaches you to eat foods that effectively regulate
your blood sugar, insulin, and glucagon. Your body will not only burn
fat and lose weight, but you will fight heart disease, diabetes, fatigue,
depression, cancer, and chronic diseases. Your body can then achieve
ultimate efficiency and optimal health."

—Richard N. Ash, M.D.
Medical Director of the Ash Center
for Comprehensive Medicine

"A sound and complete program . . . With compassion and tenderness
this book offers tools and insights to successfully deal with all aspects
of overeating. Adele has combined all the right ingredients so that the
readers come away learning how to be good to themselves, take care of
their minds and bodies, and lose weight in the process."

—Sondra Kronberg, M.S., R.D., C.N.
President of the Eating Disorder
Council of Long Island

*Formerly titled *The 5 Vital Secrets for a Healthy Life*

ALSO BY ADELE PUHN

The 5-Day Miracle Diet

HEALING
from the
INSIDE

Maintain a strong, healthy body and
a sharp, confident mind

ADELE PUHN, M.S., C.N.S.

Formerly entitled *The 5 Vital Secrets for a Healthy Life*

Vermilion
London

1 3 5 7 9 10 8 6 4 2

Text © Adele Puhn 1998

First published as *The 5 Vital Secrets of a Healthy Life* in 1998 by Vermilion
This new updated edition published in 2000 by Vermilion
an imprint of Ebury Press
Random House, 20 Vauxhall Bridge Road, London SW1V 2SA

Random House Australia (Pty) Limited
20 Alfred Street, Milsons Point, Sydney, New South Wales 2061, Australia

Random House New Zealand Limited
18 Poland Road, Glenfield, Auckland 10, New Zealand

Random House South Africa (Pty) Limited
Endulini, 5A Jubilee Road, Parktown 2193, South Africa

The Random House Group Limited Reg. No. 954009

www.randomhouse.co.uk

A CIP catalogue record for this book is available from the British Library.

ISBN: 0 09 185654 X

Papers used by Vermilion are natural, recyclable products made from wood grown in sustainable forests.

Printed and bound in Great Britain by Creative Print and Design Wales, Ebbw Vale

TO THE PEOPLE I LOVE:
MY HUSBAND, MY CHILDREN,
AND MY GRANDCHILDREN

CONTENTS

ADELE'S REGIMENS

ACKNOWLEDGMENTS

The writing of a book does not happen in a vacuum. It is instead a work that grows in the midst of daily life. During this time I have been fortunate to be surrounded by people who have generously supplied love and support. Their presence in my life has been instrumental in bringing *Healing from the Inside* into being. I wish to thank them.

To my publisher Ballantine Books: I would like to thank you for your wonderful team effort. To Leslie Meredith, whose expert editorial guidance and aid were invaluable to the organization of this book; you have my gratitude. Special appreciation goes to my editor, Susan Randol, and publisher, Clare Ferraro, for their confidence and support throughout the writing of this book.

To Wendy Weil, my agent, I thank you again for helping me widen my horizons. Your calmness, ongoing support, and advice are greatly appreciated.

My eternal appreciation goes to Karla Dougherty; you have once again taken my thoughts and ideas and transcribed them to the pages of this manuscript in your very skilled and talented way. Your work is truly appreciated; thank you. A special place in my heart goes to Leslie Messer, my researcher. Her bright mind and willingness to explore added great value to this manuscript.

A tremendous thanks goes to my longtime friend and colleague Sondra Kronberg, who graciously read the manuscript, offering insights and ideas during the busiest time in her life.

To Paul Sherman and the team at Metagenics, my thanks for your prompt answers to all our inquiries and easy access to your extensive research data on supplements.

My eternal love and gratitude goes to my husband, Arthur. Thank you for the endless hours of reading and discussions. Your invaluable input and steadfast encouragement have been so appreciated. You continue to be the loving force in my life. Without your faith and encouragement this book could never have been written.

My dearest love goes to my children, Bonnee, David, Alyson, and Margot, and their spouses, Danny, Melissa, and Paul. You managed to give me support and love even while enduring my divided attention. To my grandchildren, Charlotte, Lindsay, Jake, Zachary, and Juliane, thank you for not growing up too much. . . . Grandma is coming.

To my brother Marty Green, your love was warming, your support was aid, your own writing an inspiration. To Mary, my sister-in-law, thank you for being yourself; your love has always been a beacon.

To my uncle Hank and aunt Helen and my mother-in-law, Sydelle, thank you. I relied on you for your excitement and wisdom during the writing of this book.

To my friends Ellie Dubin, Donna Gellman, Susan Hans, Maxine Pines, Ellie Rothchild, and Margery Weinroth, thank you for your encouragement. You have endured my preoccupation, my limited time for playing and talking, and still remained supportive, dear, true, understanding friends.

The place of honor I save for my clients, for without their participation I would have no experiences to share. You all have been wonderful in your willingness to learn new ways to live healthier lives. I thank you.

The regimens described in this book are not intended to replace your standard medical care. They are depicted for the purpose of educating and introducing you to the concepts and available supplements that may help to restore your body to vital health. For optimal results, all the programs I list may need to be tailored to specific situations, taking into account any predisposition to vitamin, mineral, herbal, or food sensitivity. Please check with your physician or health practitioner before using any supplemental program.

These regimens are in adult dosages only—and they are meant for adults. See your health practitioner for an individualized program that is specifically designed for growing children.

The anecdotes I describe in this book are based on real people whom I have seen in my practice. For clarity, some of the cases I describe are composites of several clients whom I have seen with similar conditions. All names and life situations have been changed to protect the clients' privacy.

AUTHOR'S NOTE

By turning the pages of *Healing from the Inside*, you are beginning a journey to wellness and optimal health. The more you read and absorb, the more you make this knowledge a part of your daily routine.

This book is expressly designed for knowledge. It is meant to educate. My whole purpose is to help you *help yourself* feel better, get healthier, and stay well. To that end, I've introduced the various complementary therapies, supplements, and techniques that are available today in your community. I've also added the Rescue Regimens that I use in my own practice with my own clients.

I hope that the information you'll find here will provide the spark for you to learn more, to continue to explore, to become a seeker in your own well-being. My regimens are designed to work together to provide you with the best vitality and health possible. But even if you do just one regimen, one section of a program, it can help. Success can be measured in steps. If you are not ready to try every step, you can still be successful in achieving positive results—and a sense of taking charge of yourself, your body, your soul. You should go to health practitioners, nutritionists, and doctors to get advice. But in the end, you have to make the decision. You can't be led blindly. You provide the energy that comes from deciding to be well, the positive thinking that gets the carrot peeled or walks you to the health food store.

But as with any regimen or change in lifestyle, please check with your own health practitioner before beginning any of my suggestions.

And never stop taking any medication without your physician's knowledge and approval.

I wish you a wonderful quality of life. I wish you well. Enjoy my book. I hope it takes you far in healing from the inside out.

Adele Puhn, M.S., C.N.S.

HEALING FROM THE INSIDE

INTRODUCTION:
TAKE BACK YOUR HEALTH!

Wouldn't it be wonderful if you could toss out all those old bottles, creams, and ointments in your medicine cabinet? Take those antacids, painkillers, and half-used antibiotic prescriptions out of the cupboard? Forget the words "Sorry, but I can't find any physical cause for your symptoms"? And simply walk away from the next person who says, "It's all in your head"? What if all this were possible—if you could really change the way you think about food, about water, about the air you breathe?

It is within the realm of reality. *Your* reality. You can change things.

It's time to take a good, close look at your body and recognize what it is trying to tell you.

It's time to choose health!

A NEW WORLD BECKONS

Close your eyes and picture yourself the same person, but more confident and stronger. You stretch and feel how wonderful it is to be alive. You take a deep breath of delicious, clean air. Feel the warmth of the sun on your face, a soft breeze. Feel the strength in your tendons, your muscles, your lungs. You are vital, strong, and healthy. You are empowered. . . .

No, this is not a mirage or a fantasy, an impossible dream you can never attain. They are images that I portray to my clients, affirmations I use to show them that they don't have to feel weak, ill, or exhausted; they not only deserve to be well, but as human beings, they are also *supposed* to feel well.

3

However, these images are only words unless you, like my clients, find how you can take charge of yourself: by learning how to take back your body from the control of outside forces, by discovering how to make the right decisions for your *own* health.

I know. I've seen this philosophy in action. I've seen many of my clients' symptoms disappear. I've seen their skin glow, their energy revitalized, their genuine smiles of good health and vitality.

You, too, can feel this wonderful. It's simply giving your mind and body—your unique self—a different slant, a new way of looking at yourself. It's simply a matter of understanding that in order to be well you must direct your healing from the inside out.

Come closer. And listen:

CHARLOTTE AND THE SECRET BEHIND HER PROBLEM SKIN

Charlotte, an intense woman in her thirties, was a paralegal for a top law firm. She was an excellent organizer, a thorough professional who also managed to raise two children on her own. But during the last six months, Charlotte had been going through a bad time. Her skin had become dry and itchy; she had a sudden, bad bout of dandruff. She found herself scratching her legs during depositions, scratching her head in the courtroom, scratching her arms instead of writing on her laptop.

She had been to two dermatologists; she'd seen a psychologist. She took medications; she applied ointments; she even tried to walk away her symptoms with a brisk two miles every other day. But nothing seemed to work. The itching continued, now accompanied by fatigue, aches in her joints, and a very real depression. She'd been recommended to me by her primary care physician, an excellent practitioner who believed Charlotte's symptoms could be better treated through diet, nutritional supplementation, and stress-reducing techniques.

When Charlotte first came into my office, her discomfort was almost palpable. I could see her discomfort as she struggled out of her coat, trying not to scratch her red, irritated arms.

She looked as if she would give her life savings to find just a moment's peace from her itchy, dry skin.

"I have acute eczema," Charlotte told me as she gave in to her pain and scratched her arm. "Nothing works. This is my last hope."

I could understand what Charlotte was going through. I remembered my own trials, my own difficulties, with symptoms that simply wouldn't go away. In my case, it had been a chronic postnasal drip that irritated my throat; clogged ears; and a sinus problem that had troubled me throughout my school years. I knew what it was like to feel helpless, with that inner voice saying, "You might as well accept it. You will be this way for life."

BEYOND THE BODY VISIBLE

The need for relief was one of the reasons I became interested in nutrition—and it was this interest that led me back to school to study the fields of science and health. Nutrition became my focus in the years I spent studying the newest research and remedies. Eventually, my hoarse throat led me to the truth behind the cliché "An ounce of prevention is worth a pound of cure": discovering the root of a problem is much more empowering than getting rid of the symptoms.

When I tried to "cure" my sinus problems with a variety of remedies, it would stay away only for a week, a month at the most. But by looking beyond my outward symptoms, by realizing that all parts of my body were connected, I was able to "solve the mystery of my symptoms." I was finally able to find the source of my symptoms and, ultimately, prevent them from coming back.

My mystery connection involved my liver—which can be, unfortunately, an all-too-common, but rarely identified, criminal. It might sound improbable that your liver could have anything to do with symptoms that crop up in your throat and nose, but as you read this book and begin to solve your own health mysteries, you too will discover how the liver—and the gut, its "partner-in-crime"—can be major contributors to such diverse symptoms as muscle aches, chronic pain, fatigue, depression, cramps, and, yes, my sinus problems.

And, even more intriguing, I found that I could take my first step on the road to my newfound healthy life with a lemon! It had become a habit of mine to order hot water and lemon after a large meal in a restaurant; it helped me lose that "full feeling" that had begun occurring with regularity after these richer, heavier meals. I soon discovered that the lemon did more than get rid of my bloat; it actually helped me digest the food I'd just eaten. I felt cleaner, lighter. After years of experience (and drinking potfuls of hot water and lemon), I've discovered that my after-dinner drink created these comfortable feelings because it helped activate my digestion. Armed with a glass of warm water and a squeezeful, I could begin to aid my gastrointestinal tract and, ultimately, my liver—which somehow would allow my sinuses to drain. A straight connection. An easy, healthy insight. Even though I've been unable to find controlled studies to support my *lemon squeeze*, I knew through personal experience and the experience of other practitioners that it worked. It's a suggestion I've passed along to my clients over the years—one they've found successful, too.

If I had followed the norm at that time, about twenty years ago, I would never have given my liver and gut a second thought. I would have gone to my family doctor. He would have prescribed a decongestant, a cough mixture, and if the symptoms continued, an antibiotic—all of which would have further overloaded my liver and my gut, making my cough, my stuffed nose, and my hoarseness worse in the long run! There's more: the medicine might make me drowsy, out of focus, and dizzy. I'd have taken to my bed, sure I had a full-blown case of the flu.

Luckily, my interest and my fate put me on a different course. I began an internship at a nearby holistic clinic where I was introduced to complementary therapies, including herbology, deep relaxation exercises, acupuncture, massage, and the value of nutritional supplements.

Now, two decades later, I am a board-certified nutritionist with twenty years of experience working with people. Like Charlotte, they had chronic conditions that had not yet been helped by conventional methods.

THE HEALTH DETECTIVE TO THE RESCUE

Charlotte, like so many of my other clients, was about to take back her life, her vibrancy and youth. She was about to learn new concepts that would help her to begin healing from the inside out. But in order for those concepts to work, we needed to examine the clues together. We needed to find answers. We needed to be Health Detectives who could solve the mystery of Charlotte's symptoms.

I think back to that first day in my office. Charlotte sat in the upholstered chair near my desk; she appeared so vulnerable, scared. I remember her almost palpable self-consciousness as she tried to scratch her arms and legs without causing undue attention to herself. It was almost as if she'd been hiding her discomfort her whole life.

As I watched her, I realized that in order to mend, Charlotte needed hope. Like all of us, Charlotte needed to believe she could get help, that her symptoms could ease, that her mind and body really could make a powerful team. And I wanted to help her find that hope. Not false hope, but very real hope. I have found over the years, after seeing so many clients, that people need hope; they need to feel they can get better. That hope, the spark that they need to discover inside themselves, is a major step toward curing and healing.

For the first time since we started chatting, her eyes held that hope . . . and fear. She seemed almost afraid to believe me, as if she couldn't imagine life without her pain.

I started the way I always do, assuming the role of the Health Detective and seeking out the clues. The condition was obvious, but where did it come from? What were its underlying conditions? Did Charlotte have any other issues?

I asked her about her family and her medical history. Charlotte told me that no one in her family ever had a case of eczema. She didn't even know what it was until a few months ago, when she woke up in the middle of the night, scratching and itching, her skin blotchy, dry, and flaky.

I asked Charlotte what seemed to her to be unrelated questions about cholesterol, yeast infections, and diet. I asked her to think back to her past, to her parents, to try to remember if either of them had had dandruff, if meals in her household were rich, high-fat affairs. I knew we were on the right path when Charlotte told me that she loved fried foods, a taste she probably acquired from the high-fat foods her mother made every night. And that path was winding directly toward the impact food was making on her entire body.

Now we had begun to get somewhere. I was beginning to "turn the pages" of her mystery, even though Charlotte did not yet understand the clues. To her, my questions seemed irrelevant, but in my mind they were essential; her answers were helping me to focus, to come closer to understanding her condition.

But I needed more evidence to solve her mystery. I needed to find out about the medication Charlotte had taken over the years. I wanted to hear what she'd tell me about antibiotics—if she'd frequently taken them for a virus or flu as a child or even now, as an adult.

Charlotte nodded as I asked away. The past was coming back now in waves. She told me about her bad case of acne when she was young, about the dermatologist who put her on tetracycline. She'd taken the medicine for several years, one a day, all the while living with recurring yeast infections. "I thought maybe they were connected, but I didn't care. My face was so clear!" she exclaimed.

I knew what she had yet to learn: the past has a tremendous impact on the present. A regimen of antibiotics in the past could create havoc right now, today, for Charlotte.

We continued to go back to the habits she inherited from her parents, from the love of fried foods to drinking diet sodas, from a sedentary lifestyle to loading up on medication at the slightest sniffle. I told Charlotte that her body was flooding her with notices. From her dandruff to her eczema, all of her symptoms had roots that dandruff shampoo or a prescription ointment could not reach. They would be a Band-Aid at best, a catalyst for more damage at worst. As I tell my clients, treating only symptoms is like banging your head against a wall, then taking an aspirin for the pain. You have to stop the behavior *first*, the source of it all: if you don't knock your head against the wall, you won't need the aspirin!

Charlotte's dandruff problem, for example, could very well be the result of her poor diet—overly rich in simple starches, sugar, and fat—which could deplete her body of the B vitamins so critical for skin and its nerve endings, among other things.

Charlotte's eczema could also be the result of her antibiotic history, antibiotics that scientists now know kill off necessary "good" bacteria along with the bad. This "germ warfare" had contributed to the creation of a chronic yeast problem that could affect her gastrointestinal tract, altering her digestion.

"This overabundance of yeast, Charlotte, among other things, creates what is called a *leaky gut*, aiding and abetting an already overloaded *toxic liver* and . . ." I started to tell her. But Charlotte had already given me this look (one I've seen countless times until people understand where Health Detective work leads) that said, "Okay, I'll just get my coat and leave quietly. . . ."

I was used to the initial surprise. I knew that once I began to tackle the mystery surrounding these seemingly strange clues, Charlotte, like my other clients, would realize that yeast, sugar-rich foods, diet sodas, antibiotics, sedentary habits—and more—had everything to do with her gut . . . and her eczema. She would see how her skin had become the victim of this internal assault.

Later, as you read through the pages of this book, you will learn the "clues," or the symptoms, that exist because of a faulty nutritional foundation. You will discover that many roads fraught with inexplicable symptoms begin with a *leaky gut* and a *toxic liver*—and you'll also find out how to successfully restore them to good health. Without this inside healing, excellent health cannot occur.

You will also learn, as Charlotte and my other clients did, the power of the Body Bank to explain, in simple terms, the reasons why we get sick—and, even more important, how we can get healthy and *stay* healthy throughout our lives.

YOUR BODY BANK AND
YOUR GOOD HEALTH ACCOUNT

People might not understand mathematics. Scientific terms might be just too difficult to handle. But everybody, sooner or later, understands the concept of money.

Everyone, eventually, knows how to use a bank.

So I tell my clients to imagine the body as a bank. If you keep making health deposits, your Body Bank account will grow strong and healthy. But if you make too many withdrawals, you'll deplete your Body Bank account. When it comes to finances, making too many withdrawals means you'll start *running in the red*, bouncing checks and getting notices from the bank. Sooner or later, you'll be bankrupt. In Body Bank language, this means you will start getting unhealthy symptoms that can become *bankruptcy* conditions: irritable bowel syndrome, tinnitus, diabetes, osteoarthritis, polycystic breast disease, allergies, gallstones, high blood pressure, eczema.

Deposits mean good health. They repair "debit damage" and keep your life running smoothly and healthfully. And they come in many forms. The Body Bank accepts these, among others: a daily regimen of vitamin E and flaxseed oil; a Shiatsu massage and a sauna; a colorful plate of grilled vegetables; lemon sole and lentils; and a jaunt in the park on a beautiful spring day. The deposits you make in the Body Bank are the healthy things you give yourself: the ingredients you supply to create healing from the inside out.

The withdrawals are the toxic elements that deplete your account. These include drinking too much caffeine and alcohol; using artificial sweeteners; burning the candle at both ends; or keeping that fold-up treadmill under the bed, in the same carton it came in. And let us not forget the withdrawals that stress insists you make, day in and day out, from running for the morning train to bottling up your anger toward your spouse, boss, or friend.

These withdrawals can also be subtle, from drinking unfiltered contaminated tap water to taking birth control pills, from living near a highway with its constant exhaust fumes in the air to using makeup that's past its prime and has been in your drawer for years.

Whether blatant or disguised, these withdrawals will make anyone's Body Bank—yours, mine, Charlotte's—*run in the red*. Why? It's all part of the continuous connection among the different parts of the body—and how each one can impact on the others.

As yeast and toxins build up in the gut, they may be able to permeate the weakened intestinal wall and enter the bloodstream. Once "out in the open," they may travel throughout the body, causing pain and woe wherever they go. The notices that you are *running in the red* start coming fast and furious: low energy, weight gain, inflammation, lack of focus, memory loss, brittle hair. All of these symptoms raise the red flag, sending messages that the system is bogged down with toxins. These toxins, in turn, overwhelm the liver's ability to filter and detoxify, ultimately leading to varied and seemingly unrelated symptoms throughout the body. If deposits aren't made, the result is *running in the red* symptoms and, ultimately, a *bankruptcy*—in my case, laryngitis and sinusitis. And Charlotte? Her poor diet and hampered digestion gave her the "*bankruptcy* note" called eczema.

CHARLOTTE MAKES HER FIRST DEPOSIT

Charlotte stopped itching for a moment. She understood. As extraordinary as it might sound, her *leaky gut* and her *toxic liver* could have a direct and powerful impact on her skin—and, as we began to delve deeper, on her fatigue and her aching joints.

I gave Charlotte her first deposit slip that afternoon. It was to change her diet from the starchy, sugary, high-fat foods she automatically ate at her desk to fresh fruits, vegetables, chicken, and fish. I also made sure she realized that life had room for many things, including an occasional indulgence. She needed to have healthful foods for her body, but she also needed to know that healthful did not mean bad tasting. Charlotte had to be assured that there was a whole world of delicious and, yes, healthful food out there. Even better, she had to realize that on occasion she could spring for that fatty food or sugary dessert. It's good for everyone to know this "food truth": that you have choices, as long as you are eating well a majority of the time. Then you, like Charlotte, can occasionally "have your cake and eat it, too." You can feed both your body and your soul.

I designed a vitamin and mineral regimen for Charlotte. We would start slowly, increasing the dosages only if her system responded favorably, without any reactions. In later weeks I would add supplements, herbs, and probiotics (which you'll read more about in the chapters to come) to her "good health account."

Before she left, recommendations in tow, I wanted to be sure Charlotte understood what was happening. I walked her to the door.

"It's your decision, Charlotte. It's your Body Bank. You can choose health. You are in control, remember that." Just changing what she ate at lunch or making sure she took a multivitamin in the morning could make a difference, a real difference, in the weeks and months to come.

The deposits add up. They have a cumulative effect, just as the withdrawals do. I expected that Charlotte would begin to improve once we tackled the real problem, starting with throwing away the sugary snacks and her old acne medication, which did more harm than good. Instead, she deposited natural, unprocessed foods and simple vitamins, minerals, and nutritional supplements that calmed her intestines and built up her immune system. Now her health account was paying off.

I vividly remember how that first session ended. Charlotte was once again surreptitiously scratching her arm underneath her coat. She had the motivation, but I thought she still might have some uncertainty. I asked her to rate how she felt on a scale of 1 to 10, 1 being the worst and 10 being the best. Without missing a scratch, Charlotte whispered, "A negative five . . ."

But the next week that negative number turned into a zero, and over a period of a few months, the eczema had almost cleared up. Charlotte's skin now glows. She has vigor and she feels better than she has in years. The last time I asked her to rate how she felt, she gave me an incredible 9!

You've probably picked up this book because, like Charlotte, you have a condition or a series of symptoms that just won't go away. Maybe it's more serious, maybe less so. It doesn't matter. *Healing from the Inside* is an open book . . . everyone is welcome.

Unfortunately, I had no such supportive guide to help me understand my *running in the red* symptoms when I first started out. It was only through years of extensive research, continuous seminars, and much experience that I was able to pinpoint my *leaky gut* and *toxic liver* as the culprit behind my sinusitis and irritated throat. It was also during these years that I first heard Jeffrey Bland, Ph.D., speak about his exciting theories on the *leaky gut* and the *toxic liver*—and their effect on optimal health.

I want you to have more power over your health by having more information than what was available twenty, or even ten, years ago. I want to help you uncover the information that will dispel the mysteries within your own body—and know that you can truly understand, once and for all, the vital ingredients for a healthy life.

This book is designed to help you not only get well but also prevent illness from ever settling in. To that end, the first section involves gaining empowerment. It describes in detail the ways to reclaim your health, to take back your body, and to choose well-being. You'll learn in detail how the Body Bank concept will help you achieve this control, including the specific good health deposits that can prevent illness, as well as the sometimes subtle, dangerous withdrawals that can lead to *running in the red* symptoms and *bankruptcy* conditions. You'll also find the necessary knowledge that breeds strength as you discover how your body works, and how your systems are connected to one another, making a greater whole.

The second section involves the "fun" part: learning how to solve your own Body Bank mystery. Here you'll discover how to be a top-notch Health Detective, as well as find the sometimes startling, sometimes surprising *health-links* that can provide real clues to your condition. Do you know, for example, that a buildup of wax in your ears can be a sign of a high cholesterol level? Or that poor circulation can contribute to hair loss? You'll also find easy-to-follow instructions for taking the various vitamins, minerals, herbs, and probiotics I discuss throughout the book. By the time you learn *How to Solve Your Own Mystery*, you'll find yourself better educated and less overwhelmed the next time you check out the shelves of supplements—or feel a symptom flare up!

The third section is all about knowing the "mastermind" behind your symptoms: the *leaky gut*. You'll see exactly how, and why, this condition and its ramifications could interfere with your foundation for incredible health, paving the way to solutions to mysteries we've just begun to explore. You'll discover how this *running in the red* account can lead to a whole slew of seemingly unrelated conditions, as well as to ways to help that ensure your body has the best chance of staying healthy, strong, and efficient.

The fourth section involves understanding the gut's partner-in-crime: the *toxic liver*. Here's where you'll find out exactly how the liver works and how you can determine when it's congested or sluggish. You'll see how it collaborates with the *leaky gut* to create a great many symptoms and conditions—and how it works against the benefits of that fresh food you eat or those vitamins, minerals, and herbs you take.

Finally, my last section involves preventing "crime in your neighborhood," providing ways to make sure your health investments are secure. In this section, you'll find help for respiratory bankruptcies; skin, hair, nail, and mouth bankruptcies; joint, muscular, and skeletal bankruptcies; psychological and stress-related bankruptcies; allergic bankruptcies; and more.

Within each *bankruptcy*, you'll discover a mini-quiz to see if you have symptoms that match the ones in these areas—symptoms that, if not heeded and corrected, can result in some of the common conditions my clients have had.

In addition, each chapter contains my own Rescue Regimens. Here, following a program similar to what I have used in my office, you will learn the types of herbs, supplements, foods, vitamins, and minerals that can contribute to good health and help prevent your symptoms from becoming full-fledged *bankruptcy* conditions. But even if a condition is in place, you may be able to reverse its symptoms by exploring the specific recommendations I've outlined for each *bank-ruptcy* state.

Soon you'll find yourself looking forward to a health account that's "in the black." But remember, as with any other self-care regimen, my Rescue Regimens are not intended to be started without first checking with your physician or health practitioner. For optimal results, the programs may need to be tailored to specific situations, taking into account a predisposition to vitamin, mineral, or herbal sensitivity. They are depicted for the purpose of educating and introducing you to the concepts and available remedies that can help restore your body to vital health. They are designed to give you hope—and good, sound ideas and information that will guide you to look at your body in a whole new way.

Healing from the Inside is unique. Instead of offering a list of supplements you should take, symptoms and conditions in a dry tome that reads like a textbook, this interactive book invites you in, inspiring you to participate in your own health and your own life. You'll notice the difference as soon as you begin to read about your Body Bank's deposits and withdrawals, as you try out a few quizzes, as you assume the vital role of Health Detective to solve the mystery of your own symptoms and ill health.

To help you better understand and use concepts in *Healing from the Inside*, I've also added boxed inserts—quotes, snippets of inspiration, statistics, and new research results. You can browse through them at your leisure, as you turn your withdrawals into deposits, as you take charge of your good health.

In short, I want you to feel comfortable, to feel as if I am with you, in your kitchen or your living room, at your desk or at your health food store. I want you to gain knowledge and confidence so that you can choose health!

Congratulations. You're about to embark on an exciting road of self-discovery and health. Like Charlotte, you'll be better equipped to live with more youthful energy, vitality, and optimism.

I'm eager to welcome you, to help you solve the mystery of your body, to help you find the right investments to earn real health. I want you to feel what I feel: the empowerment that comes from knowledge, understanding, and action.

No more mysteries. Let the healing begin!

Section I

Gain Empowerment—Reclaim Your Health, Vitality, and Energy Through Knowledge

1

THE MYSTERY OF THE BODY BANK

There are more things in heaven and earth, Horatio,
Than are dreamt of in your philosophy.
　　　　　　　　—William Shakespeare, *Hamlet* (Act I, Scene 5)

Shakespeare penned these immortal words almost four hundred years ago; they are spoken by Hamlet after he first spies his father's ghost on the castle walk. The young prince is talking about the inexplicable mysteries of life and death, the unfathomable connections between his own life and death—and the world around him.

You might be wondering why a nutritionist might invoke *Hamlet*—or anything written nearly four hundred years ago. What do these words have in common with the clients I see every day, the people who come to me with their pain that won't go away, their discomfort, and their fear?

Plenty. I too work with the mysteries of life and death, and "things in heaven and earth" that were not dreamed of twenty, ten, or even five years ago. As anyone who has kept up with the advances in science, nutrition, and medicine knows, we live in a time when things once only dreamed of can help cure disease and remedy chronic conditions. Our brave new world contains promising programs for health that have nothing to do with white lab coats, pharmaceutical pills with questionable side effects, and diagnostic tests that ignore underlying conditions.

There's more. Who would have imagined that we would once again research ancient herbs or that we have successfully synthesized them in the laboratory to heal the sick? Foxglove, an ordinary herb, is the active ingredient in digitalis, a medication widely used to prevent cardiac arrest. Eucalyptus, a soothing herb, is one of the main ingredients in cough medicines and drops.

And who would have believed that we would once again rely on the use of homeopathic principles invented over two hundred years ago? Or that we would realize more than ever that "we are what we eat," despite the fact that forty years ago people didn't have an inkling about the link between saturated fat and heart disease? Or that—strange, but true—even when we eat an apple or a green salad fresh from the garden, we *still* might not be getting the nutrients we need, thanks to an undernourished, overused, and depleted soil?

The solution to the mystery is not in the cure, as in traditional medicine, but in the *reasons* someone gets sick, in searching out the clues "in heaven and earth" that this book will help you discover and change.

In knowledge there is strength. In education there is the start of empowerment. Together, you and I will glean facts inherited from your past and from those assimilated in the present. You will learn the ways, both mysterious and obvious, in which your symptoms are connected to the faraway places in your body where they began. By knowing how your body works, how its systems are all interrelated, and what your symptoms are telling you, you have a better chance to help *prevent* those aches and pains from becoming osteoarthritis, that fatigue from becoming chronic, that diarrhea from becoming irritable bowel syndrome, that allergic reaction from becoming asthma. With the right information, you can take the right action—toward health. On your own. By yourself. In charge and in control. It's called empowerment.

There is a vast array of natural, health-supporting products out

---

HERBS ARE GOOD MEDICINE

Read all about it! More pharmaceutical drugs that come from natural herbs!

- *Vincristine and vinblastine:* Two anticancer medications that come from the periwinkle plant.
- *Aspirin:* One of its main components, salicin, comes from willow bark.
- *Taxol:* An anticancer drug that comes from the yew tree.
- *Atropine:* An antispasmodic medication that contains belladonna.
- *Over-the-counter laxatives:* Most contain the natural herb senna.

there—and once the mystery underlying the origin of the symptoms or condition is solved, it becomes a matter of choosing the right products to deposit into your Body Bank to make and keep you well.

THE MYSTERY OF THE LEMON AND THE TISSUE

When I was growing up, our kitchen cabinets were filled with cupcakes, candy bars, chips, and boxes of chocolate cookies. My mother would buy a head of iceberg lettuce, a tomato or two, and a cucumber, but that was about it. And lemons? Never around. Why bother buying a lemon when you can buy a plastic version filled with juice? It even *looks* like a lemon!

I not only became inducted into the "Sugar Hall of Fame" but, throughout my childhood, I continued to believe that a lemon was an exotic fruit, equivalent to a pomegranate or a Persian melon.

All that changed when I became an adult. A whole new world opened up. I was soon eating bountiful salads, enjoying rich wholegrain bread, and sprinkling my Cajun catfish with lemon.

Thanks to an introduction to the cornucopia of healthful, delicious foods that I never knew existed, I was eating better, feeling better, and reading more about diet and health; I was soon drawn into the field of science and nutrition. Whenever possible, I would go to my university library, researching the latest advances, writing copious notes on health and illness, and reading everything about the body that I could. It was there, during those long hours among the stacks, that I began to formulate a blood-sugar control program that came to be known as *The 5-Day Miracle Diet*, as well as my ideas about prevention and wellness.

HEALTH BY ANY OTHER NAME . . .

Don't be confused if you've never heard of complementary therapies. Until recently, they went by the name of *alternative therapies*. Thanks to the surge in these new modalities, they are now more aptly considered a complement to traditional medicines, rather than a separate entity.

WITH ADELE'S COMPLEMENTS!

Empowerment: it's the feeling you have when you take back your health, when you decide to be in control of your own life, your own destiny, your own body. And it starts with that first healthy deposit you make, whether it is taking a multivitamin and mineral supplement, putting on your walking shoes and opening the door, or eating a fresh, crisp green salad at lunch.

CHOOSE HEALTH!

Unfortunately, even though I was learning a lot about wellness, I had not yet unlocked all the clues to *being* well, especially when it came to myself. I was always making excuses for my hoarse voice whenever I asked the librarian for a book, or whenever I moved my chair to avoid the nearby odors of perfumes, floor waxes, even the scented tissues my neighbor was using. Worse, my throat was almost always sore. I now know that my symptoms were the result of my overwhelmed liver and gut. My sore throat, my hoarseness, my sensitivity to odors—all these were a result of the way my *leaky gut* and *toxic liver* reacted to stimuli, from the weather to my stress levels, from the aromas that surrounded me to what I happened to eat and drink a few hours before.

My symptoms were something I lived with; they did slow me down, of course, but I tried not to think about them. However, as I read the literature on natural healing, I began to realize that I should not have to accept living with my laryngitis. There was some exciting information becoming available about vitamins, minerals, homeopathic regimens, and herbal research. Could it be true, I wondered? Could I possibly be able to live without a sore throat?

One study led to another. I'd soon left my laryngitis research and delved into a plethora of other conditions, all of which seemed to involve organs far from the condition at hand. I grew fascinated with the idea of searching out the real villains behind the symptoms of my throat ailment. I felt like an explorer embarking on an amazing voyage. The more I learned, the more I needed to know.

Even more exciting were the remedies. Instead of antihistamines and nasal sprays, there were herbs with names like little thistle and wil-

WITH ADELE'S COMPLEMENTS!

Complementary therapies are proactive. They offer a total approach. While they may sometimes treat individual symptoms, they never lose sight of the fact that the mind and body are a whole. Further, complementary therapies offer preventive measures before an illness occurs.

As sound and practical as that might seem today, it wasn't too long ago that Americans considered complementary treatments as something exotic and separate.

And, as accepted as they are beginning to be in our culture, complementary therapies are still not as popular here as in other parts of the world. Visit a chemist in London and you'll see a wide variety of natural remedies mixed right in with the pharmaceuticals. Just ask an Asian about acupuncture—a relative newcomer to our sacred halls of medicine—and he or she will tell you that acupuncturists have been practicing for centuries. They are as common in China as internists are in the States.

low bark, and homeopathic remedies whose names reminded me of Hippocrates and ancient Greece.

And there, in the midst of clearing my throat, I found the answer that would help relieve my laryngitis. It wasn't "one pill and call me in the morning." It wasn't "take two capsules on an empty stomach." It wasn't "spray into each nostril when you can't breathe."

The first step to healing was surprisingly simple and convenient—and it made sense. It was a combination of healthful eating, eliminating anything with artificial sweeteners, specific nutrition supplementation, herbology, and relaxation techniques—all of which could relieve the conditions that initially caused my laryngitis. It was then, during my early initiation into natural healing, that I realized how a simple lemon could begin my restoration process.

Through a proper regimen, I soon started to build up a healthy reserve in my body.

Reserve. As in Federal Reserve. As in statement savings accounts. As in savings accounts linked to checking accounts. As in CDs, solid investments, and retirement funds. Reserve. That was it. My idea for the

Body Bank was born, my system of deposits and withdrawals that affect you now and in the future.

The Body Bank was a concept I could understand, and a way of creating wellness that I could pinpoint and visualize. Just as I wanted money in the bank, I wanted to be healthy. But both need routine deposits to build up that reserve.

I plunged into my work with a new zeal, using my Health Detective work to help my clients, my family, my friends, and, later, my children heal their aches and pains—and prevent future ailments—by keeping their Body Bank accounts healthy.

THE BODY BANK'S MYSTERIOUS ASSETS EXPLAINED

Two or three decades ago, nutritionists and natural healers could be found primarily in trendy places that sought out new ideas. Holistic centers, where I began my internship, were few and far between. To-day, you can find some natural remedies in your local pharmacy, right next to the chewable antacids. But this accessibility doesn't make the field any less intimidating if you, like most people, have never used these remedies or have read conflicting reports about them.

Traditional healing has been set up to be *reactive*: medications are prescribed once symptoms are present. Health changes are requested only when the hypertension, diabetes, or obesity is already in place. More and more medical schools and health institutions are recognizing the importance of nutrition and are taking a preventive approach to treating patients—but there is still a wide gap.

It's no wonder that computer owners are on-line to each other with questions about complementary medicine. People just don't know where to go to find the answers to health questions. And the vast array of new vitamins, minerals, herbs, homeopathic medicines—and sci-fi–sounding probiotics—almost makes it worse. The entire world of complementary therapies feels confusing and unapproachable. How do we know what we need? How do we know what products to use? What will work? Whom to trust? Should we take separate doses of all the vitamins? And what about herbs and possible allergic reactions to them? Help!

SO EXACTLY WHAT IS THIS
ANTIOXIDANT, FREE RADICAL THING?

Picture this scenario: Several inebriated guys are hanging around a bar, relentlessly harassing a woman. She ignores them. They continue to taunt and annoy her. She starts to panic. Suddenly, the doors swing open and a strong, vibrant, confident man enters. He quickly makes short shrift of the drunken fellows, even though it means sacrificing himself for the woman's safety.

Now think of those drunks as free radicals and the self-sacrificing hero as an antioxidant, and you'll have an idea of how the process works.

Antioxidants are the substances found in foods that intercept free radicals (potentially damaging materials that are created by cell metabolism and environment activity), destroying them even as they destroy themselves. Antioxidants actually bond with the free radicals; they "cling" to them and they are then unable to be used by the body for other purposes—the ultimate sacrifice.

These antioxidants, found in many fruits, vegetables, and other plant-based foods, have been found to fight cancer, soften the effects of aging, increase immunity, and lessen cholesterol buildup.

Just visit any health store. For the uninitiated, it can be as overwhelming as visiting Macy's, "the largest department store in the world," for the first time.

Before you can solve the mystery of your Body Bank, or truly understand the concept I've created, you need to know how to make all this new complementary material your own. It might sound like a foreign language, but it is only the unfamiliarity that makes you feel this way. Once you've mastered this new approach to health, you can conquer the feelings of inadequacy, of confusion. And at last you can feel true, vital, energizing empowerment.

And that empowerment begins by becoming familiar with the assets that constitute a healthy Body Bank. These are the complementary regimens, including "hands-on" massage and stress-reducing modalities, that are only now beginning to have an impact on general society; these are the supposedly "alternative" treatments that studies are finding to be effective. And as we move forward into the future, there will most likely be even more studies, more exacting research, about these modalities. The evidence is burgeoning and the message is clear: Complementary regimens can no longer be ignored.

In brief, here are the complementary assets found in a sound Body Bank. You'll need to make deposits gathered from these regimens to strengthen your healthy body account and prevent future problems. They are a major component in helping you to gain empowerment.

"FOOD, GLORIOUS FOOD," OR DIET AND NUTRITIONAL SUPPLEMENTS

We are all familiar with the ingredients of a good, balanced diet, one that is low in fat (preventing the buildup of cholesterol, a leading cause of heart disease), high in fiber (preventing colon cancer and diverticulitis, as well as hypertension and heart disease), and rich in vitamins and minerals (aiding the fight against many forms of cancer, metabolic disturbances, infections, and birth defects). But sometimes we have to help Mother Nature along, choosing foods more wisely and providing supplements to our meals and snacks to build up a heartier immune system, stronger bones, and better internal health. Here are some examples:

• Beta-carotene, the precursor of vitamin A (meaning it converts as needed to the vitamin once inside the body, which makes it less toxic), is found in fruits and vegetables such as carrots, spinach, sweet potatoes, collard greens, and cantaloupe. It can help reduce the chance of stroke and heart disease. A longitudinal study of 87,000 nurses over eight years found that those who took between 15 and 20 milligrams of beta-carotene per day (the equivalent of three carrots or one sweet potato) had 40 percent fewer strokes and 22 percent fewer heart attacks than those who took less than 6 milligrams.

And taking only slightly more than 100 milligrams of vitamin E every day gave these same heart-healthy nurses a 36 percent decrease in cardiac arrest. (Vitamin E can be found in wheat germ, oatmeal, brown rice, and peanuts.)

• Cranberry juice has been found to be an effective preventive measure for many women who develop frequent urinary tract infections. Dried cranberries come in capsule form for those watching sugar intake or calories.

• Red-hot chili peppers, such as jalapeño peppers, are high in capsaicin, an ingredient found to be effective in treating rheumatoid arthritis and general pain. You can also purchase capsaicin capsules. *(Warning: Do not take capsaicin or hot peppers if you have ulcers.)*

• Folic acid can help prevent birth defects and possibly reduce the risk of cervical cancer, heart disease, and stroke. Folic acid can be found in cantaloupe, oranges, asparagus, broccoli, and corn, among other fruits and vegetables. Combined with vitamin B_{12}, folic acid is being recommended to prevent memory loss.

• Vitamin D, found in eggs, dandelion greens, fortified milk products, and sardines, and vitamin C, found in citrus fruit, sweet peppers, asparagus, cantaloupe, and broccoli, have been found to slow down osteoarthritis. A study of 556 elderly Framingham, Massachusetts, residents found that those who took a supplement of both vitamins since the 1980s have had a much slower rate of osteoarthritis progression.

• Omega-3 fish oil has been shown to significantly reduce the amount of triglycerides and the blood-clotting factors that lead to stroke in people who took 6 grams daily—the equivalent of approximately 10 ounces of salmon or 6 ounces of lake trout. *(Warning: Do not take fish oil if you are on blood thinners.)*

• Phytochemicals—non-nutritive plant substances found in fruits and vegetables that give them their odor, color, and flavor—also help prevent disease and infection. The phytochemicals in garlic, onions, and chives, for example, have been found to lower cholesterol and help prevent breast cancer. Those in tomatoes may prevent blood clots.

• Antioxidant substances found in grapes and berries, such as quercetin, have been demonstrated to help eliminate toxic, cancer-producing chemicals from the body. They may also help reduce blood cholesterol levels and keep urinary tract infections from coming back.

• Potassium has been found to help cut the risk of high blood pressure. Seek out foods such as apricots, spinach, tomatoes, potatoes, and oranges.

• Zinc has been found to shorten the duration of a common cold if dissolved in the mouth. You can find it in fish, legumes, mushrooms, meats, and poultry. *(Because too much zinc can suppress the immune system, it should be taken properly, as instructed in Appendix C of this book.)*

And these are only the tip of the iceberg (created from filtered water, of course)! Nutritional supplements can literally enhance every aspect of your life, because they provide vitamins, minerals, amino acids, enzymes, antioxidants, and fatty acids that you don't always get enough of from your food. They are invaluable health tools—and a vital element of healing from the inside out.

"DON'T FORGET TO STOP AND EAT THE FLOWERS," OR HERBS AND BOTANICALS

American women might have been branded as witches for picking herbs in the forest to stave off an illness a mere two hundred years ago, but today these same women would be considered entrepreneurs: herbology is a $700 million-a-year industry in the United States.

Using herbs to ward off illness has been and still is a major element of traditional Chinese medicine (TCM), combined with acupuncture and hands-on therapies to help restore balanced energy to the body.

Herbs are prepared in many different ways. Sometimes they are steeped in boiling water and sipped as a tea, ground into a powder, diluted into a syrup, made into a pill, or used as a poultice on the surface of the skin.

Herbs work. It's long been common knowledge that ginger can aid in motion sickness, while current research keeps showing that feverfew has been effective in preventing migraine headaches. And an amino acid substance called alliin is released from garlic when eaten, which triggers the enzyme allinase into creating an antibiotic (allicin) as potent as 1 percent of penicillin—without its potential for damaging the gut.

Bach Flower remedies, or botanicals, are primarily used to help reduce emotional and psychological distress. The liquid crushed from flowers, heavy with dew, is distilled in water to form a concentrate, or essence. Clinical research has found that a person's psychological state can affect his or her body functions by stimulating or suppressing the body's immunity and hormone production. The flower remedies I've introduced to my clients over the years have helped them cope better with stress and emotional pain—and, in turn, helped reduce their vulnerability to disease. *(One word of caution: Although extremely rare, adverse allergic reactions to herbs and botanicals have been documented. See Appendix C for details on possible toxicity of common herbs.)*

WITH ADELE'S COMPLEMENTS!

The mind–body connection is a powerful entity and a basic tenet of complementary healing. I'd like to share something I tell my clients when I first explain the power of the mind and the body working in concert.

I'm a jogger; it's the exercise I love to do, especially out in the fresh air. But like everyone else, there are days when I'm not feeling up to it. I'm a little tired and out of sorts. If I go out to run and ruminate about not wanting to do it, I feel my body behaving just like my head: I can't run.

But when I give a pep talk to my brain, telling myself to "just put on those running shoes, open the door, that's it, just get moving!" suddenly I not only jog but soar! I feel great and my body feels whole and healthy. Talk about the power of the mind–body connection!

"YES, THERE IS SUCH A THING AS GOOD BACTERIA,"
OR PROBIOTICS AND PROACTIVES

Today's studies have found that antibiotics produced by the pharmaceutical firms cannot keep up with the bacterial mutations they are supposed to kill. Antibiotics, whether taken yesterday or last year, not only kill "bad" germs but good bacteria as well—the ones in the intestine that produce vitamins and help ensure proper digestion. You can also take in antibiotics in every bite you eat of poultry or beef, which, except for organic varieties, have been "shot up" with antibiotics and hormones for better production value and longer shelf life. Combine these facts and there is no question that we have become an "over-antibiotized" society.

Probiotics are exactly what they sound like: the antithesis of antibiotics, which are reactive. Antibiotics might cure, but they don't prevent. Probiotics are different. These live bacteria help restore friendly bacteria to your digestive tract, bacteria so necessary for protecting your body against invaders.

Bacteria flood our digestive tract by the time we are only four days old. As adults, we have some 400 strains of bacteria living in our gut, some of them good, some of them bad. Achieving the correct balance of bacteria can improve the digestive process, may prevent colon cancer, and can help relieve gastrointestinal distress.

Unfortunately, over the years, you can literally lose your balance, giving a toxic environment the edge. Thanks to such withdrawals from the Body Bank as a regimen of antibiotics, a high-sugar diet, too much alcohol, unrelenting stress, or even drinking chlorinated water, bacteria—the good, the bad, and the ugly—can be destroyed, creating havoc in your Body Bank.

Eating yogurt and drinking buttermilk (if you aren't lactose intolerant) can help maintain that equilibrium, but if you've lost some of your good bacteria you'll need something stronger to entice them back: probiotics.

Probiotics are live, good bacteria that you ingest with water. Some people might equate them with old-fashioned "traveling tonic shows," but probiotics (also called proactives) have been found to do what tetracycline and all the new antibiotics cannot: prevent invasion by bad bacteria in the first place, whether the bad guys are a new, mutated, or old-fashioned form.

Studies have also found that, in the elderly and in seriously ill patients, probiotics can be safely used in preventing diarrhea and yeast infections caused by the use of strong antibiotics.

"A GENTLER, KINDER MEDICINE," OR HOMEOPATHY

The strange-sounding Latin formulas of homeopathy might sound intimidating, but they are actually very body friendly and can be effective in soothing aches, pains, and the discomfort from flu and colds.

Europeans have long embraced homeopathy. The British royal family has had a homeopath on staff for decades! Americans have been slower to accept these remedies, but today even the venerable National Institutes of Health, a branch of the Department of Health and Human Services, is conducting experiments to determine homeopathy's efficacy.

Homeopathic remedies are similar to the concept of a vaccine, which uses a small dose of the cause of an illness to create an immunity to it. Homeopaths use dilutions that mimic the conditions in question; the quantities are so small that they cannot harm, only heal.

Homeopathy was the brainchild of Samuel Hahnemann, a German physician who lived in the 1790s. In those days the treatment of choice was either bleeding or purging, so the more humane realm of homeopathy was, as you can imagine, an overnight success. "Like cures like" was one of Hahnemann's beliefs and, to that end, he would dilute, dilute, and dilute further still the active ingredients found in a specific condition. In a process he called "potentizing," he put the solution through a series of forceful, fast-shaking actions. Ultimately, the doses he used would be so dilute that the original ingredients would be almost nonexistent but still very effective. Today, the same principles apply, and the same process of potentizing is done in laboratories around the globe.

Homeopathy is the medicine of listening. Remedies are chosen based on an individual's emotional and physical constitution, not just the particular ailment. Each potion is chosen based on highly specific symptoms, such as "a headache that occurs after a sunburn, accompanied by eye fatigue" or "a headache made worse by riding in the car," or "a headache that begins after overeating and improves with a leisurely walk."

One remedy at a time is tried. If one doesn't work, another is used until the right formula is found. Although you can buy homeopathic remedies in health food stores and more conventional drugstores, it is always best to go to a licensed homeopath for the most accurate diagnosis and treatment. The one exception is in purchasing oscillococcinum, a common homeopathic remedy that has relieved flu symptoms in many people. It is so mainstream that you can easily find it in pharmacies next to the cough syrups and decongestants. Follow the directions on the bottle. (In Appendix A, I've listed several sources to help you find a good homeopath where you live or work.)

"THE EYE OF THE NEEDLE," OR ACUPUNCTURE

When you think of acupuncture, you probably get an image of needles sticking out all over your body. Ouch! Well, your impression is not entirely wrong. Needles are involved, and you might feel a slight prick as they are inserted, but acupuncture is not the horror you might imagine it is. Acupuncture actually takes the pain away. In fact, it's been scientifically proven that acupuncture releases chemicals in the brain, including endorphins, that are natural painkillers. Indeed, acupuncture is widely accepted as a remedy for chronic pain. Studies have demonstrated that acupuncture will help relieve nausea, control drug

addiction, and aid stroke victims during rehabilitation when combined with traditional medicines. And in China, acupuncture has been
used in lieu of traditional anesthesia for brain surgery! Not only did
110 patients studied feel no pain under the knife, but their recovery
was much quicker and had fewer side effects.

Acupuncture is an exact science. Sterilized, extremely fine needles,
inserted by licensed acupuncturists, are not "stuck" at random. They
follow meridians, or energy pathways, that run throughout the body;
these pathways flow from head to toe. Inserting needles (or applying
hands-on pressure in acupressure) at specific points on these passageways will provide relief from pain.

If you have pain when you urinate, for example, needles might be
inserted at the base of the neck, on the torso, and at the back of the
legs, all of which are on the same meridian, or energy pathway, as the
bladder. Although your pain might be centered in the bladder, its
source can be anywhere along the meridian path. Although seemingly
far from the problem area, these needles in your neck or back can ease
your bladder pain because they help clear the entire path.

"TOUCH ME, FEEL ME," OR HANDS-ON THERAPY

There's a reason you feel good when someone gives you a hug. It's
calming, comforting, and a moment of compassion. You get the same
feeling on the giving end: frayed nerves feel better when we hold our
babies, when we pet our dogs and cats. (There's a reason why chicken
soup is so good for flu and colds, and it's not just the natural antibiotics in the simmering soup. It's the warm, nourishing food made by
a caring person who is feeding your soul as well as your body.)

If we are not nurtured when we feel sick, our emotions can prevent
a speedier physical recovery. If we are depressed, we're not going to
fight as hard to stave off infection. Research has shown that people
with depression can have a deficiency of tyrosine, an amino acid that is
necessary for balanced mood, proper brain function, and the body's
ability to handle stress. Without tyrosine, stress can build and create
havoc in our bodies—ultimately suppressing the immune system.

Hands-on therapy is one way to treat the whole person. It's soothing, nurturing, and stress reducing; in purely physical terms, it can
relieve pain as well.

The most common form of hands-on therapy is *massage*, that won-

---

THE BIGGER PICTURE

One of the tenets of natural healing is working with the whole person—
a holistic approach. It's providing the time and patience to help a person with his or her physical problems and the emotional vulnerability
that crops up from the pain or the stressful mental state that made
that body vulnerable to pain in the first place.

---

derful, deeply relaxing manipulation of the soft tissue that used to be
an exclusive luxury of the rich. Today anybody and everybody can have
a professional massage by a licensed therapist. (If you're pressed for
time or money, you can even get a fifteen-minute beneficial backrub
for about $10 at storefronts across the country.)

A good massage runs the gamut from general forms that calm and
soothe the nerves, relaxing and releasing tension in tight muscles, to
more specialized forms such as Shiatsu and acupressure, which concentrate on isolated points of the meridian to relieve specific pain or
emotional states.

Reflexology is a massage where all the work is done on the feet (and
sometimes the hands). Reflexologists concentrate on specific areas on
the soles that correspond to various parts of the body. By stimulating
an area of the foot, the blocked energy in the specific organ can be released, initiating positive changes in ailing areas.

When a stream of water is used, the massage becomes *hydrotherapy*.
It makes the massage more potent and relaxing. Hydrotherapy can
also mean ten minutes in a relaxing whirlpool bath, a steam room, or a
sitz bath (in which a person sits in a shallow tub of lukewarm water).
Hydrotherapy helps to eliminate toxins by changing the body temperature and stimulating the immune system.

All of these hands-on techniques are geared to prevention. They
are designed primarily to relax frayed nerves, soothe aching muscles,
and reduce stress, in addition to helping cure various ailments. And
health practitioners and scientists have been gathering evidence that
these techniques can help you reclaim your health, vitality, and energy:

• A study of children and infants suffering from premature birth, HIV,
cocaine exposure, and a family atmosphere of clinical depression,

found that anxiety and the production of stress hormones—as well as visits to the doctor—were decreased when hands-on massage therapy was used.

• Women suffering from PMS were given reflexology therapy for a period of four months in one particular study in England. The women's symptoms dramatically decreased, as compared to another group who did not receive the actual therapy.

• When therapeutic massage was used on hospitalized cancer patients, their anxiety and feelings of pain were significantly reduced.

"THE SCENT OF THE MATTER," OR AROMATHERAPY

It was fourteen years ago, but I can still remember the scene as if it were yesterday. All four children were living at home and there was never a quiet moment. In fact, it was complete bedlam! I'd come home from work, exhausted, wave hello, and, before getting involved in everyone else's day, I'd close my bedroom door: aah, my sanctuary. I'd start the water running in my bath, mixing certain oils and pouring them into the warm water. As the scent surrounded me, I would feel immediately relaxed. It didn't matter how long my bath lasted, five minutes or twenty. I'd already got what I needed: the wonderful aroma. The smell of my bath reminded me it was *my* time. Subconsciously, my whole being knew that this was my space, my quiet, my serene place. The smell was all I needed to trigger relaxation; the bath was merely an extra plus. Soon I was ready to go downstairs and tackle anything, including dinner!

Our sense of smell is the only one with a direct, immediate passageway to the brain's emotional center. This is why a quick whiff of perfume from a passing stranger, the smell of home-baked bread, or in my case, the scents permeating my bath can almost instantaneously trigger an entire scene in the mind, a memory that can bring a jolt of nostalgia, sorrow, or joy. Because smell is so very powerful and "fast acting," aromatherapy can be extremely effective.

Basically, aromatherapy is the science of scent. Although you can use aromas in a simmering pot, or in candles, perfumes, and room sprays, it works its "magic" best when combined with the deep relaxation of massage. A therapist uses essential oils designed to relax you or relieve pain in specific areas. Depending on the scents used, you might feel energized after a massage or ready for a nap.

PREVENTION IS WORTH AN OUNCE OF CURE:
THE BODY BANK IN ACTION

I remember a client, a woman in her forties, very well. Unfortunately, she was very overweight. Her lifestyle was a huge withdrawal—to the point where she had developed diabetes, high blood pressure, moderately dangerous levels of cholesterol and triglycerides, and was now dealing with cancer.

She had come to see me on the recommendation of her physician: she needed a dramatic change in lifestyle and diet. I knew that the very foundation of her Body Bank needed to be overhauled and "redesigned." I suggested we start slowly. I began teaching her how to eat to control her blood sugar with the diet plan I use in my office, in addition to a regimen of vitamin and mineral supplements.

The woman interrupted me with a disapproving look on her face. She shook her head. She told me that she'd never taken a vitamin in her life, that she'd never needed them. I almost fell out of my chair! She completely ignored the fact that she had high blood pressure, diabetes, and cancer.

It was my turn to shake my head. I'd never seen such denial. If my client had been making healthy deposits to her Body Bank all along (which, of course, would include vitamin and mineral supplementation), she might not have gotten sick in the first place!

A whiff of peppermint can make you feel ready to take on the world. A combination of rosemary and juniper will calm frayed nerves. And lavender oil has been shown to help reduce insomnia and restore a full night's sleep, without medication.

Smelling is believing. Aromatherapy can be so powerful that, in Japan, corporations use lemon or other citrus-scented aromas in the office air to keep workers alert and focused.

"OMMMMMMM," OR RELAXATION TECHNIQUES

Lindsay, a client in her mid-thirties, went to a hypnotist before going into the hospital for minor surgery. She was anxious about the procedure (the removal of polyps from her vocal cords), as well as getting "knocked out." I suggested she see a hypnotist to help ease her anxiety.

Instinctively, people "fight off" an incision, but with hypnosis the mind is less combative. People "allow" the surgeon to do the job.

It worked. Not only was Lindsay calmer right before the operation, but she also recovered in record time. She was out of the hospital in less than a day, with no residue of anesthesia grogginess or disorientation.

Hypnosis has also been used to help people lose weight, quit smoking, gain self-esteem, and more. Although research in these areas is ongoing, there is ample proof that self-hypnosis can help a person relax. One particular study of adults who suffered from chronic headaches found that simple self-hypnosis techniques helped ease the pain more efficiently than more complicated therapies. Another study, this one of children undergoing chemotherapy, found that self-hypnosis helped relieve the nausea and anxiety that accompany it.

Other forms of deep relaxation include:

• *Meditation.* This age-old relaxation technique is almost an institution. For effective meditation, you'll need a quiet space and a comfortable chair, or you can simply sit cross-legged on a mat, arms stretched out over your knees, palms up. Close your eyes, take several deep breaths, and try to concentrate on a sound or a mental picture, either an object or a wall. Whenever your thoughts wander, try to bring them gently back. Meditating for at least fifteen minutes a day can revitalize you; it can help focus your energy and keep you centered.

I've been practicing meditation for years. It clears my head and helps me take things as they come (which is especially helpful when I'm stuck in rush-hour traffic). I never truly appreciated its results until several years ago. I'd been too busy to do my usual meditation. One night I woke up with a vague "gnawing in my stomach," a feeling of hunger that wouldn't go away. I wandered around the kitchen looking for something to eat. I was concerned when this occurred two nights in a row: I am usually a sound sleeper and nothing wakes me except an extremely loud alarm. The next day, after yet another sleepless night, I began my meditation again. That night, I didn't wake up—I slept soundly. The "gnawing" feeling in my stomach was gone. I suddenly realized that the descriptions my clients gave me about their ulcer discomfort was what I had been feeling. I now understood firsthand the tremendous impact meditation had on my life and my stress levels. Now I make sure I practice meditation almost every day, no matter how hectic my schedule!

ACID RAIN

Antacids, those chalky or flavored tablets that were synonymous with upset stomachs in every ad or television series featuring a Type A personality, were considered curative several years ago—and a good source of calcium, to boot.

No more. Heartburn is not always caused by too much acid. It can occur in a full stomach as well as in one with nothing in it. Acid can "repeat," or reflux, back up to the esophagus, causing heartburn as you chew your food.

But acid can also build up when your system is empty, waiting for food; there is an overflow of digestive acids, or enzymes, that have been produced but have nothing to do.

In reality, there's very little stomach acid that really needs to be alkalized, or neutralized. Instead, those antacids alter the acid environment necessary for enzyme function, and the body then needs to produce even *more* acid.

• *Guided imagery.* This form of meditation involves a safe scenario—a valley, perhaps, or a beach or a meadow—where, eyes closed, you can let your mind wander and let your cares literally slip away for a few minutes. Whenever I can, I like to slip away to a nearby park where there is a beautiful arboretum. All I have to do is look at the open sky and the trees, and I calm down; I feel immediately at rest. When I do my imagery, this park is the place I conjure up; it calls up the peaceful contentment I feel when I actually visit.

• *Deep breathing.* Exactly like it sounds, this is deep, long breathing—counting to 5 as you breathe in through your nose, and counting to 5 as you breathe out through your mouth. You can either lie down or sit in a comfortable chair. As with meditation or guided imagery, your eyes should be closed. Performing this brief exercise once or twice a day, either in your office (with the door closed) or at home, can help you feel calm, strong, and in control of yourself.

• *Biofeedback.* This is designed to help you relax, but it is done via computer. Here you learn to recognize the times when your heartbeat accelerates or when your breathing becomes rapid so that you can control anxiety before it controls you.

WITH ADELE'S COMPLEMENTS!

There's something innate in us—something like one of those little devils that sits on one shoulder whispering in our ear: eat this, forget that, skip class, don't go to work. Thankfully, they're not whispers we heed every day. Most of the time, we like to think that the angel on our other shoulder is winning, that we are doing the best we can every single day.

But when life gets tough, when stress levels get high, the devil's voice gets louder. Just when we need the self-help most—the exercise, the massage, the relaxation breathing, the quiet time, the small little gift that will make us smile—we fight it. We don't do it.

As with the meditation that fell by the wayside when I was too busy, stopping the very things that can help you through a tough time is a common reaction. But it doesn't have to be that way. Just as I was reminded that the gnawing in my stomach could be relieved by the meditation I hadn't been doing, you too can realize that the good things you do for your health are not luxuries, not things to push away, but special rewards you can embrace. Let your self-help activities do their job: to help *you* be healthier, calmer, and more in control.

In all these natural therapies, there is one thing missing: *you*. Your needs. Your symptoms. Your history. Your present lifestyle. For complementary therapies to be most effective, they need specific clues from you, the patient and the healer. You need to believe in yourself and your ability to examine the clues and take action. You need to believe that you can prevent a symptom from becoming a condition. You need to believe that you can help your body heal itself, that you know your body and you can do what needs to be done to keep yourself well.

Yes, you need to know exactly what the complementary approach is. But you also need that human element. Call it the excitement of learning, an adventure into wellness. It's what my practice and my book are all about.

I believe that health, knowledge, *and* pleasure are positively and completely intertwined. Now, that's what I call empowerment.

But empowerment doesn't happen overnight. You cannot wish for empowerment: *you* have to make it happen. With every new fact you learn, every connection that you make, every snip of insight you incorporate into your life, you move further and further along. Soon, heeding your body's signals, understanding what it is saying, and knowing where its first cries are heard becomes second nature—and that's when true empowerment begins.

To help you on your quest for knowledge, you need to unravel the mystery of the body beautiful and see what makes it work. . . .

THE PRINCIPLES FOR HEALING FROM THE INSIDE: ALL IN ONE BOOK

Healing from the Inside is that "personal touch," helping you understand your unique body, its needs and its desires. Once you recognize the withdrawals you're making against your body's foundations—the gut and the liver, and your Body Bank as a whole—you can stop them and prevent your present conditions from coming back.

But there's still more to know before you can put on your Health Detective "badge." You need more clues—about what makes a healthy deposit, what culprits can turn out to be subtle and not-so-subtle withdrawals, and how each affects your body.

Let's start with the mysterious body beautiful.

THE BODY'S MYSTERIES REVEALED

When I had a cold, I thought head and nose. When I had a stiff knee, I thought leg. When I got a rash, I thought skin. No more. Now I know that every part of my body is connected, all the systems are joined. If I make a healthy deposit, it goes right to the source: my whole body.

> —A 52-year-old insurance broker whose chronic
>   shoulder pain eased after two months of healthy
>   deposits

Running was Danny's passion. As soon as he'd come home from work, he'd peel off his suit and tie, don a T-shirt and shorts, and slip into his well-worn running shoes. He'd gotten the routine down to five minutes.

Then he'd run. To the right, down his suburban street, to the nearby reservoir. No matter the weather—rain, freezing cold, snow, or relentless sun—nothing stopped Danny from running. He'd even run in a few local marathons—until the pain began.

Danny's sudden cross to bear was a severe stabbing pain that ran down the side of his leg. He'd already been to several general physicians, internists, neurologists, and orthopedists, and the response was always the same: we don't know why you are having trouble running. Everything appears fine. Your blood work shows nothing.

By the time he'd come to see me, Danny was in bad shape, both physically and mentally. He'd traded in his running hours for too-frequent naps on the couch. His running shoes were pushed to the back of his closet. He was pale and stressed out.

Worse, whenever he tried to jog after what he considered a sufficient amount of time off his feet, he still felt the horrible pain down the side of his leg. Five weeks had gone by since his last attempt to run and he was afraid to try again. He was afraid of the pain. He was afraid it would be there for good.

On his first visit to me, Danny showed me a well-worn snapshot. It depicted him wearing a number, racing past a crowd of cheering bystanders in the Boston Marathon. He was lean, sinuous, happy.

To help Danny *gain* empowerment and get back to that place—to where he was healthy, vigorous, a winner—we had to go into the past. We had to look beyond the running track to his family's history, their teachings and habits, which Danny learned and made his own. We had to learn exactly what had happened to Danny that led to his leg pain.

I remembered a discussion I'd once had with an acupuncturist colleague of mine. We were discussing how acupuncture is similar to the work I do with my clients. Both deal with ailments and areas of the body that do not seem to have any connection to one another, such as, in acupuncture, the elbow to the throat and lungs, the wrist to the heart, the leg to the kidneys and bladder. So leaving no stone unturned, I asked Danny about his bladder—whether he had pain when he urinated, if he had a frequent need to relieve himself.

Danny looked a bit puzzled, but what I asked hit home. Danny had some problems when he urinated, especially after he'd gone for a jog. He hadn't made the connection between his painful leg and his bladder, but I did.

As far as Danny was concerned, he now had two problems: leg pain *and* bladder irritation. Wrong. I sensed that they were not two separate conditions, which is why I asked him the questions I did. I suspected the bladder irritation was integrally connected to the pain in Danny's leg.

It isn't that astounding a stretch once you understand the links between the different parts of your body, once you see how one set of circumstances can lead to another. It simply takes learning and understanding.

With this all-important information, the mystery of Danny's leg was not difficult to understand. It was no longer obscure and the solution to his pain was not a dark, deep secret. The ball of his foot hit the concrete with every step he took as he ran. The pounding impact of his foot went up through the ankle, along the leg, to the kidneys and bladder. To most people, that particular route means nothing. But to those practiced in natural healing, it is fraught with meaning.

IN THE OLD DAYS

*Thousands upon thousands of persons have studied disease. Almost no
one has studied health.*   —Adele Davis, *Let's Eat Right to Keep Fit,* 1954

Acupuncturists know that the course, or meridian, that moves
from the ball of the foot, alongside the outside of the leg, then up
and inward to the back, kidneys, and bladder, is the important energy
zone of the kidneys and bladder. They know that if they place a nee-
dle at the meridian's source—the ball of the foot—it will affect the
kidneys and bladder.

By the time Danny had come to see me, the continuous assault from
his running had done its damage. As he himself discovered the more he
learned in our work together, his mileage kept him lean, at a price—
pain. The pounding he gave his body every time his foot hit the pave-
ment affected the bladder and kidney meridian: it became irritated from
the constant "hit." The bladder's reaction to this relentless assault was irritation, which in turn created the pain in Danny's leg, the "energy zone"
that started at the ball of his foot and traveled up his leg.

Danny was surprised at my connection, but he couldn't deny the
evidence. He felt that the pain had something to do with his running,
but he thought he had bruised, pulled, or injured his leg. But now he
realized that to understand a problem you have to trace it back to its
source. You have to follow the trail of clues your body leaves, the outward clues that tell you about the inward workings. As with any other
mystery, the signs are there if you only know where—and how—to look.

He agreed to try my remedies, which concentrated on soothing
the bladder and preventing the assault on his kidney and bladder's
meridian zone. I recommended parsley tea and corn silk to strengthen
and calm his abused bladder.

I also suggested that Danny start running on softer surfaces than concrete to decrease the pounding his body received. I told him, too, about
wearing cushioned socks to help absorb shock. These ongoing deposits
helped stop the assault on Danny's bladder, which in turn prevented the
constant irritation. The result? The pain is gone. Danny is running again,
vital and strong, and preparing himself for the next Boston Marathon.

B IS FOR BODY

Everything in your body is connected. There's the obvious mind and body connection. Then there are the less obvious connections—the energy zones we cannot see but that can create a healthy balance or, as in Danny's case, a jarring assault that can cause imbalance and pain. Finally, there are the links between the various biochemical processes in our body, the automatic functions of our various systems, and how they all depend on one another to work, to create a strong, sturdy foundation for the Body Bank to be built and stay solid.

In order to help you heal yourself, the connections in your body must be understood. You need to know how your body works—the mysteries it holds. Your body language can reveal all the clues you'll need to eventually make the right deposits for your life.

IN THE BEGINNING . . .

Unless you're a scientist or a nutritionist like me, you most likely think of denim when you hear the word *genes*. But for us body-oriented folks, *genes* immediately evokes deoxyribonucleic acid (DNA) and that beautiful red and blue double-rung ladder you stared at in Elementary Science.

The genes that determine the color of your eyes or the shape of your nose are within a section of a particular DNA molecule. So are the genes that govern the texture of your hair and the size of your foot. In other words, DNA makes you who you are. It holds your hereditary material, your strengths and weaknesses, the activities that go on within your countless cells.

Its structure, in scientific terms, is a double helix, or a twisted ladder. The genes provide the codes that tell various proteins to come together to perform a function, whether it be to take care of waste in the kidney or breath in the lungs, to join the "think tank" in the brain or look out at the world with perfect vision.

PROTEIN: THE STUFF OF LIFE

A secret of creation is revealed: Chains of amino acids join together to form proteins, which become specific cells. These cells, in turn, join

WITH ADELE'S COMPLEMENTS!

It's hard to imagine the inside of your body when you're putting on makeup or shaving in front of the mirror. But without a conscious thought from you, the different systems inside are working in concert, delivering oxygen-rich blood to your entire body, breaking down that breakfast you had before your first morning meeting into simpler substances. Food by-products and waste filter through your liver and kidneys so that around 11:00 you may begin to squirm in your seat, needing to relieve yourself. Then there are the digestive juices, rumbling in an empty stomach, telling you it's time for lunch.

There's more, so much more instinctive behavior—instinctive connections between symptoms that you need to survive: Your skin gets goose bumps from the cold; it's time to put on a sweater. Your immune system begins to fight off the germs from that coworker by the water fountain; she's sneezing away. Your endocrine system directs traffic, producing adrenaline (the boss wants to see you), estrogen (it's your time of the month), or digestive hormones such as insulin to help "devour" that candy bar withdrawal you just had to have.

All this and you haven't even given it a thought. Your heart beats faster when you see that attractive person walking down the street. The yawn signals it's time to sleep. The laugh starts deep in your belly, bringing with it a sense of peace.

Shakespeare said it best: "Oh, what a piece of work is man!"

together to become tissue. Tissue becomes a part of an organ, be it the heart, lung, or the folds of your skin. And the tissue becomes part of a vast whole—an entire system encompassing blood passageways, nerves, and functions. These systems—the circulatory, the central nervous system, the respiratory system, and more—make up the miracle called the human body. Your human body. All is connected, and all comes from the very first infinitesimal cell's DNA transmitted at inception.

The coded instructions contained in the DNA ladder do not give birth to your cells directly; a skin cell or a nerve cell does not spring immediately to life. Nor does it mean that your feet or hands magically appear like a bunny out of a hat. Instead, the instructions control the production of proteins, which are the ultimate building blocks of life. Every part of you, every tissue, every organ, gets its characteristics from protein. But these proteins themselves must be made.

Proteins begin life as small chemical units called amino acids. The DNA's coded instructions tell these amino acids to "get in line" in a certain order. The amino acids soon build up into a chain of proteins. Eventually, the coded instructions become reality: the type of protein they specifically call for is now intact, whether it be a protein that governs the curl of your eyelashes or one that determines the color of your hair.

Ultimately, depending on the original message, the chains of proteins join with others to become your eyes, your heart, your graceful movement in a dance.

HEREDITY VERSUS ENVIRONMENT: NOT EVERYTHING IS ETCHED IN STONE

Because of the "power" of that first cell, of genes at work, knowing your family history is crucial in determining your deposits and withdrawals. But heredity is only part of the picture. Although there is an almost infinite number of patterns, there are only twenty amino acids that get called into play when replicating DNA. Not every "switch" is turned on. You might have coded instructions to grow more hair on your face, for example, but that lies dormant, like an unplugged lamp, as other instructions gain control. In short, not all the messages encoded on DNA strands will be used.

But the switches can move from "off" to "on" if something triggers them. Research has shown that stress produces a "rush" of chemicals (or hormones) into the system. The chemicals in your brain, the compositions that are played, can swerve off course. A DNA strand that could cause illness can be ignited.

On the other hand, if you live a healthy life, making consistent deposits into your Body Bank, different—and beneficial—switches could be turned on. Perhaps the coded instructions for your immune system are made more powerful; although your heart and lungs were originally coded with a circulatory system "glitch," this glitch is not triggered. In short, heredity is not destiny; environment plays a strong role, too. You might not be able to make your brown eyes blue (without tinted contacts,

A PRESSURE PRIMER

The next time you have your blood pressure taken, you can know exactly what those numbers mean:

- The upper number is called *systolic pressure*. It reflects how forcefully blood is being pushed through your arteries by the contractions, or beats, of your heart.
- The lower number is called *diastolic pressure*. It reflects the amount of pressure your arteries feel in between beats, while the heart is resting.

A normal reading can be anywhere between 110/70 and 140/80. If you have a reading any higher, it's important to implement a blood pressure reduction program right away with your doctor's approval. You could have hypertension.

If your first reading is high, do not be alarmed. You could be suffering from "white jacket syndrome." This phrase was coined from the white jacket physicians wear when they see patients. It's normal to feel anxious when your doctor (in her white jacket) comes into the examination room. The result? Your blood pressure goes up—quickly. A second reading should be taken twenty minutes later, after you've had a chance to calm down.

that is), but you may be able to prevent a heart attack or emphysema by changing some habits, such as quitting smoking, beginning an exercise regimen, and eating a diet rich in fresh fruits and vegetables containing antioxidants.

THE DIFFERENT SYSTEMS OF THE BODY AND HOW THEY COME TOGETHER TO MAKE A WELL-RUN BANK

A wise sage once said that the whole is much greater than the sum of its parts. Nowhere is this more true than in the human body. It's time to leave the minute world of the cell and enter the bigger picture—the whole picture, in fact. Let's take a tour through your Body Bank building.

THE RESPIRATORY AND CIRCULATORY SYSTEMS:
"THE BRANCHES THAT PICK UP, STORE, AND DELIVER LIFE"

Blood is much more than a prop in a horror movie. Every cell in our body depends on it. Red blood cells travel through the body via a series of arteries, providing the oxygen and other nutrients that every organ needs to survive. When the cells are satiated from their "meal," they need to get rid of their waste products. The blood circulating in the veins takes care of "the remains."

The main branch of the Body Bank for this blood is the heart, a hard, feisty muscle that's no bigger than a fist. Pressure from the heart forces the blood out into the body. This is how we get blood pressure readings.

Although we receive many of our nutrients through the food we eat (and I'll be talking about the digestive system next), we also receive necessary nourishment from our lungs and our hearts. Thus, the respiratory and the circulatory systems work hand-in-hand. They "meet" deep within the recesses of the lungs: When we breathe in oxygen-rich air, it journeys to the lungs via the bronchial tubes. Here it comes into contact with oxygen-depleted blood that is waiting for a "pickup." Oxygen from the freshly inhaled air is exchanged for the carbon dioxide waste in this blood. Then, as quickly as you can say "exhale," the now oxygen-rich blood travels back to the heart via the bloodstream.

Infection can occur in the bronchial tubes, interfering with breathing and the body's supply of oxygen. Smoking, for example—a major Body Bank withdrawal—can eventually destroy the tiny air sacs in the lungs, to the point that the "exchange rate" between oxygen and carbon dioxide becomes imbalanced.

If a person doesn't have a terrific diet (another walloping withdrawal), the heart receives a double hit. Pressure can build up because the artery walls can become clogged with fatty plaque. The heart itself might be working too hard if, for example, you are struggling with obesity (another major withdrawal). Circulation becomes sluggish. The heart has to go into overdrive to deliver already poorly oxygenated blood to your body's cells.

But healthy deposits can change this equation. The heart can remain strong via aerobic exercise. You can eat healthy foods, low in fat and rich in other nutrients, and you can stay away from cigarettes.

And speaking of nutrients, let's take a "lunch break" on our tour and visit . . .

THE DIGESTIVE AND URINARY SYSTEMS:
THE BRANCHES WITH THE BEST RETURN ON YOUR
DEPOSITED INVESTMENT, WITH A MINIMUM OF WASTE

The food we eat provides us with the nutrients we need to live. Nutrients—the components of food—are broken down during the digestive process and are used for energy, growth, tissue repair, and ongoing cell function, among other things. In short, nutrients enable us to survive and thrive. The nutrients we consume, in both food and supplements, are a primary Body Bank deposit.

When people hear the words *digestion* and *elimination*, they usually think stomach and rectum. But the digestive system is much more involved than this; it includes complex biochemical processes and a variety of organs. It also depends on the workings of the other systems, such as the circulatory system, to help deliver its "goods."

Let's take a simple apple spread with peanut butter and follow it through this Body Bank branch:

You take a bite of that delicious, crisp apple and crunchy peanut butter, chewing it with your teeth, which grind that bite down into smaller and smaller sections. The hard chewing and the presence of the food increase saliva production, which helps to liquefy the food and start the breakdown of carbohydrates in the apple and peanut butter. That almost liquid bite passes through the esophagus to the stomach. Here, digestion really "digs in." Gastric juice, produced by the gastric glands in the stomach's lining, tackles that apple with a relish—literally. In this case, it's not Heinz but digestive enzymes like pepsin that get the gastric juices going. Once the gastric juices have done their jobs, that juicy bite of apple smeared with peanut butter will start to become a simpler carbohydrate, glucose.

But there's still more "breaking up" to do. The onetime bite of apple and spread leaves the stomach and travels to the small intestine. Here, the unrecognizable piece of fruit mixture gets a "hit" of bile that's produced by the liver and stored in the gallbladder. This bile breaks up fats. Soon, the breakdown is complete, and glucose, among other nutrients, waits to be transported by the circulatory system throughout the body. While these nutrients are sent to the cells of your Body Bank, undigested particles, including fiber and waste, are pushed through the large intestine. The waste is stored in the lower colon and, eventually, passes out through the rectum as stool.

Urea, a waste product made from the breakdown of amino acids, goes a different route. It travels to the kidneys (which regulate body fluid content and levels) along with other waste products, including creatinine, excess water, and excess minerals, where it is eventually passed through the bladder as urine.

The entire digestive-urinary system is a potential place for withdrawals from the Body Bank to take place. In fact, the gut and the liver may be the silent villains behind most symptoms that have made you *bankrupt*. Consistent, cumulative deposits in the liver and the gut are so important to a healthy Body Bank.

THE SKIN (INTEGUMENTARY) AND SKELETAL SYSTEMS: THE "BARE BONES" BRANCHES

The skeleton is what you have left when the organs and other systems of the body are stripped away. It is the structural framework for the body, protecting important organs and working with the muscles to make it possible for you to walk, run, jump, or simply drum your fingers. Bones might be hard, but they are live cells—tissues made of calcium and other minerals. Tendons hold muscle and bone together, and connective tissue called ligaments join whole sections, such as the knee to the leg.

Skin, on the other hand, is the protective surface of your body—the very first layer you show the world. (Well, not *exactly*. My world, and most likely yours, usually sees coats, sweaters, turtlenecks, scarves, and maybe a necklace or two draping that skin.) But however we cover it up, skin is crucial for our good health. It is composed of three layers, the uppermost layer actually made of tough, dead cells. Skin tissue becomes harder and "old" as it grows from the lower depths to the top. In fact, we shed these dead skin cells continuously, day in and day out, as new cells take their place. Skin helps to:

- Protect organs from damage
- Regulate body temperature
- Excrete toxic waste in the form of sweat
- Produce vitamin D, which contributes to a strong skeletal structure

SOME TIES THAT BIND

Those who discover the concept know that the Body Bank doesn't stand alone, that its branches are connected not only in health but also in *running in the red* symptoms. Here are some examples:

- If, while you are under stress, your adrenal glands produce too much adrenaline, your immune system can become weakened. This can deplete your body of important nutrients and cause stress-related conditions.
- If you don't have the right proportion of substances in your gastrointestinal tract, your body may not be able to carry out its digestive breakdown job effectively. The result can be partially undigested food that eventually seeps out of the intestines into the bloodstream, possibly causing toxins to affect your muscles and joints, your liver, and your skin.
- If the right hormones are not triggered in the brain, you might exhibit unusual behavior. You might not be able to do such simple tasks as adding 2 and 2 or getting from your house to work. Your personality might change; you can become moody and depressed, even violent. For messages to be carried to the parts of the brain that order a specific action, electrical impulses that are triggered by these hormones must be able to move. If your endocrine system is not up to par (which may be linked to a digestive system that is not providing the nutrients your body needs), these hormones will not be released. The pathways in your brain stay inert and messages are not delivered.

THE ENDOCRINE AND REPRODUCTIVE SYSTEMS:
THE BRANCHES WITH ALL THE CONTROL

Hormones are the powers behind the throne, the assistants CEOs would be lost without, the silent partners in a business venture. Hormones are, in actuality, chemical messengers that trigger specific activities in the body. The various glands that make up the endocrine and reproductive systems stimulate their production:

- The adrenal glands, located near the kidneys, are part of the endocrine system and produce hormones that are crucial in the "fight-or-flight" response. Long ago, when tigers jumped out of trees, when wild boars sprang from the bushes, when warring tribes ambushed without warning, the "fight-or-flight" response was a necessity. The hormones produced by the adrenal glands made the heart race, the breath come faster, the blood vessels constrict. The body was primed and ready to fight—or flee as fast as possible. As soon as primitive people responded or the danger passed, the rush of adrenaline would subside; the physiological changes would return to normal and the glands would quiet down.

Today, however, the closest we probably come to a tiger is the one in the corner office, and these heightened physiological processes can do more harm than good. The stress we feel on an ongoing basis, from financial worries to downsizing to aging parents, keeps the adrenal glands "pumped." Eventually, the eroding effects of stress are felt throughout the body. In short, you run down and develop a condition—unless you have made some healthy deposits in your Body Bank.

• The pituitary gland plays a pivotal role in the reproductive system. Without the hormones secreted by the pituitary gland, a woman's menstrual cycle would be irregular; she might not ovulate, creating infertility, or she might have an inability to nurse if she did get lucky enough to give birth.

The reproductive systems of men, too, are affected by hormonal activity. Testosterone, which is produced in the testes and is partially regulated by the hypothalamus in the brain and by the pituitary gland, helps keep sperm fertile. As men age, testosterone can become more active, changing to dihydrotestosterone (DHT), which can lead to an enlarged prostate and prostatitis.

Here's a tip: The pituitary gland produces adrenocorticotropic hormone (ACTH), a hormone that helps set the digestive process in motion in the liver. It also triggers the thyroid into producing thyroid-stimulating hormone (TSH), which, in turn, helps regulate metabolism, growth, and heart rate. The pituitary gland also stimulates the production of its *own* hormone, somatotropic hormone (STH), which triggers the growth of tissue and muscle.

So if your pituitary gland goes out of whack, it can also mean that your adrenal glands or your thyroid won't work efficiently, which in addition to affecting your tissues, muscles, and metabolism can affect your immune system. Combine this with a liver that's congested and a digestive system that's not up to par, and you can end up with a destructive, endless cycle of imbalance.

Think of a pebble that hits a still pond. The ripples reverberate, the circles growing bigger and bigger. The connection between hormonal secretion and your body is very much like that pond: one disturbance can create far-reaching ripples. Happily, deposits, too, can have far-reaching—but healthier—effects.

THE NERVOUS SYSTEM: THE BRANCH THAT "MINDS THE STORE"

If you thought the brain stood alone, "heads" above all the others, think again. In order for the brain to receive, assimilate, store, and respond to stimuli from the outside world, the message must get there. Whether it's a scene, a smell, a touch, or a sound that starts the ball rolling, it's the combination of bursts of electrical charges and chemical impulses that moves the message along. And once again, it's hormones that trigger the entire event.

The next time you smile at the face of someone you love, remember that the burst of joy in your heart, the flush of color on your cheeks, the rapid heartbeat, and the rush of memories in your cerebral cortex are all brought to you by hormones. What better reason to keep those healthy deposits coming?

THE IMMUNE AND LYMPHATIC SYSTEMS:
THE BRANCHES WITH THE SECRET PASSWORDS

The immune system is basically a "mixed bag" of cells; organs, especially the spleen, which keep an emergency store of germ-fighting red and white blood cells; glands, such as the lymph glands and the thymus gland; and blood vessels that ward off foreign viruses and bacteria.

But the switch that ignites the spleen, the thymus in the brain, and the lymph nodes to produce, store, and transport "fighter cells" is dependent on those chemical messengers, hormones. An imbalance in the body, especially the gut or the liver, can upset that balance, keeping a messenger asleep or making him work too hard. Either way, the immune system is compromised and your Body Bank account becomes *bankrupt.* You might wind up with asthma, depression, an ulcer, arthritis, a skin rash, or Epstein-Barr virus.

The first wealth is health. Sickness is poor-spirited, and cannot serve any one; it must husband its resources to live. But health . . . runs over, and inundates the neighborhoods and creeks of other men's necessities.

—Ralph Waldo Emerson, *The Conduct of Life,* 1860

There is good news: Your immune system grows stronger with every sip of vegetable soup, every bite of apple, every forkful of salad, every yoga posture, and every swallow of nutritional supplements. Each time you make those health deposits, you are working on restoring homeostasis, the stable internal environment—the ultimate body balance.

The tour of the Body Bank building is now complete. You've been introduced to the mysteries that lurk inside and you've learned one basic fact: All the systems are related; all depend on the others; all need to be balanced for good health.

By learning how to "read" your body and your Body Bank account, you are on your way to making the concepts of *Healing from the Inside* yours to keep. You are becoming empowered—and starting to *reclaim your health, vitality, and energy through knowledge.*

But to ensure that you put health deposits in and do not deplete your Body Bank account with too many withdrawals, you need to know what's right for you—and what's been wrong.

Knowledge must be used for true empowerment. You must delve beyond the facts and use what you have learned to solve your own body's mysteries, to determine what your symptoms are trying to tell you, to know what deposits and withdrawals have been affecting your health. In the next chapter, I'll show you how to be your own Health Detective so you can review your own personal history. Soon you'll be making positive changes and reaping the empowering, glowing, energized rewards!

Section II

LEARN HOW TO SOLVE YOUR OWN MYSTERY

3

THE CONTRIBUTING
HEALTH CLUES

I not only feel better than I ever have in my life, but I tracked down my problems myself. I did it. Me!
—A 25-year-old student who has recently learned to ease the symptoms of his longtime chronic fatigue in a new way

For just a moment, I'd like you to imagine yourself someplace else: my office. I'd like you to pretend that you are there with me, sitting in the comfortable armchair across from me or leaning back on my leather couch.

I smile and welcome you.

You smile back, but it's hard. Maybe you are nervous, about to begin some changes in the way you live and the way you eat. It isn't a completely comforting thought. You may have been in pain a long while or suffering from an ailment that just won't go away. But still, change is never easy. And what if this doesn't work?

And yet, you have no energy. Perhaps you're depressed. Or maybe it's the medicines for your allergies that just don't work, despite the rounds of specialists you've seen and the potions you've downed that have left you drowsy.

I see it in your eyes: you don't know what else to do. You don't know where to turn or what will ever help. I've seen it countless times, in many clients, and I am filled with compassion. But I'm also filled with determination.

We can work together, you and I. It will take some time. And it will take some changes. But it will be worth it. We can work to find out what ails you and maybe stop it in its tracks.

I'm not proposing that I have all the answers, that there is a "quick fix" to heal your pain. But as I would tell you if you were sitting right here in my office, with the sun filtering through the blinds, I will help educate you. I will help provide solid, easy-to-understand information. I will help you *help yourself.*

I take out a pad and pen and hand it to you. You are ready to write. You are ready to begin your Health Detective work. You are ready to learn.

Let's begin.

THE SECRET'S OUT

By now you should begin to understand the basics of your body structure, the Body Bank concept, and the different arenas that make up natural remedies. But information like this can take you only so far. To truly grasp the importance of empowerment in your search for a healthy life, you need to delve even deeper. Action, not passivity, is key. Rather than depending on lists of herbs, supplements, and homeopathic remedies, I rely on finding connections, some subtle, some intricate, some as plain as the light of day.

How do you find these connections? Simple. You put into action the concepts from Section II, "Learn How to Solve Your Own Mystery," and become the Health Detective.

It's a role that is completely interactive, involving both my experience and your desire to solve the mystery of your ailments. By learning how to sift through the clues, by checking the facts and asking the right questions, you too can become a top-notch detective. By looking below the surface, as I always do, to examine the links between your different systems and your different symptoms, you can see your condition in a completely new light. And you just might find peace, discovering the real root of your problem and dealing with it once and for all.

The way to start at home is identical to the way we would begin if you were visiting my office. In person, we would examine your symptoms and complaints. I'd explain my Body Bank concept. I would help

---

BANK S-TELLARS

The doctor of the future will give no medicine, but will interest his patients in the care of the human frame, in diet, and in the cause and prevention of disease.   —Thomas Edison

---

you understand that the deposits and withdrawals you choose will affect your good health and vigor, and that your present ailment is most likely an accumulation of years of withdrawal, of *running in the red.* At home, you will have me within these pages, explaining all this as if we were face-to-face. The more you read, the more you will begin to see that you, *yes, you,* can be in control of your body, your health, and your life.

And the first place to start your Health Detective work is with these withdrawals, which are outlined on the "application form" that follows.

THE APPLICATION FORM

Take out your own pad and pen, or simply write the answers on these next few pages. This is your Body Bank "application form," and it has three components:

- Everyday environment and inherited lifestyle
- Diet
- Genealogy and personal medical history

These three elements make up the areas of your life where possible withdrawals have been made—with or without your knowledge. And any withdrawals in these areas are cumulative: they add up to an account that begins *running in the red,* possibly creating the *leaky gut* and a *toxic liver* (which will be covered in depth as Chapters 6 and 7). If you do not start adding deposits at this point, you will receive more and more notices of *running in the red*—symptoms of fatigue, headaches, aches, pains, and more. Ultimately, you may become *bankrupt*—when these symptoms become actual conditions, whether they be arthritis, sinusitis, or athlete's foot.

That's why it's important to be accurate on your application form. Take the time to give thoughtful consideration to each area. Read the explanations and examine the questions I ask. Use them as a spring-board for seeing other withdrawals you've made. You're learning a new way to look at your body and your ailments. Remember, there's no right or wrong answer. There's only information and reasons. Your good health awaits!

PART ONE: EVERYDAY ENVIRONMENT AND INHERITED LIFESTYLE
Like the gambling father who runs through the family's money, your family's habits can affect you without your having done a thing. It's not just a matter of genetics. We also inherit a lifestyle and an eating style (like my love of chocolate chip cookies) that, later in life, produces a not-always-welcome end product, a condition that many of us think "came out of the blue." Wrong. That first withdrawal, made either before you were born or in your infancy, set a precedent for withdrawals from your Body Bank—ones that can continue to pile up until you become ill or until you start making some healthy deposits.

Unless you have studied science and nutrition, you probably didn't know that you might have begun your withdrawals during those days in the womb, or that the sugary foods you have eaten mirror the way your mother ate, compelling you to continue a cycle of *running in the red* symptoms that will ultimately *bankrupt* your good health. I can understand. Before I began my research, I would never have made a connection between my love of chocolate chip cookies and my throat problems.

Astonishing, but that's the way things can happen. It's hard to believe that when you get that athlete's foot in your twenties, those recurring yeast infections, the itchy rash, they could be connected to your early introduction to a sweet, high-starch diet or to just passing through your mother's yeast-rich birth canal. It might seem extraordinary, but there is indeed a direct line from *A* to *Z*.

Here's an example of inherited lifestyle; it shows how mother and child can be physically attached long after birth: One of my clients, a thin man in his early thirties named Jake, had restless leg syndrome. He'd shake his leg or tap his foot incessantly while working, while eating, while conversing. He couldn't stop, even when someone told him that he seemed nervous or that his leg was making the table shake. He would always shrug; he thought it was just a habit, something he always did. We began the task of the Health Detective and, through our dis-

WITH ADELE'S COMPLEMENTS!

We never like to say good-bye to old friends. But sometimes these friends are enemies in disguise, ready to sabotage our good health and vitality. You might miss that cigarette in the beginning, that once-a-day burger and fries, that drunken spree, but remember that it's only temporary. These things aren't good for you. They are the despots of withdrawals, the knaves who will keep you down and relish your fall.

Instead, fight them. Stand up to them. Choose health. Believe it or not, their power will soon disappear. They will be seen for what they are: weak, spineless habits.

Saying good-bye to your enemies is the single most powerful deposit you can make. Turn to health, to prevention. That's celebrating life.

cussion, Jake began to identify his problem. He recalled that his mother suffered from aches and pains in her joints. She suffered countless headaches, had a history of kidney stones, and could never seem to get a good night's sleep. Jake's mother didn't have a "shaky leg," but the investigator in me felt that those aches and pains, those headaches and those sleepless nights, could be directly connected to his "shaky leg."

If Jake didn't pay attention to the fact that his mother had had kidney stones, owing to her inability to keep calcium in solution in her body, he could wind up with them, too. He needed to concern himself with the possibility that he had inherited a predisposition to this condition, something to which he'd given little thought until now, when he began his Health Detective work.

Jake's symptoms could also be linked to this metabolic malfunction, which usually creates a calcium-magnesium imbalance. In addition to strengthening bones, calcium and magnesium are needed for proper muscle contraction and relaxation.

Why the imbalance in mother and son? Jake, like his mother, drank too much diet soda, which, thanks to the phosphorus in every sip, helped deplete his calcium reserves. They also shared a dislike for green vegetables, such as calcium-rich kale and magnesium-rich salad greens, and the only time Jake went near dairy foods was for ice cream. No wonder his mother's restless muscles created those sleepless nights, and he also had muscles that knew no rest. Even worse, without the right amount of magnesium being absorbed and with too much phosphorus, a metabolic malfunction went into action and the little calcium received wasn't properly absorbed.

The withdrawals had been piling up for Jake and he hadn't even been aware of them! Worse, a calcium-magnesium imbalance could eventually lead from his *running in the red* symptoms of restless leg syndrome and fatigue to *bankruptcy*: kidney stones or osteoporosis.

But Jake's story has a happy ending. As soon as Jake made some deposits to his Body Bank, cutting back on his diet soda and repairing the damage by adding vitamin B_6, calcium-magnesium supplements, and fresh foods, his leg stopped shaking—for good.

If you answer yes to any of the following questions, you might have inherited an unhealthy lifestyle and daily routine along with your eye color.

1. Do you find yourself reaching for starchy, sugary food when you are emotionally upset, just as your mother or father did? _____
   _____

2. Were artificial sweeteners considered a staple in your household?
   _____

3. Were your meals a ho-hum routine, always the same color, mostly brown and white, and always overcooked, leaving you without proper nutrients? _____
   _____

4. Was your family's idea of outdoor exercise a Sunday drive in the car? _____
   _____

5. Do diet foods filled with chemicals accompany every lunch and dinner, and you always find yourself running out to get more?
   _____

6. Do you stay up half the night watching old movies, while munching on greasy potato chips, depriving yourself of the sleep necessary for cell repair? _____
   _____

7. Have you always needed a glass of orange juice every morning at breakfast for that "hit" to get you going, and without it you find yourself dragging your heels? _____
   _____

8. Do you continue that family tradition of having a daily cocktail and crackers and cheese, instead of dinner? _____

  _____

9. Would you consider either one of your parents depressed, not sleeping enough, or sleeping too much? _____

  _____

10. Were salads a boring chunk of iceberg lettuce and thick, creamy dressings at dinner while you were growing up? _____

  _____

Whether they are things you learned as a child by watching and imitating your parents or things you've gravitated to as you grew up, poor sleep habits, irregular eating patterns, and a sedentary lifestyle all come with a "negative credit report." But like real credit, your good health can be repaired with the right deposits in your Body Bank account.

PART TWO: DIET

A high-fat diet, usually containing a lot of artery-clogging saturated fats and simple sugars, is easily learned at our mother's knee, or later at school, at the office, or around the dinner table. (Do you love chocolate chip cookies, too?) The high amount of fat we consume can eventually overwhelm the mechanics necessary for proper digestion. Other effects? Blocked arteries, obesity, a straining heart, and undigested toxins that build up over time, helping to create those *running in the red* conditions, a *leaky gut* and a *toxic liver*.

But whether inherited or marked by habits begun after years of watching food ads on TV, your diet can play havoc with your Body Bank account. If you don't get the nutrients your body needs, your cells can weaken. Your immune system can be compromised. Your hormones won't be stimulated correctly. In fact, your entire body may well be unbalanced. That old wives' tale about an apple a day keeping the doctor away was prophetic!

If you answered yes to any of the above questions, your diet needs some healthy deposits—fast.

Here are the questions for part two of the application:

1. Do you drink several grande-size espresso lattes a day, with such a "hit" of caffeine that you can deplete your body of calcium and weaken your bones? _____

  _____

THE FRAMINGHAM STUDY:
YOU CAN CHANGE YOUR LIFE

For over twenty-five years, scientists have been researching the citizens of Framingham, Massachusetts. They've already discovered that the risk factors of coronary heart disease (CHD) are almost all based on habits. Yes, bad habits—a dangerous withdrawal that you can change into a health deposit:

- Cigarette smoking
- Sedentary lifestyle
- Too much stress
- Obesity
- Elevated cholesterol
- Diabetes
- High blood pressure

Granted, you cannot control your genetic makeup. But with quitting smoking, a proper diet that's rich in fiber and low in fat, and an active lifestyle, you can reduce your chances of developing not only CHD itself, but many of these risk factors!

2. Do you skip breakfast, ordering in a muffin or a bagel and butter at work, leaving yourself in a weakened, aggravated, low-blood-sugar state? _____

3. Do you consider a rare steak, onion rings, salad with blue cheese dressing, and homemade pie a fabulous—and frequent—night out? _____

4. Do you not have a clue when it comes to where you can buy organic fruits and vegetables in your neighborhood? _____

5. Do you use potentially contaminated tap water to fill your ice cube trays, make coffee and tea, or make soup? _____

6. Do you feel a salad is only edible when you add chunks of cheese, ham, or oil-drenched croutons, and top it off with a thick, creamy dressing, with just a few shreds of carrots for a garnish? _____

7. Does your idea of fresh fruit include only watermelon in the summer and a few apples in the fall? _____

_____

8. Do you only like your fish swimming in a bowl with a plastic palm tree, passing up the essential fatty acids you could get if you ate the real thing? _____

_____

9. Did you stop taking vitamin-mineral supplements when you graduated from those fruit-flavored, critter-shaped, chewable tablets for kids, relying instead on deficient foods to protect you from a toxic environment? _____

_____

10. Do you eat the same foods over and over again, even straight from the fridge, never giving yourself the variety of nutrients you'd find if you tried something fresh and new? _____

_____

Examining your diet in black and white makes it easy to see where you've gone wrong. When you're eating almost unconsciously, out of habit, day in and day out, you might not realize that you're not getting the nutrients you need. Maybe you didn't realize that you were missing out on salads or fresh fruits, or that fish came in forms other than tuna in a can. A poor diet can easily be rectified, however, with the proper healthy "bites."

PART THREE: GENEALOGY AND PERSONAL MEDICAL HISTORY
This is the portion of the application form that is the most universal, with questions you'd hear at the first visit to a doctor's office or on an insurance questionnaire. Of course, personal medical history involves heredity. Genes are in place as the fetus begins to grow. Immune systems are determined by genetic patterns. *But you can change certain factors.* Not everything is etched in stone. You might have a predisposition, thanks to heredity, but with consistent healthy deposits to your Body Bank that predisposition might never be triggered.

As you will soon see, your diet may be almost as responsible for your hair loss as the genetic code you were born with. You will learn that your debilitating, cranky fatigue may be the result of an inherited lifestyle and not part of your individual makeup. And, most important, you'll find out that you've been making too many withdrawals from your Body Bank account and that you have to make a deposit soon. But don't despair if you answer yes to any of the questions that follow. After all, you're starting to see your symptoms in a totally new way, as you become your own Health Detective, changing your so-called destiny and your unhealthy path.

If you answer yes to any of the following questions and make the appropriate changes as you go through this book, you can be the *first* in your family to stop making unhealthy withdrawals from the Body Bank. And remember: like cash in the bank, health deposits begin to work immediately!

1. Have you taken antibiotics for bacterial infections, never replenishing the "good bacteria" that got wiped out as well? _____
   _____

2. Did either of your parents develop late-onset diabetes, following a lifetime of sugary, starchy eating? _____
   _____

3. Does anyone in your immediate family take high blood pressure medication? _____
   _____

4. Does nervous energy seem to run in your family, resulting in a lot of stress-driven colds, flus, and fatigue? _____
   _____

5. Do you have a high cholesterol or high triglyceride count, and still eat those french fries like they were candy? _____
   _____

6. Is your hair beginning to thin at an unusually young age? _____
   _____

7. Could your whole family stand to lose more than a few pounds?
   _____

8. Do you break out in a rash whenever you eat strawberries or shellfish, making you a bona fide member of your family? _____
   _____

9. Does asthma keep appearing in your family tree? _____
   _____

10. As you get older, do you find it more difficult to digest raw vegetables, forcing you to carry a roll of antacids in your pocket just in case? (Not yet your father's ulcers, but getting there.) _____
    _____

11. Did your parents travel extensively, bringing back a surprise package of parasites along with the T-shirts, beads, and souvenir globes that fill with snow? _____

_____

GO NO FARTHER THAN YOUR BATHROOM SHELF

There's a clue that you might have a deficiency of selenium, and it's called dandruff. If you suffer from the flakes, one reason can be a lack of selenium in your diet. Just look at the label on your dandruff shampoo. One of the major ingredients is selenium.

Genetic codes can be broken. Many of your predispositions can be left in the dust if you change your eating habits, if you lose some weight, if you go to a health practitioner to be checked for possible parasite contamination.

That's it. You've completed an application form to open your Body Bank account. If you've answered yes to any of these questions (or have thought of similar ones that apply to you), it's possible that:

- Your digestive system is dealing with an excess of toxins (that ubiquitous *leaky gut*), which are leaking into your bloodstream and creating a variety of symptoms, from fatigue to aches and pains, irritability to nausea.
- Your liver is overburdened and cannot perform its detoxification process properly. Hormonal imbalance, a *leaky gut*, and a glut of high-fat, sugary food hinder its ability to strain the toxins from the nutrients in the foods you consume.
- You have an excess of yeast and a depletion of important enzymes, amino acids, and nutrients essential to proper digestion and good health.
- Your withdrawals have led to any number of *bankruptcy* conditions, affecting every system in your body, from respiratory problems to allergies, from heart trouble to depression.

ADELE'S OWN HOME SHOPPING NETWORK

Here are some new products and household tips that focus on food safety. You might want to try them.

- You can find a recent addition to your regular cleansers on your supermarket shelf. This one is made from baking soda and citric acid. It scrubs away chemicals and dirt from tomatoes and potatoes more effectively than plain water.
- Gone are the days of the damp, moldy sponge, which salmonella and other bacteria love. There are now specially treated sponges designed to kill those nasty germs before they hit the dish.
- Many of our kitchen cleansers contain powerful petrochemicals that can be toxic. To avoid chemicals in your food, on your counters, or mixing with the delicious aromas of cooking, try natural cleaners such as baking soda for scouring and vinegar and water for cleaning your kitchen windows.

But help is on the way. A good Health Detective does more than solve a problem. He or she points out the withdrawals you are making and the deposits you need to make to build your health and exceptional wellness. Only then will you be in charge of your life, able to recognize your *own* symptoms and make your *own* choices.

Here's a sampling from my "A-Files":

WITHDRAWALS *WILL* CATCH UP WITH YOU

Some account withdrawals are easy to recognize. Too much drinking. Smoking. Too much high-fat, sugary, starchy food. Burning the candle at both ends. We all know these lifestyle habits have a cumulative effect. We know they hurt your body. Think of them as the megawithdrawals, the cold cash you take out even though you know you're going to go way into debt.

Just stopping these habits—or even cutting back—is enormously healthy and a move your Body Bank will thank you for in the years to come.

But there are other withdrawals, ones that are more difficult to determine. These are the ones that separate a rookie Health Detective from an experienced professional. Here are a few surprising withdrawals for you to think about, some you inadvertently make and some that are being made for you, but they are all ones you can easily stop, too.

SUBTLE WITHDRAWAL 1: SELENIUM WHO?

The soil that bears your food used to contain selenium, a hardworking cancer fighter. Unfortunately, today's fields, especially in the Northeast, have been overused and ill-treated, resulting in soil that can be sorely depleted of selenium—and other minerals, for that matter. Onions and garlic, for example, are considered two powerful natural antibiotics. But without enough selenium in the soil, they may not contain the substances that make them so healthy. In order to get the nutrients that are missing from your fruits and vegetables because they were grown in depleted soil, you have to go to supplements. Make sure you get the selenium you need on a daily basis in capsules or tablets. (See page 92 for my Basic Health Regimen for Vitality and Well-Being.)

SUBTLE WITHDRAWAL 2: DANGEROUS FOOD

The foods you eat—from beef to fish—can be filled with antibiotics or pesticides. Unless foods are officially labeled "free-range" or "organic," toxins can be absorbed, build up, and filter through your vulnerable gastrointestinal tract (the *leaky gut* again!), sneaking into your body and creating debilitating symptoms.

But food safety is more than purchasing cleaner meats and produce. It also involves preparation. There are many things you can do to keep your food—and your health—squeaky clean. You can remove many surface toxins by scrubbing fruits and vegetables carefully with pure vegetable soap and a clean brush.

Unfortunately, proper cleansing is not the only issue. Grilling foods at such high temperatures that they can become burned, thereby releasing carcinogens in those burgers, vegetable kabobs, or barbecued ribs, is a danger, too. Even if you opt for stovetop cooking, danger might lurk in the very pots you use to heat the sauce or the soup. Stainless steel, glass, and iron are the best materials for cookware. Aluminum can be particularly damaging. Acidy foods such as tomato soup can absorb some aluminum from the pot. When you eat this "tainted" soup, the aluminum is absorbed by your body, which eventually can accumulate in the brain. In fact, studies have shown that there is a relationship between Alzheimer's disease and excess aluminum in the body.

Tap water, too, can contain pesticides, parasites, and bacteria. Studies have even found traces of arsenic! Water can also contain chlorine, which is potentially helpful but may do more harm than good. Although chlorine kills "bad bacteria" in the water, it can also be carcinogenic.

You might feel good about getting in your eight glasses of water a day, but if you're getting it along with high bacterial counts, you'll need a team of biochemists to determine all the types of toxins that may exist in just one sip. "Tainted" tap water can compromise the immune system, introducing toxins into an unsuspecting gut. It can literally poison your system. A better bet is to make a healthy deposit by drinking certified bottled or filtered water.

SUBTLE WITHDRAWAL 3: THE S-FACTOR

Stress uses up a lot of energy, and not just from the soul. Ask anyone interviewing for a new job, auditioning for a role, or breaking up a relationship. In addition to using psychic energy, stress depletes your supply of calcium, vitamin C, zinc, magnesium, and other brain food needed for good health. Deficiencies of these nutrients, in turn, can affect your entire body, particularly your immune system—the only "insurance carrier" your Body Bank has.

SUBTLE WITHDRAWAL 4: YEAST ON THE RISE

You can wind up with allergies, jock itch, athlete's foot, and digestive disturbances when there is excessive yeast in your system. Taking antibiotics kills off the "good bacteria"—which provides the perfect environment for yeast to proliferate. Eating a starchy, high-sugar diet encourages yeast growth. This excess yeast and other substances start accumulating on the mucosal walls of your small intestine, ready to break through and leak undigested toxins into your cells, creating that "over the top" withdrawal: the *leaky gut*. (And I'll be discussing this at length in Chapter 6.)

SUBTLE WITHDRAWAL 5: PRESERVE FURNITURE, NOT FOOD

You might feel virtuous when you drink a "lite" juice or low-fat frozen dinner, but you're withdrawing "cold cash" just the same. A main preservative in processed foods, sodium benzoate, creates extra excretion work for the liver, contributing to *running in the red* and *toxic liver*, and ultimately causing a whole slew of *bankruptcy* conditions.

SUBTLE WITHDRAWAL 6: REPLACEMENT PRICE

When you decide to do hormone replacement therapy (HRT) during menopause, you might avoid the hot flashes, the mood swings, and the flushing, but you lose something in the process. HRT's estrogen may be linked to increased rates of ovarian and breast cancer, as well as greater risk of developing lupus. Synthetic estrogen can have the added risk of interfering with the body's metabolism. It is not as easily broken down as natural estrogen and it can accumulate in the gut, causing liver congestion and, in turn, such *bankruptcies* as high blood pressure and edema. Studies have also linked estrogen to an increased risk of blood clots in the veins and gallstones.

Research has shown that progesterone and estrogen combined can be more beneficial than estrogen alone. Using natural progesterone cream not only relieves some of the symptoms of menopause but actually increases the production of natural estrogen. That's a wonderful example of turning a withdrawal into a long-term deposit!

DEPOSITS MEAN GOOD HEALTH

If your withdrawals seem to be adding up on your application form, don't despair. You can correct most damage to your Body Bank account with a few well-placed health deposits. You don't have to be a detective to figure out some of them: fresh fruits and vegetables, fiber-rich food, lean proteins, sensible meals at sensible times.

But there are other deposits that might not be as clear-cut. Think of them as the "new venture investments" or "soy futures." These are a few of the obvious—and not so obvious—health deposits that I recommend, ones that have helped many of my clients. Remember, with the right motivation and commitment, they can work well. The sooner you start making these healthy deposits, the sooner you'll start to experience the benefits!

HEALTH DEPOSIT 1: EXERCISE YOUR OPTION

Okay, this is an obvious one. Exercise has been found to increase the "good" cholesterol in your body, or high-density lipoprotein (HDL), which dismantles the "bad" cholesterol, or low-density lipoprotein (LDL), that clogs your artery walls. If left to accumulate in your arteries, LDL can eventually plug up your arteries, literally stopping the passage of life-sustaining blood throughout your body. The more HDL you have, the more "cleanup" activity there is in your arteries and the more LDL is carried away and returned to the liver to be properly broken down.

Exercise also helps:

- Ease depression
- Strengthen your heart, bones, and muscles
- Facilitate weight loss by burning calories and increasing your metabolic rate
- Provide renewed energy and feelings of youthful vigor

And the best news? Simply getting off the couch and walking to the front door will set this healthy deposit in motion. In fact, the Framingham study found that the most benefits from exercise come to those who have just begun a regimen.

Just in case you needed another reason to make this particular deposit: When you sweat during an exercise routine, you also release some of the dreaded toxins from your body!

HEALTH DEPOSIT 2: THE HIGH AND LOW—THE RIGHT COMBINATION
It might be hard to believe right now, but I can tell you from experience that my mouth waters at the sight of a plate of grilled vegetables, lightly browned and crunchy. Add some wild grains and I'm in heaven. It's true. Eating a diet low in fat and high in fiber can be delicious. I teach a style of eating that places your body at a good blood-sugar level. Once your blood sugar is stable, you lose your cravings for sugary, fatty foods. Even better, meals like the one I just described taste absolutely wonderful! When your blood-sugar level is good, your taste buds change direction—you find yourself interested in choosing a healthy menu in a restaurant or healthy foods at the supermarket.

A BODY BANK ACCOUNT THAT'S *RUNNING IN THE RED*

DECEMBER 28TH

WITHDRAWALS

10 dinners out in classic French restaurants. Ordered much wine.
Couldn't sleep for three days in a row.
Worked 16-hour days for the past two weeks.
Ate the entire box of cookies I bought for my son.
Sewed on buttons without direct light.
Ate salad only once this week.
Took a series of antibiotics for my urinary tract infection and didn't
    replace the "good" bacteria.
Forgot my vitamins.
Worried all week about my promotion.

DEPOSITS

Made an appointment with a nutritionist.
Ate an apple every day in the afternoon.

A good diet helps to provide the vitamins, minerals, and protein your body needs for health, vitality, and balance. Healthy foods, when broken down during the digestive process, provide the ingredients your cells need to grow, replenish, and repair.

HEALTH DEPOSIT 3: THE FAT THAT IS ESSENTIAL—EVERY DAY

Fat is not a four-letter word. You need a certain amount of fat in order to live. This doesn't mean you should dive into the butter dish. Essential fatty acids (EFA) are not the rich, thick fats you'll find attached to deep-fried chicken or embedded in chocolate frosting. They are, specifically, the fats that you need to get from food—the Omega-3 and Omega-6 oils that not only keep your skin glowing and your hair shiny but also help reduce high blood pressure, triglyceride levels, and blood clot formations. EFAs should also help the brain function at its best, providing some of the fuel necessary for neural messages to be transmitted. They aid in various body processes, including metabolism and digestion, and enable cells to grow, restore, and replicate.

You can get some of your EFAs from foods, especially flaxseed oil and deepwater fish such as salmon, sardines, and mackerel. Evening

---

A HEALTHY, BALANCED BODY BANK ACCOUNT

JANUARY 10TH

WITHDRAWALS
Ate egg rolls three times this month.
Drank three glasses of champagne at the anniversary party.
Stayed up to watch that late-*late*-night movie.
Worked two weekends.

DEPOSITS
Splurged on a massage.
Took my regimen of supplements every day.
Ate a salad at lunch during the week.
Avoided junk food, even though Jane offered me one of my favorite
varieties of doughnuts at work.
Drank a cup of chamomile tea when I needed to get a full, good night's
sleep.
Took my dose of whey protein probiotic every morning.
Joined my local Y.

---

primrose oil, an Omega-3 EFA supplement, has been reported to help ease the pain of arthritis, as well as help lower blood pressure, ease premenstrual symptoms, and decrease LDL cholesterol levels.

In fact, one study takes Omega-3 EFAs a step further. Researchers found that boys between the ages of 6 and 12 had more learning disabilities, temper tantrums, and sleep disorders if the level of Omega-3 essential fatty acids in their bodies was low.

HEALTH DEPOSIT 4: CONSUMING PHYTOCHEMICALS
You know they're supposed to be good for you, these phytochemicals, because studies have shown that they fight cancer. They gobble up carcinogenic molecules before they can do damage to your cells. But do you know what they are? In order to make this healthy deposit, you need to know that phytochemicals are natural compounds, like vitamins and minerals, found in fruits and vegetables, grains and legumes. They give food their flavor, color, and smell. Foods chock-full of "phyto dough" include tomatoes, garlic, hot peppers, tofu, carrots, kale, oranges, blueberries, and raspberries.

HEALTH DEPOSIT 5: DE-COMPRESS YOUR STRESS

Hands-on therapy is an important component of complementary therapy. A massage will help you relax and reduce the stress that depletes your body of nutrients. For example, in a Shiatsu massage, the therapist uses only the thumb and one other finger on specific points of the body, clearing blocked passageways in the respiratory system, promoting circulation, and allowing vital energy (or *ki*, as the Japanese call it) to flow properly.

A sauna after the massage has the added benefit of sweat. As with exercise, the more you perspire, the more toxins you release through the pores of your skin.

HEALTH DEPOSIT 6: SUPPLEMENT YOUR DIET

Depending on your specific symptoms or full-fledged *bankruptcies*, there are many beneficial remedies. There are also basic nutritional supplements to help prevent symptoms and maintain your good health. (My Basic Health Regimen for Vitality and Well-Being and other restorative regimens are in the chapters to come.)

Food alone doesn't supply the amount of vitamins, minerals, and other nutritional supplements you need on a daily basis for prevention of health problems. Soil depletion, social habits, loss of nutrients through overcooking—all take their toll. Even if you think you are healthy because you don't have a full-blown *bankruptcy* condition, reconsider your complaints, the messages that your body is sending, telling you things could be better. Don't wait for disease to happen. You can do something now!

HEALTH DEPOSIT 7:
CHAMOMILE AND OTHER HERBS ARE NOT JUST FOR COOKING

The mention of chamomile probably gives this health deposit away: it's all about taking herbs to help you feel better. Chamomile, in particular, is noted for its ability to soothe frayed nerves and calm the psyche. It can help to prevent insomnia, anxiety, and gastritis. Chamomile can be taken as a tea, as a relaxing bath, or as a mouthwash for gingivitis.

Such therapeutic herbs can help get rid of the everyday kinks in your system. They can help you balance your body, unwind, and regain your strength.

HEALTH DEPOSIT 8:

TAKING PROBIOTICS—THE ANTITHESIS OF ANTIBIOTICS

As you have seen in Chapter 1, probiotics are beneficial bacteria that you mix with water. One particular study shows that probiotics help combat new, mutated viral infections, especially in the colon. Another study found that lactobacilli, a type of probiotic, helped strengthen the body's immunity against "Montezuma's revenge," or traveler's diarrhea. Another study found that some probiotics produce the enzyme lactase, which can help alleviate the symptoms of lactose intolerance.

Yogurt made with live cultures is a good source of *L. acidophilus*, a potent "good" bacteria. But read your labels! Not every yogurt on the dairy shelf contains live cultures.

It takes a good police detective to discover the perpetrator of a crime. In order to be successful, you need to know where to look and what questions to ask. Similarly, it takes a good Health Detective to discover the real culprit behind a symptom. Using your "application form," you can understand the roles your inherited lifestyle, family medical history, and diet play in your health. You can make deposit after deposit into your Body Bank, but the "illness interest" will simply gobble up your profit unless you recognize the true villains. You can put these villains out of commission and then your deposits will add up to good health and long life.

I hope this chapter gave you some ideas of how to begin healing from the inside out by becoming your own Health Detective. It's time now for you to begin making your deposits and getting rid of the withdrawals that have prevented you from living a rich, full life.

It's time to make this information your own. It's time to start your Health Detective training as you begin to solve the mystery of your own body and its symptoms. Remember, you have the ability to change, and incorporating these concepts into your everyday life will make that change possible. But change doesn't just happen with a wish. My principles cannot become your reality overnight. Before you can become a top-notch Health Detective and eventually live a healthy, strong life, you need more clues, more suspects to "interview." Read on. . . .

4

Amazing Stories:
Hidden Links, Important Clues

It's like unraveling a great mystery: me . . . and my health. I feel so confident about my future, it's like I can't wait to turn the page!
> —A 42-year-old mother of three who'd suffered from fibromyalgia until she understood her condition's surprising links: the who, what, where, and why

Think of the ramifications of your financial state, how it reflects on every facet of your life—what you can buy, what you can do, how and where you can live, and even though it doesn't seem to be related, how well you can sleep at night! In other words, the state of your bank account can be a straight, simple transaction that's as easy to connect as getting change for a purchase—or as complex and varied an exchange as sharing stories with the people you meet in life.

Your Body Bank account is no different. Some of the connections are easy to see: smoking and bronchitis; high fat and high blood cholesterol; stress and migraine headaches. But some links are intriguing, even amazing, and understanding them now can save you from debilitating conditions down the road. These links are the less obvious ones because, even though they seem to involve only one organ, they are affecting the whole body. These conditions are a signal that something is wrong in your body. If you have chronic fatigue syndrome, you might have a *toxic liver*; if you have adult-onset acne, you might have a *leaky gut*; if you suffer from arthritis, you might have a food allergy and both a *leaky gut* and a *toxic liver* . . . conditions that can be healed only from the inside out.

You can look at your body in a whole new way, fitting pieces together. There are clues that must be unearthed and examined, from all angles and all points of view. It's like an intricate puzzle you will feel so accomplished to have solved.

And that's where the Health Detective comes in.

THE LINKS THAT LIE DEEP

Here's a brief sampling of the links that I have extensively researched and seen firsthand in my practice. Some will surprise you, some will amaze you. But all will demonstrate how important your role as Health Detective is to your body and your good health. These *health-links* are designed to get you thinking about yourself—to look, listen, and understand in ways that might not have occurred to you. They will guide you as you read the pages of this book, as you learn about the important roles of the liver and the gut, as you discover possible symptoms that can lead to *bankruptcy* conditions if they are not addressed.

Being a Health Detective can be as exciting as embarking on a great adventure, one that might seem scary at the onset as you venture into the unknown, but that you will learn to love the more you explore and the healthier you get. It can be the beginning of a whole new attitude, a whole new way of looking at yourself. And these *health-links* are the start, ultimately leading you to the knowledge you need to re-create your strong, vital body, and to regain control of your life and your health, teaching you to make some deposits into your Body Bank account.

HEALTH-LINK:
DRY SKIN, DRY EYES, DRY HAIR—ARE YOU TAKING A
CHOLESTEROL-LOWERING MEDICATION?
You can buy all the creams and conditioners you want, from generic drugstore brands to designer concoctions sold only in exclusive shops—but if you have a vitamin A deficiency, your skin will stay dry, your hair brittle, and your eyes like sandpaper.

"That can't be me," so many clients have told me. They take a multivitamin pill. They eat their fruits and vegetables. They even take an antioxidant supplement, one that contains beta-carotene, which is converted into vitamin A by the liver.

So where's the problem? It just might be in your medicine cabinet. Cholesterol-lowering medication can interfere with vitamin A absorption. Even if you take megadoses of vitamin A, the medication can inhibit your body's ability to use it. (Vitamin A absorption is further hampered if you are taking antibiotics.) Ask your physician about your cholesterol-lowering drug. Perhaps you are ready to try a different approach, one based on natural remedies. But do so under the supervision of a physician or health practitioner if you are already on medication.

Then there are those people who figure that since they are on cholesterol-lowering medication, they can eat anything they want. Why not? They're protected. Unfortunately, the steaks, desserts, and salad dressings they begin to eat contain a high amount of saturated fat, potentially offsetting the balance of the essential fatty acids their body needs. The result can be dry eyes, skin, and hair.

HEALTH-LINK:
FORGETFUL? FOGGY THINKING? IT'S A MYTH
THAT THEY ALWAYS COME WITH AGE
When you eat too many high-protein foods, and if you are not processing them well, you may wind up with an excess of a protein by-product called homocysteine. Studies, including those published in the *New England Journal of Medicine* and the *Journal of the American Medical Association*, show that too much homocysteine in the body can result in cardiovascular problems and Alzheimer's-like symptoms in the brain.

For proper metabolic function *sans* too much homocysteine, the amino acid methionine must be converted into another amino acid called cysteine. This process is helped along by vitamin B_{12}, found primarily in animal foods. What's the result of this well-run conversion? A healthy heart, a strong body, and a brain that's clear and focused.

But this important process can go awry if you have low levels of vitamin B_{12}, owing to either eating a strict vegetarian diet or improper absorption of vitamin B_{12}. Older adults in particular have less intrinsic factor (a substance in your stomach needed for vitamin B_{12} absorption). And without enough vitamin B_{12}, their bodies cannot properly produce folic acid, which in turn means that their homocysteine levels go up.

Because of this situation, many people have linked old age to problems such as heart attack or memory loss, when it's really improper vitamin B_{12} absorption and a deficiency of folic acid that's to blame!

HEALTH-LINK:

SPINACH—TOO MUCH OF A GOOD THING?

Popeye ate his spinach and he was able to pack a wallop. And, yes, spinach is chock-full of nutrients, especially calcium. We all know that women, especially those approaching menopause, need more calcium. But say you find yourself eating all sorts of good things, including lots of spinach and other calcium-rich food, and your bones still ache. Maybe you've broken a hip and you exhibit all the signs of the *bankruptcy* osteoporosis. Maybe you also have problems sleeping at night (a possible result of calcium that's been driven down) and you are under a great deal of stress (which depletes calcium reserves). All signs point to a calcium deficiency, even though you're taking your calcium supplements and eating your yogurt on a daily basis. What's going on?

Look closely at the spinach you pile up in your salads and the glass or two of carbonated beverages you drink with your high-protein meals, accompanied with the tremendous stress in your life. Don't even count on the spinach, because it contains oxalic acid, a substance that is attracted to calcium—so much so that it binds with the mineral in your intestines, producing insoluble salts that are excreted in the feces. And the high phosphorus levels found in carbonated beverages can also cause calcium wastage. This means that all that calcium you think you are getting with every bite is not going to your bones. Your cells simply cannot absorb these insoluble salts, and your calcium literally gets thrown out with Popeye's tin can.

HEALTH-LINK:

ARE YOU LOSING YOUR HAIR? CHECK YOUR HEART

You've noticed that over the past few weeks, there's been more hair in your drain than usual. In fact, you've asked your hairdresser to layer your hair to offset that receding hairline that seemed suddenly to appear. Hair loss can be attributed to more than old age. Your hair follicles are one of the last areas to get oxygen-rich blood pumped from the heart. If your circulation is sluggish, erratic, or weak, the blood might not make it all the way to the follicles. Without oxygen, your precious locks fall out.

If you've been noticing hair loss, do more than go to your hair salon. Visit your health practitioner. Read Chapter 7 on the *toxic liver.* A strong, healthy body needs a solid foundation: an equally strong, healthy liver. If your liver is overburdened or congested, it can interfere

TO SEE YOUR VEGETABLES, YOU HAVE TO EAT THEM!
A HEALTHY FOOD *HEALTH-LINK*

Lately, you've needed to squint at the pages of a book, even with your reading glasses. Things aren't in as sharp contrast as they used to be. Letters look alike; the television gets blurry; needlepoint has become an impossible task. Your eyesight seems to be getting worse, but it's a slow process. You know you're straining your eyes; you know something's wrong, but you're not quite sure what. You just don't have the clarity of vision you once had.

Both cataracts and macular degeneration are linked to aging. Cataracts are, in actuality, a clouding of the lens of the eyes until blindness occurs. The lens of the eye sends the image perceived through our pupils to the retina. Macular degeneration is a gradual deterioration of the central part of the retina, which is the innermost area of the eye. The center of the retina is called the macula, hence the name.

Eventually, macular degeneration, too, can cause blindness. It has been linked to aging, hypertension, and artherosclerosis. But research has found a very real *health-link* in both cataracts and macular degeneration—and the foods you eat.

If you eat a diet that's lacking in fresh fruits and vegetables, it's possible you are not only doing your entire body damage but your eyes as well. Antioxidants have been found to be important in helping keep eyes healthy and strong. So are other important nutrients, vitamins, and minerals.

A study that lasted two years in Cuba, where people ate mostly rolls and rice, with little in the way of fresh meats, fruits, and vegetables, found that failing eyesight was prevalent, as were deficiencies in the B vitamins, particularly B_{12}, thiamin, riboflavin, and niacin, as well as vitamin A and vitamin E. The Cubans' eyesight improved when supplements were given.

Another study, in California, found that these nutritional supplements improved the vision of people with cataracts by 88 percent!

Choose health and help prevent macular degeneration and cataracts by:

- *Avoiding caffeine*. One study found that drinking too much coffee actually affected the way the eye focuses. (It may also harm the liver!)

- *Eating a healthy diet, rich in antioxidant-packed fresh fruits and vegetables,* such as broccoli, kale, asparagus, berries, dark green leafy lettuce, onions, oranges, spinach, sweet potatoes, tomatoes, peanuts, Brussels sprouts, carrots, garlic, and fish.
- *Taking a vitamin E supplement.* This is a powerful antioxidant that may help prevent cataracts and macular degeneration. But start slowly! Build up to 400 IU daily over a period of a few weeks.
- *Taking bilberry,* an herb in capsule form that contains bioflavonoids that help inhibit the aging process and decrease toxins in the retina. Take as directed.

with adequate circulation. Your heart and a possible underlying *toxic liver* could be the "mane" problem, one that some health deposits can help.

HEALTH-LINK:
BEWARE WHAT YOU MICROWAVE

Most nutritionists agree: buy fresh and eat fresh. Raw vegetables are the way to go, but if cook you must, blanching or steaming is best. And if time is of the essence, there's always the microwave oven, where most of your veggies can cook, simmer, and stew without losing that freshness.

But if you have a sore tongue, an upset stomach, or an anxious feeling without any real reason, you just might look at that very same microwave for the answers, especially if you are a vegetarian. Microwave ovens do keep most nutrients intact, except for one that packs a mighty nutritional wallop: folic acid. Simply put, microwave ovens can destroy folic acid, causing a withdrawal from your Body Bank that can create all these symptoms—even if you're eating a healthy amount of fruits and veggies every day.

Where's the *health-link?* In the beef. Vitamin B_{12} is found primarily in animal protein, and vitamin B_{12} is necessary for proper production of folic acid. If you're a vegetarian, you are not eating beef and might not be getting the vitamin B_{12} you need, resulting in a folic acid deficiency. Add a lot of microwaved veggies, and your folic acid "quotient" drops even lower. Don't be surprised if you find yourself with a nervous stomach and generalized anxiety.

BANK S-TELLARS

There is no medicine like hope, no incentive so great, and no tonic so powerful as expectation of something tomorrow.   —O. S. Marden

---

HEALTH-LINK:

WHAT YOUR GALLBLADDER HAS TO DO WITH YOUR SKIN

You're resigned to having psoriasis. It's been in your family for as many generations as your blue eyes, brown hair, and gallbladder disease. But what you really might have inherited is an inability to properly use fat, which can set psoriasis in motion.

If you frequently burp after eating a lot of fats, if you get stomach pains accompanied by nausea, and if you find your symptoms increase after a particularly rich meal, you could very well be dealing with gall-bladder disease.

A stronger *health-link* to this organ can be psoriasis, those silvery scales growing over an inflamed, red rash. Outbreaks of psoriasis can be exacerbated by stress and the toxic amino acids called polyamines in the bloodstream, thanks to a possible overburdened liver and a gall-bladder that cannot properly filter out the polyamines in the blood. The connection is liver and gallbladder problems—and psoriasis.

The best bet for avoiding this condition is to eat a high-fiber, low-fat diet. In fact, one study found that people in countries that have low-fat diets have much less chance of developing psoriasis. Another study, performed in Sweden, also found that vegetarian diets considerably improved psoriasis, possibly owing to a high fiber content.

Taking an Omega-3 essential fatty acid supplement, also known as alphalinolenic acid, may reduce the outbreak of psoriasis and keep an essential fatty acid deficiency at bay. Flaxseed oil is a prime source of Omega-3 oil. A study done at the University of California at Davis found that after taking Omega-3 essential fatty acid supplements in the form of fish oil, 60 percent of the patients suffering from psoriasis showed at least a moderate improvement.

HEALTH-LINK:
THAT FIRST FLUSH YOU FEEL MIGHT NOT BE EARLY MENOPAUSE
You're nearly at that age when menopause can make an appearance—
and perhaps you think it has. Maybe you seem to always have a bloated
feeling. Maybe you're always extremely tired. Maybe you feel disoriented. Or maybe you intermittently feel flushed. Although these symptoms might suggest otherwise, you are not necessarily going through
menopause.

Perhaps you drink a lot of coffee or a lot of caffeinated sodas and
teas. Maybe you eat a high-fat diet of steak, ribs, and burgers. Or
maybe you regularly use one or two medications for your broken-out
skin. You can trace each of these conditions back to the liver, overtaxed and overburdened so it cannot properly do its job. Instead of
that "silent (and not-so-silent) passage," you could very well have a
toxic liver, a liver congested, overwhelmed, and crying out for help,
that needs to be detoxified and relieved before you can truly feel
young, vital, and healthy (see Chapter 7).

HEALTH-LINK:
HOLD THE Q-TIP! HEAR THIS ABOUT THAT WAXY BUILDUP IN YOUR EARS
You don't understand it. You shower every day. You are scrupulously
clean. But somehow, someway, wax builds up in your ears. Although
you are careful to clean your ears, you have trouble hearing what's being said around you. You keep cotton swabs in your desk drawer. It's
becoming embarrassing.

Hold that washcloth. Throw away those Q-Tips. That waxy buildup
can mean something more than poor hygiene. Wax in your ears can be
a sign of high cholesterol, caused by eating too many dietary fats. Your
clogged arteries are not able to drain properly. (Check that liver again;
it can be congested, too.) Hence the buildup.

If you have an excessive amount of wax in your ears, make a health
deposit to your Body Bank account by taking a blood cholesterol test.
Consult your health practitioner to know if you need to do anything
about this condition.

WITH ADELE'S COMPLEMENTS!

Prevention has always been my message. It goes a lot further than a "cure" and it helps ensure long-term health. Think how wonderful it would be to get rid of that tired feeling before it becomes chronic fatigue syndrome, that hypoglycemia before it becomes diabetes, that sniffling cold before it becomes bronchitis.

In short, by making health deposits now you are helping to create a healthy future. Yes, you have to understand your Health Detective "guidelines" to know that destiny is not carved in stone. But once you begin to see the connections between your symptoms and your body's systems, you can begin to realize that destiny can be changed—and that you really can do something about it on every level. You'll soon realize that no *bankruptcy* condition is a *fait accompli*. You don't have to develop high blood pressure, osteoporosis, and more. You can change your life with a little hope, a little action, a little soul. You can make a difference in your *own* health "case."

Now, that's excellent Health Detective work—and a real learning experience!

HEALTH-LINK:
WHEN IT COMES TO COLDS, LOOK BEFORE YOU ZINC

There's been a great deal of press lately about the wonders of zinc. At the first sign of a cold, pop a zinc lozenge. You'll feel better in no time, so it is claimed. But as with most things in life (and in your body), there is much more than meets the eye. It's true that zinc has been shown to enhance and strengthen the immune system, but taking an overdose (over 100 milligrams a day) may give the opposite effect: a *weakened* immune system.

Yes, zinc can help keep the symptoms of a cold at bay, but beware. Check the amount of zinc in your multivitamin and mineral—and the lozenges you take for your cold. But make sure you're not ingesting more than that 100 milligrams daily. (See my Basic Health Regimen, page 92.) Otherwise, your cold might not just linger, it might get worse. Instead, consider zinc a preventive tool. Taking a proper dose—not too high and not too low—is a wonderful deposit in your Body Bank for your immune system. Zinc can prevent a whole host of symptoms and conditions, including that ubiquitous cold that, with proper immunity, you might not have gotten in the first place! And consider what other health deposits should be made to strengthen your immune system, supporting it and protecting yourself against frequent infections. That way you may not need the extra zinc lozenge!

These are only a few *health-links* to get you thinking, to help you understand that there's always more than meets the eye—in mystery novels, in relationships, and in your body. For true empowerment, you need to understand your whole body, its links and its connections. Only then can you know exactly what vitamins, minerals, foods, supplements, and herbs you need to take for good, long-term health.

By the time you turn the last page of this book, you'll have a much greater understanding of your own body—the symptoms you experience and, most important, some of the healthy deposits you need to make for your own vitality, wellness, and strength. You'll be well on your way to discovering, implementing, and embracing the concept of healing from the inside out.

5

But First: The "How-Tos"

So I'm sitting in my kitchen staring at these bottles of vitamins, these packages of herbs. What do I do with them?
—A 60-year-old health food store novice

Remember the instructions that came with your camcorder? Or your dishwasher? Your VCR? For most of us, those white, carefully folded, printed-in-small-type instruction booklets are usually stored in the top left-hand drawer of a kitchen cabinet, never to be looked at—except to find a service number.

Call it human nature. Those instructions are so boring, so technical, that no one, even if he or she took the time to read them, would even understand them (or they would quit with a yawn before page 3).

It might not matter too much with a household appliance, but sometimes instructions are important, especially when it comes to your health. With the vast array of vitamins, minerals, supplements, and herbs out there, it's a wonder how anyone even begins, let alone takes off the safety wrapping!

This chapter is designed for all of you who don't want to spend a lot of time decoding. It's a brief, simple, and to-the-point guide for taking the supplements you'll be learning about in the rest of the book. (See Appendix C for a complete A-to-Z explanation of each one of the supplements I discuss in the book, including function and warnings.)

THE LITTLE INSTRUCTION BOOKLET

In the previous chapters, we explored some of the links a Health Detective needs to recognize in order to know what to work on and how to prevent *bankruptcy* conditions from taking hold. You've started to become familiar with, and are beginning to discover the importance of, the terms *leaky gut* and *toxic liver*—those *running in the red* conditions that can sabotage your healthy deposits unless they are addressed. You've also found some facts, insights, and descriptions into the actual remedies for making healthy deposits.

Slowly, step by step, you are beginning to understand the power you have to change things. The knowledge you are starting to incorporate into your daily life is helping you recognize what it *really* means to take care of yourself, to take control and help your own body, your own well-being, your entire self. This is, ultimately, the purpose of this book: education for you to stand up and take charge of your life.

Within these pages, you'll continue to discover some of the potent power behind:

- Vitamins, minerals, and other nutritional supplements
- Herbs
- Homeopathic remedies
- Probiotics

(See Chapter 1 for the details on exactly what these remedies are.)

But information is good only if it can be used. Now it's time to learn the nuts and bolts of your Health Detective work: how to follow the regimens you've read about. Let's begin your instructions now.

AN EASY PILL TO SWALLOW: VITAMINS AND MINERALS

Vitamins come in two categories: fat soluble and water soluble. Fat-soluble vitamins need fat to be absorbed. They are stored in the body and accumulate over time, and can become toxic if taken in too-large, continuous dosages.

In contrast, the body takes what it needs from water-soluble vitamins and usually excretes what it doesn't need. Although not as common as with fat-soluble vitamins, some water-soluble vitamins can also be toxic; do not take more than the recommended dosage range.

WITH ADELE'S COMPLEMENTS!

I can't think of anything more frustrating than wanting to get well but not knowing how to do it. You like the idea of natural healing and you want to try complementary remedies, but as soon as you reach your health food store you're ready to run right out the door. There are so many choices, so many varieties, and so many brands of the same item. Who knew there were so many different types of B vitamins? What kind of calcium supplement should you get? And what about green tea? Bee pollen? Should you just close your eyes and choose a multivitamin and mineral supplement? Each one claims to be the best. Help!

Don't worry. You're not alone in this brave new world. After all, when you get a prescription filled you go to a pharmacist. Behind the high counter are shelves of pills, capsules, and powders that would be just as overwhelming to you if you had to choose. Luckily, your pharmacist does the work for you. He or she knows exactly which one to pick. It's written on the prescription.

That's what I hope this book will do for you. It will supply you with ideas and suggestions for remedies to help you get well, stay well, and *be* well for the long term. Tucked in your bag for easy reference, this book will arm you with knowledge. You can walk over to that health food store shelf, examine the bottles, and home in on exactly what you want. You'll be able to ask the right questions and understand the answers. Confidence—that's what it's all about. Controlling your own life and your own body. You'll have the knowledge of *Healing from the Inside Out.*

You'll usually see RDAs listed on a vitamin bottle; these are the *recommended dietary allowances* determined by the Committee on Dietary Allowances. They cover the basics. Everyone has his or her own prevention needs and individual withdrawals, and the RDAs just aren't up to the job. I prefer to use the term WDAs, or *wellness daily allowances.* It's hard to make a case for RDAs being sufficient for everyone; amounts simply cannot be the same for each person. It would even be hard to prove that my WDAs cover everyone. After all, we all have different requirements, from lifestyle to work and stress levels, from sickness to health, from youth to the senior years.

But my WDA's higher levels do help compensate for some genetic predisposition you might have, for the way you might eat, for the environmental toxicity you might be exposed to, and more. Using what you learn from *Healing from the Inside*, implementing my Rescue Regimens, and acting as your own Health Detective will help you supplement the WDAs to meet your specific needs. You'll find that my programs all start with WDAs, adding specific remedies based on your specific *running in the red* symptoms or *bankruptcy* condition. (See Chapter 8 for a full explanation of how my Rescue Regimens in Section V work.)

Many supplements work in concert, with one nutrient enhancing the function of another. For example, bioflavonoids help vitamin C do its job more efficiently.

Vitamins and minerals come in tablets, capsules, powders, and liquids. Capsules and powders are usually the most easily digested. In addition, powders can be mixed with water or sprinkled on food—a plus for people who can't swallow pills.

Minerals also come in different forms, which can have different rates of absorption. The chelated form of a mineral has a good absorption rate and is fairly reliable; these are readily available at health food stores. *Chelate* means that the mineral is bonded with protein molecules, helping it enter the bloodstream faster and become more efficiently absorbed. Minerals must always be taken in the proper ratios because, instead of working together, some fight for absorption, ultimately creating great imbalances. (My programs in the following chapters will help you know how to take supplements in the proper amounts for prevention and symptom relief.)

Take your vitamins and minerals with food, unless instructed otherwise. Start slowly; do not begin with the maximum amounts. Introduce a new vitamin only every few days. Give your body a chance to become accustomed to the supplement; observe any reactions that may occur. If you experience any stomach discomfort, headache, or any other condition that wasn't there before, stop. Wait a few days, then resume very slowly. If the symptoms begin again, you'll know that it isn't simply a coincidence. It is possible that you have a sensitivity to that vitamin or mineral, or a metabolic or digestive problem. Stop the

---

GOOD MEDICINE

Although the regimens I discuss here are designed to help you find a new, natural approach to prevention and sound, complementary ways to heal your symptoms, there are times when conventional medicine must not only be heeded but appreciated. If you are on medication for a particular condition, continue to take your medicine while you add my natural programs (with your doctor's or health practitioner's supervision, of course!).

---

supplement completely and speak to your health practitioner before restarting. He or she might be able to suggest a different brand or offer a good reason why your body can't handle the supplement.

Split large dosages into two or three equal portions, taken throughout the day. By cutting the dosage, you give your body the greatest chance to absorb the supplement and the least chance of having a stomach reaction or other symptoms.

Make sure you buy your vitamins and minerals in airtight, dark containers; heat and light can spoil their effectiveness. I store mine in a cool, dark cabinet in my kitchen.

FOOD FOR THE SOUL, TOO: OTHER NUTRITIONAL SUPPLEMENTS
In addition to vitamins and minerals, there are many other nutritional formulas available to help you achieve better health. *(Warning: Be certain to see Appendix C for any warning regarding specific supplements, and please check with your physician before taking any supplements.)*

Amino acids can be purchased as powders, capsules, liquids, or tablets. Amino acid supplements must be taken on an empty stomach. Look for packages that have USP (U.S. pharmaceutical grade L-crystalline amino acids). The "L" identifies the chemical structure that is usually the one best accepted by humans. Amino acid supplements should be taken only for limited amounts of time; discontinue their use after two months. The only exception are my Foundation Regimens for a *leaky gut* and a *toxic liver*; they have specific limits already set. And any extended amino acid regimen beyond those listed in my programs should not be undertaken without the supervision of your health practitioner.

BANK S-TELLARS

Look to your health; and if you have it, praise God, and value it next to a good conscience; for health is the second blessing that we mortals are capable of—a blessing that money cannot buy.

—Izaak Walton (1593–1683)

Enzymes help carry out essential body functions, such as wound healing and metabolism. Most of these enzymes are found in the body, coming "alive" during the process of food metabolism. They enhance the breakdown of the food you eat. Some can also be found in raw fruits and vegetables, but as soon as you cook these foods, the enzymes begin to lose their effectiveness. Enzyme supplements are usually a combination of various types. They usually come in capsules and powders. Store them in a cool, dry place, such as the pantry.

Essential fatty acids come in capsules and liquids, and should be refrigerated once opened to prevent rancidity. Two of the most important types of essential fatty acids are the Omega-3s and the Omega-6s, which can be found in various fats and supplements, including fish oil, flaxseed oil, canola oil, borage oil, and evening primrose oil.

A BETTER BREW: HERBS

There was a time when people who harvested medicinal herbs were branded as witches. In actuality, herbs are the oldest remedies around; they were used in ancient Egypt, Greece, and China. Even today, many traditional medicines contain specific herbs at their (excuse the pun) root.

You can purchase dried herbs in bulk at a health food store or even in the supermarket; they've become that mainstream! They also come in tea bags, capsules, and tinctures.

Tinctures better preserve the herbs; they are also a more concentrated form of the herbs. These are best used for symptoms that have become severe or that need relief fast. Follow the directions on the bottle.

In general, herbs are better taken away from food. This means no less than fifteen minutes before a meal or two hours after eating.

ALL IN THE FAMILY

There's a lot of confusion around about vitamins, minerals, and nutritional supplements. Because people recognize the names of certain vitamins and minerals, they believe they are separate from more "exotic" nutritional supplements, such as amino acids or enzymes. In reality, vitamin A is as much a nutritional supplement as shark cartilage. Iron belongs in the same neighborhood as coenzyme Q10. In short, a nutritional supplement is any supplement to your diet that enhances your body's function. This includes vitamins, minerals, and other nutritional supplements. When I discuss my Rescue Regimens, you'll see that they are all grouped together.

"HOW DO YOU FEEL?"—HOMEOPATHIC REMEDIES

Homeopathic remedies usually come in pellets, with full instructions on the bottle—or guidance from your licensed homeopath. You should start taking these pellets at the first small signal of a problem; homeopathic remedies are more effective when taken before a symptom or condition gets acute. And remember patience. As with many good things, homeopathic remedies take time to work if you have an ongoing, chronic condition; it may take months to see changes. But if you are in a crisis situation, homeopathic remedies, according to Dr. R. N. Talukdar, a homeopathic physician, will begin to work within three hours—if they are the right ones for your condition.

If you are really serious about trying homeopathic remedies, see a licensed homeopathic physician. Because diagnosis and treatment remedies are so very detailed and specific, only a trained homeopath can decide which combinations of remedies, and in which amounts, are best for you.

NICE GERM, NICE GERM: PROBIOTICS

In general, probiotics help replace the "good bacteria" in the gastrointestinal tract. They come in powders that should be mixed with water or in capsules. There are also products available in your health food store that combine all these "good bacteria" in one concentrated form.

BASIC HEALTH REGIMEN
FOR VITALITY AND WELL-BEING

If you are looking for a general program and have no *running in the red* symptoms, follow this regimen.

DIET AND LIFESTYLE

- Eat a healthy, well-balanced diet, including at least *five servings of raw fruits and/or vegetables every day.*
- Eat *fiber-rich whole-grain breads and grains.*
- *Choose fish* several times a week to get those important essential fatty acids.
- Add an *aerobic exercise at least three times a week* to your healthful diet and at least *one or two stress-reducing activities*, such as yoga or throwing a Frisbee with your dog.
- *Drink eight to ten 8-ounce glasses of bottled or filtered water* every day.

VITAMINS, MINERALS, AND OTHER NUTRITIONAL SUPPLEMENTS

The following basic regimen is not intended to replace your standard medical care. It is depicted for the purpose of educating and introducing you to the concepts and available supplements that may help restore your body to vital health. For optimal results, the program may need to be tailored to your specific situation, taking into account any predisposition to vitamin, mineral, herbal, or food sensitivity. Please check with your health practitioner before using any supplemental program.

If you see △ in front of a vitamin, mineral, or herb, please check Appendix C for further information.

The following are daily adult doses only! Take a good *multivitamin and mineral formula rich in antioxidants* every day with a full glass of water. There are many supplement formulas that are acceptable, even though they may vary slightly. This formula should include:*

Vitamin A	5,000–10,000 IU (International units)
Beta-carotene	5,000–20,000 IU
Vitamin B_1 (Thiamine)	25–100 mg
Vitamin B_2 (Riboflavin)	25–100 mg
Folic acid	200–600 mcg
Vitamin B_3 (Niacin)	10–30 mg

Vitamin B_6 (Pyridoxine)	25–100 mg
Vitamin B_{12} (Cobalamin)	100–200 mcg
Pantothenic acid	50–100 mg
Biotin	200–300 mcg
⚠ Vitamin C with bioflavonoids	100–500 mg
Vitamin D	200–400 IU
⚠ Vitamin E	200 IU
⚠ Vitamin K	50–100 mcg
Boron	1–2 mg
⚠ Calcium	150–500 mg
Magnesium	75–500 mg
Potassium	50–99 mg
Molybdenum	100–150 mcg
Selenium	100–200 mcg
⚠ Zinc	15–30 mg

In addition to your multivitamin and mineral formula, take these vitamins and minerals daily:

B Complex	100 mg
Vitamin C, ester or buffered	1000–3000 mg
Calcium/magnesium	800–1000 mg (calcium)
(in combination or separate)	100–500 mg (magnesium)

Calcium/magnesium comes in a combination supplement form and can be taken together.

Take 2 flaxseed oil capsules every day.

*The higher levels may be found in multivitamin and mineral formulas that instruct you to take more than one a day, or you can use individual vitamin and mineral supplements to achieve the total amounts you want to take.

Many probiotics are dairy-based products. *L. acidophilus,* for example, is one of the active cultures in yogurt, which, if not overly processed, is a good source for getting a dose of this particular probiotic! If you are lactose intolerant, there are nondairy powders and capsules made from plant fiber.

As with any new supplement added to your diet, start slowly and build up to a maintenance dose. Store your probiotics in the refrigerator— except for whey protein, another type of probiotic, which should be stored in the pantry. Do not take your probiotics at the same time of day as a prescribed regimen of antibiotics. Follow the directions on the package for taking them over a period of time. Most important: don't rush. You'll be taking the probiotics for a while.

You now have some details, explanations, "how-tos," and insights to move ahead on your journey toward healing from the inside out. You have some of the raw materials and you are ready to go.

Think of how you would create a beautiful sweater. The end product is only as good as the elements that you put into it. If you want to end up with a wonderfully soft, fabulously made sweater, the wool must be first-rate, the working area must be up-to-date and well-lit, and the knitter must have experience. Similarly, a body is only as good as the materials you put into it. If you want a body beautiful, *you* need to put in wonderful items—in this case good food, nutritional supplements, and knowledge. The power of these health deposits will help ensure a strong, healed, healthy body—and a long life.

Section III

Know the Mastermind Behind Your First Offense

6

THE NEW VILLAIN: INTRODUCING THE *LEAKY GUT*

I know my hipbone's connected to my thighbone, but the fact that my intestines can be connected to my aching joints is astonishing!
— A 27-year-old sales associate and mother of two who came to see me about pain in her right hand and wrist

Chris never seemed to have it easy in life. His father had died at an early age, and he assumed responsibility for his younger sister and his sick mother while still in high school. Chris worked at a local shop to earn spending money. He helped with the chores around the house, he mowed the lawn, and he fixed the plumbing. Despite all he had to do at home, Chris managed to get excellent grades and go to a good university on scholarship.

But even then Chris worked, cramming his part-time job at the library with studying, going to classes, and somehow getting to know the woman he would later marry.

By the time Chris had finished graduate school, he had already gotten his first promotion at the advertising agency where he worked. He became an account executive. The years passed. Chris and his wife had two children. They moved to a small but charming turn-of-the-century house in the suburbs. He liked his life, even though he continued to work hard. He knew how to make time for pleasure, too. He'd spend every Sunday, no matter what came up at the office, with his children. He was close to his family.

After ten years with his firm, Chris became a victim of downsizing; he lost his job. But he never gave up. He never said, "Enough!" And he never complained. It took Chris a stress-filled year to find another position, this time at a small ad agency near his home. His salary was less, and both Chris and his wife, a legal secretary, had to work harder to support their family and their home.

But still there was Chris smiling, all energy, his eyes twinkling. There was Chris on Sundays, at the public tennis courts, teaching his two daughters his favorite sport.

And then it happened. It wasn't something that occurred in the middle of the night, a sharp twinge or a feeling of nausea. It wasn't a sudden cramp or blinding headache. It happened over several months: pain. Chris's "tennis elbow," which hadn't bothered him since college, began acting up. So did many other parts of his body; his aches and pains were almost insufferable. He was extremely tired, barely making it to his office and back home. He had no energy, no drive. He never considered the need to heal from within.

Chris's physician had put him on an antiinflammatory drug for his tennis elbow, but this made his stomach hurt; he grew even more listless. Chris was afraid he had cancer; he didn't know what was wrong. He stopped playing tennis completely and, instead of spending time outdoors with his family, he now spent his spare time watching TV or taking a nap.

Even his work was suffering. Although he now worked for a small firm, Chris still had a great deal of job-related stress. He was responsible for three major clients at his agency and five subordinates, three of whom were becoming "rising stars" while his own energy, creative zeal, and confidence were waning.

His wife, supportive at first, became frustrated. She and Chris began to bicker. Their two children responded to the tension in the house by fighting between themselves. Life for Chris was becoming a disaster and, despite countless visits to specialists, he had no idea what was wrong with him. Every test he took came back negative.

Chris felt completely out of control; he wondered if he was losing his mind. I could only imagine the torture that this hardworking, vital man who was not yet in his forties was feeling: to know something is radically wrong inside his body but not to have a clue as to what it is.

Before I even began my Health Detective work with Chris, I suspected that he was trying to function as usual in a body that was sorely depleted. His Body Bank account had been *running in the red* for so long that it was tremendously overdrawn. By unwittingly abusing his

STOMACH (ONE) LINERS

1. The skin that covers your body (epithelial tissue) is the *same* tissue that covers your digestive tract. (You just don't have to worry about using an SPF block.)
2. Saliva is 99 percent water, with a bit of mucus and a dash of enzyme thrown in.
3. In a healthy stomach, half a million lining cells are replaced every minute!
4. When empty, your stomach looks like a deflated balloon. It can stretch to accommodate about 4½ quarts of food. When full, it looks like a large water balloon.
5. The entire gut, from esophagus to large intestine, is about 2,000 square feet. But it's curved and folded to fit inside; it looks something like the lunar landscape.

body for years, Chris had become *bankrupt*. He had a variety of symptoms that could only get worse—unless he stopped making withdrawals and began to make health deposits instead.

How did I know? The symptoms themselves were prime notices of a body out of balance: aching joints, a lack of energy. I asked him about my "usual suspects": his routine diet, his sleeping habits, his levels of stress, his medications, and the habits learned at his mother's kitchen table. His answers confirmed my suspicions. His Body Bank application had all the signs of a "credit risk."

The pressure at work had increased. Chris had begun working even harder. One of his clients, a telecommunications firm, had been pushing his creative talents to the limits. The stress was building and the little sleep the poor man managed to get was filled with nightmares.

Chris's palate hadn't seen a fresh vegetable in weeks. Because shopping and cooking, on top of a troubled marriage, was too much to deal with, the family was living on fast foods, such as not-so-happy burger meals and pizza. This onetime happy and healthy man wasn't even supplementing his diet with a one-a-day multivitamin and mineral pill.

There was more. The antiinflammatory pills he was forced to start

---

BANK S-TELLARS

Let thy food be thy medicine, and thy medicine be thy food.

—Hippocrates, 500 B.C.

---

taking again for his pain were playing havoc with his stomach, making it even more difficult for his body to adequately digest his food. And to add to his misery, Chris came down with a stubborn case of athlete's foot.

These seemingly unrelated "offenses" helped to create his symptoms. "Your account has been *running in the red* for so long that you've developed these various symptoms," I explained to him that first day he walked into my office. "You're headed for *bankruptcy.*"

I knew that Chris and I could work together to remedy his faulty system. It was not too late for him to become the man he once was. He could even become stronger and more vital than he had ever been in his life—if he would allow himself to take charge.

I asked Chris to sit down, to settle down in the armchair.

I told him, as I'm about to tell you, the Story of the *Leaky Gut.*

A "LEAKY GUT" QUIZ

Do you have any of these symptoms? If so, it's possible you are *running in the red* and could have a *leaky gut* that needs fixing.

- I feel bloated and gassy right after I eat.
- I suffer from indigestion and heartburn—a lot.
- I'm never regular. I always seem to have constipation or diarrhea.
- My fingernails keep breaking off. They are much too soft.
- My bottom always itches. I think I have hemorrhoids.
- I have acne—and I'm over thirty!
- I feel nauseous whenever I take a vitamin.
- I need to burp even when I've eaten something very easy on my stomach, like green tea or plain toast.
- My flatulence is embarrassing me. I find that I'm concentrating more on trying to control it than on participating in important meetings or enjoying the food in a luxurious restaurant!

THE *LEAKY GUT* FOUNDATION

You rarely think about your gastrointestinal tract—or your gut, for short—in "romantic" terms. In fact, you probably don't think about it at all unless you have an upset stomach, gas, bloating, or discomfort. But your gut performs some of the most important functions in the entire body. And it is critically important for a healthy Body Bank account. The gastrointestinal tract, officially a fifteen-foot "tube," runs from your mouth, down your esophagus, and through your stomach, your small and large intestines, to your rectum. It provides not only the arena for food to be broken down and digested by your cells (see Chapter 2 for more details on the digestive process), but also a protective wall, a barrier, from the rest of your body. In a healthy gut, this inner wall is similar to a bank vault, impenetrable and strong, enabling waste and food by-products to go out through the rectum or the kidneys. This "steel vault" keeps food matter, toxins, and bacteria from leaking outside the gut into your bloodstream, where they do not belong.

Normally, food particles would not be considered "venomous." But when the digestive system has been compromised, the flora balance is upset. This is the beginning of *dysbiosis*, a state in which food does not always get broken down as it should. The toxins build up, the intestinal walls weaken, and the gut is no longer able to differentiate between what should be allowed to pass into the bloodstream and what should not. The toxins seep out into the bloodstream, through that "steel vault," and send a loud alarm to the body's immune system. Allergic reactions, in the form of inflammatory responses starting in the joints, can begin to proliferate from these circulating food "toxins," causing even more damage to your body. Add these undigested food particles to the waste by-products and toxins from the food you eat permeating the intestinal wall and you have a *leaky gut* that can, like Chris's, give you very clear, very real symptoms.

THE SNEAKY LEAK

The digestive process is simple and effective, a miracle of the human body—at least when it's in good working order. True, the gut might not be glamorous, but it is the busy, complex hub of our body. There's a lot of activity from beginning to end. And by the time food is swallowed and makes its way to the stomach and then out the swirling tunnels of the small intestine, anything can happen. You might not read about it in Biology 101 textbooks, but that critical process of life-sustaining digestion can be thrown off course at any time with a little help from some subtle and some not-so-subtle withdrawals from the Body Bank.

Digestive enzymes are hard at work as soon as food is eaten, breaking down the food, turning it into smaller and smaller packages until it can be wolfed down by hungry cells. These enzymes are vital for proper digestion; they are the chemical catalysts that trigger the breakdown of food, enabling nutrients to be absorbed by the body. Unfortunately, sometimes the process does not go as planned. Thanks to a poor diet, genetic predisposition, or nutrient-robbing stress, among other factors, the enzymes throw few sparks, and the foods aren't properly broken down. The result is a *leaky gut,* which has been researched by Dr. Jeffrey Bland and HealthComm International, Inc. Dr. Bland has found that as people age, their gastrointestinal tract goes through changes. Its functions are diminished and more toxins are released into the body at large. He reports that many of the conditions we suffer from as we get older—arthritis, inflammatory joint disease, poor digestion, overwhelming fatigue, and more—are not a product of aging but of that ubiquitous, all-encompassing *leaky gut.*

Dr. Bland's research also linked the *leaky gut* as a cause of inflammation and arthritis-like pain. When toxins leak into the bloodstream, they alert Kupffer cells—immune system warriors stored in the liver— to spread the word: aliens are invading the body! Unfortunately, the immune system goes into overdrive, contributing to such autoimmune conditions as arthritis. When that same arthritic pain is treated with antiinflammatory medication and painkillers such as aspirin and acetaminophen, the *leaky gut* becomes even more vulnerable, allowing more and more toxins to permeate the intestinal walls. A damaging cycle begins.

More research:

- Studies have found that people suffering from Crohn's disease have problems absorbing fats; there is a saltwater imbalance in the fluids of the intestinal tract. Why malabsorption? Why fluid imbalance? Possibly because abnormal cells have colonized the mucosal walls of the intestine—a *leaky gut* in full swing.

ENZYMATIC ACTION

It doesn't just work for "scrubbing bubbles" or cleaning teeth. Enzymes are crucial for the digestive process to work and to keep your gut healthy and strong.

Here are four enzyme heroes you might want to become familiar with. They're important to your system, and, at the very least, you can toss the names around at parties and impress your friends!

- *Amylase.* Found in saliva and intestinal and pancreatic juices. Its main purpose is to break down those carbs.
- *Lactase.* Found in the small intestines, its job is to break down the sugar in milk.
- *Sucrase.* Another small intestine enzyme, it breaks down refined sugar.
- *Lipase.* Found in pancreatic juices and the stomach. This enzyme is crucial for properly breaking down fats.

- The coenzyme A, an important enzyme in the digestive process, has been found in insufficient amounts in patients suffering from colitis and chronic ulcers. A *leaky gut* can alter enzyme activity.
- A random study of 434 outpatients at an American clinic found that 314 of them had a gastrointestinal disorder and 55 percent of them also had a *leaky gut.* Sixty-four percent of the 434 patients with pancreatic conditions also had a *leaky gut.*
- Research has found a *leaky gut* in conjunction with hemorrhaging, shock, infection, and malnutrition, and it has been suggested that strengthening the mucosal wall of the gut before major surgery would prevent postoperation infection.

TOXINS BY ANY OTHER NAME

The small intestine is the most susceptible area for *dysbiosis* and a *leaky gut* to develop, because it is where the majority of digestion takes place. When foods are improperly broken down, digested, then ingested by cells, toxins build up on the mucus-coated inner walls of the small intestine. Bacteria and parasites thrive. Yeast forms colonies. This veritable jungle of microscopic toxicity eventually makes the "bank vault"—the mucosal walls of the small intestine—weak and vulnerable. Gradually,

---

WITH ADELE'S COMPLEMENTS!

The most exciting thing I've learned from all my research is that individuals can make a difference—you, me, each person can take charge of his or her health. You have the power inside yourself to be healthy. I might give you information, the ideas and nutrients that will help make you strong, but it's *you* who will decide to try them. It's *you* who will wake up tomorrow morning, or the day after, or the week or month after, and make the conscious decision to change for health's sake, to opt for a better quality of life. It's yours for the taking!

---

over time, the integrity of the walls weakens and microscopic toxins literally begin to "leak" through the walls into the bloodstream and cell tissue outside the gut. This process is called *translocation*, whereby toxins ultimately infiltrate the entire body.

But a definition is only an explanation; it doesn't make things come alive. In order to truly understand the toxins involved in the mucousy inner walls of the gastrointestinal tract, we need to take a closer look. As they do in the classic sci-fi movie *Fantastic Voyage*, let's travel down, past the esophagus and the stomach, to the small intestines and see its environment firsthand.

Bacteria flourishes in your gut; some are "good," necessary to help digestion take place. These are the symbiotic bacteria, which go so far as to eventually help heal tender walls. Then there are the neutral bacteria; they are the "slackers," the ones who hang out without causing any flurries as long as the bacterial environment is balanced. Then there are the other bacteria—strong, fast, and powerful—that, given the right set of circumstances, can overrun your gastrointestinal tract. These are the "bad" bacteria, ready to attack at the first sign of weakness. And as they build their power base, the bacterial environment becomes imbalanced—disturbed, confused, and hostile. The walls weaken, their strength pushed to the limit.

On the outside, *Fantastic Voyage* aside, it's impossible to see these bacteria battling it out or that vulnerable, stressed intestinal wall. But you can see their manifestations. Like Chris's situation, this *leaky gut* may eventually lead to other conditions, from aches and pains in the joints to serious

---

PARASITES: THEY'RE HERE!

It used to be that parasites were something you brought back when you went to a foreign country, especially Mexico. You were always instructed to be scrupulous in what you ate and drank, and even what water you used to brush your teeth.

But this situation is no longer limited to travelers. Today, America has also been visited by parasites. In fact, over 1,000 people got sick from an exotic parasite called cyclospora, which apparently came from imported raspberries.

Then there is the parasite lurking in rainbow trout. It was reported that fish caught in the Missouri River were found to be infected with *Myxobolus cerebralis*, which could be passed on to trout-eating enthusiasts.

Yes, parasites and their "close friends," bacteria such as salmonella and staphylococcus, are here to stay, and we must learn to take all the proper precautions to keep them from entering our gastrointestinal tract.

- Wash all fresh fruits and vegetables carefully. Use a scrub brush.
- Use a separate cutting board for meats. And always wash your hands before and after handling food.
- Cook all meat and poultry until well done. (Sorry, rare-burger lovers; it's just too easy to catch a parasite when it isn't killed by cooking.)
- Don't cook meats in a microwave. That heat doesn't destroy parasites.
- Use only filtered or bottled water. Parasites can lurk in tap water.
- Promptly refrigerate food that isn't eaten, especially in summer.
- Always, always wash your hands before—and after—handling food.
- When in doubt, throw it out!

---

fatigue and irritable bowel syndrome. Worse, a *leaky gut* can make your healthy deposits almost worthless.

But you can turn your Body Bank account around. And recognizing that you're in trouble is the first step toward better health.

A WEAK LEAK: WARNING SIGNS

Chris could try ginseng for three millennia; he could even try stretching exercises and take a multivitamin to no avail. Unless he fixed his *leaky gut* problem, his persistent tennis elbow would ensure that he'd never play the sport again.

You need never join Chris. You can move forward to health if you heed the warning signs that suggest a *leaky gut*. Here are some "clues" that point to a *leaky gut* that even the most novice Health Detectives can recognize:

- Extreme fatigue
- Severe allergic reactions or sensitivity to certain foods and/or your surroundings, including a skin rash, coughing, or a dry throat
- Constipation or diarrhea
- Undigested food particles in stool
- Bloated feeling
- Heartburn
- Gas and belching
- Aches and pains in your joints
- A general lack of strength in your body
- Chronic yeast infections, athlete's foot, or jock itch
- Frequent headaches
- Feelings of confusion, fogginess, or disorientation
- Frequent bouts of illness, including colds or flu
- The beginnings of many *bankruptcy* conditions, including gastrointestinal disorders and some full-blown allergies

If you think that a *leaky gut* might be what's undermining your good health, it's time to restore, repair, and strengthen your foundation before trying to remedy anything else. And that's where your Health Detective work really gets going.

SOLVING THE MYSTERY OF THE *LEAKY GUT*

In order to build the foundation for your Body Bank, you need to know *why* you have this *leaky gut*. To help you solve your mystery, here are some clues connected with this particular brand of *running in the red*.

A SNEEZE ISN'T JUST A SNEEZE: THE CASE OF THE ALLERGIC REACTION AND THE *LEAKY GUT*

You don't have to be a famous detective to truly understand the relationship between an allergy and a *leaky gut*. You simply have to think like a longtime Health Detective. I know it's "elementary" that allergies can be present without creating symptoms as the gut begins to fill with toxins. You can continue to eat, drink, or breathe the allergy-provoking substance and experience absolutely nothing for a long time. But suddenly you start to cough. Your eyes burn. Your throat tightens up. It might feel as if your allergy sprang out of thin air, but in reality it was a long time in coming. Your allergy reached a threshold, a place where it would no longer be ignored. Like "the straw that broke the camel's back," your allergy went over the line and the symptoms, long dormant, came to life out of an overburdened and overloaded body.

OFF-TRACT 1: KILLER ANTIBIOTICS

When Sir Alexander Fleming discovered the mold called *Penicillium* in 1928, he had no idea of the medical revolution he would ignite. The first antibiotic, penicillin, was soon dubbed a miracle drug. Others soon followed, and many infectious diseases were finally stopped in their tracks, including tuberculosis, typhus, bacterial pneumonia, and gonorrhea.

But sometimes there can be too much of a good thing. By the mid-1940s, bacteria had learned how to resist the antibiotics in use; harmful bacteria began to proliferate in people's bodies. So doctors began to prescribe more and more antibiotics. Add the unexpected antibiotics in the meats, poultry, and dairy products we buy and we are bombarded by these medications—to the tune of approximately 35 million pounds a year!

Unfortunately, antibiotics kill off not only harmful bacteria but also the necessary, good bacteria we need for digestion and immunity. Once intestinal bacteria are wiped out, the body simply doesn't have a line of defense. More germs come along, challenging the immune system and hindering the digestive process more and more. In addition, this environment creates a system where our enzymes cannot be

A BOUNCED CHECK: YEAST INFECTIONS

Any Health Detective worth his or her badge knows by now that excess yeast may cause a whole host of problems, including the ubiquitous *leaky gut.*

One of the conditions created by yeast that runs unchecked is a yeast infection—that itchy, burning problem in the vaginal area also called *Candida albicans.*

Although there are over-the-counter medications to treat yeast infections, if the yeast population itself is not cleared up, you'll just keep getting them again and again.

Here's a diet I give my clients who suffer from too much yeast. It helps attack the yeast where it lives and takes care of it once and for all.

- *Stay away from sugar, simple starches, and fruit.* They help feed the yeast. Try nongluten grains, such as brown rice and mullet. They will be less damaging to your intestinal environment than wheat, oats, barley, or rye.
- *Avoid dairy products.* Milk and other dairy products encourage the growth of yeast. The only exceptions: butter and plain yogurt.
- *Limit your intake of potatoes and corn.* They, too, feed the yeast.
- *Keep your household air vents clean and dry.* When you breathe in molds in high concentrations, it may weaken your body's ability to fight the "yeast beast."
- *Avoid eating any pickled or cured products.* Microscopic molds can grow on deli meats, pickles, bacon, dried fruits, cheese (except for cottage cheese), chocolate, maple syrup, and honey.
- *Limit your Thanksgiving Day turkey.* It contains tryptophan, which comes from yeast. Also stay away from any vitamin or mineral supplements that contain tryptophan.
- *Eliminate any foods that may contain yeast, mold, or fungi.* These include commercially prepared breads, cakes, and soup, alcohol, barbecued potato chips, vinegar, dry-roasted nuts, salad dressings, soy sauce, sauerkraut, relish, natural root beer, and cider.

produced properly. In short, the digestive system can't do its job. When the helpful bacteria go, the harmful bacteria grow and grow, until toxins permeate the intestinal walls and the *leaky gut* is born.

This effect of antibiotics can be so influential that repeated doses can be instrumental in creating a *leaky gut.* Unfortunately, once the

FIBER OPT-ICS

We all know that fiber is an important component of the digestive process, preventing complaints such as constipation and conditions such as diverticulitis. But do you know why?

Soluble fiber dissolves easily in water and passes through the gut slowly, adding bulk and softness to stools. It facilitates stool transit and elimination, slows absorption of glucose, and makes you feel full after a meal. Studies have also found it helpful in lowering blood cholesterol. You can find soluble fiber in oatmeal, peas, fresh fruits and vegetables, and legumes.

Insoluble fiber, on the other hand, doesn't dissolve in water. It absorbs fluids, filling with water, as it passes quickly through the gastrointestinal tract, adding weight and volume to your stools. Insoluble fiber comes out intact; it helps keep you regular. Studies have found that insoluble fiber reduces the risk of colon cancer. You'll find this fiber in wheat bran and whole-grain breads and cereals.

All this good insoluble fiber needs water, lots and lots of water. Just as a cellulose sponge gets big, soft, and puffy when it's filled with water, so does insoluble fiber. But if you don't drink a lot of water, the fiber doesn't get big and soft; it stays blocked in your gut, literally blocking the passageway.

Newspapers reported a story of a man who had to have surgery to remove unexpanded oat fiber from his gastrointestinal tract—the result of eating too many oat bran muffins and not drinking enough water!

damage is done, you are continually working with a faulty system unless you take specific steps to correct it.

One of those steps is something many physicians are starting to recommend to their patients on antibiotics: "active culture" supplements or yogurt. The active cultures in some yogurts help restore the bacterial balance in your digestive tract. But be warned: some varieties on the market have been sterilized, destroying the positive, "active" bacteria. You might think you're making a healthy deposit, but your body still isn't getting what it needs. Try one of the organic yogurts; you can buy them in health food stores and even in certain supermarkets. They generally have more active cultures.

SPRING CLEANING FOR YOUR BODY

Aaah . . . the green buds on the trees, the blooming flowers, the warm, blue skies. It's springtime, and time to give the house a good, thorough cleaning. Spring cleaning means washing the windows, dry-cleaning those drapes, organizing the closets, shampooing the carpets, and polishing the floors.

Finally, after all your efforts, you have sparkling results: a clean, beautiful home that looks and smells wonderful. But wait—what about the basement?

You slowly walk down, noticing how dusty and dirty it is. You cough. Your eyes tear. You run back up the stairs.

You lean against the closed door. Right now, you have two options. You can either ignore the basement, leaving the dust and dirt to get worse while you live in your sparkling clean house and not knowing when that toxic atmosphere might seep up the stairs, into the air ducts, affecting your quality of life. Or you can take a deep breath; don a mask, rubber gloves, and old work clothes; grab scrub brushes, buckets, and disinfectants; and clean up that dusty, moldy, dirty basement once and for all. You may cough and sneeze as you clean. It might be hard work, but you know that it will be well worth it. Your foundation will be as sparkling as the rest of your house. You truly live in a clean environment, top to bottom—and you can enjoy the spring.

Think of your body as that house and your *leaky gut* as that messy basement. If you ignore the gut's warning signs, it won't matter what supplements you take for what ails you; your basement is toxic and you'll never know when it will affect your health. But if you take care of that *leaky gut* once and for all, cleaning it up and restoring it to its former vigor, your entire body—from the foundation up—can feel remarkable.

OFF-TRACT 2: BAD FOOD!

Yes, it's true. Those ice cream sundaes not only make you overweight but give you a *leaky gut*, a withdrawal that can lead to a *bankruptcy* condition. The foods we love to eat—the starch and sugar found in high-fat desserts, sauces, and dressings—can feed the yeast in the gastrointestinal tract. A diet built of an excess of simple sugars and starches also doesn't give the body enough fiber, which can create constipation and gas. Eventually, the withdrawal of a poor diet will lead to a vulnerable intestinal wall and a *leaky gut.*

A profusion of yeast can be transferred from mother to child in the birth canal, making you prone to excess yeast. But this excess yeast can also come from a poor diet, especially if you overload on carbohydrates, such as flour products, and simple sugars.

Although linked to a *leaky gut,* the "yeast beast" all by itself can initiate and contribute to many kinds of symptoms, including extreme exhaustion, bladder infections, jock itch, athlete's foot, and asthma.

OFF-TRACT 3: STRESS MESS

Stress creates imbalances in the entire body. Acid production is increased, helping to stir up havoc in your gastrointestinal tract. Eventually, stress can affect your overall quality of life. When it is constant, there's not much left for other bodily functions, including digestion.

If you don't feel well when you are eating, it's possible that stress has made you lose your appetite. It can literally "eat up" your nutrients, including the B vitamins, vitamin C, and zinc. Stress needs constant, unrelenting attention from your body. Your stress mechanisms, from your adrenal glands (which secrete the "fight-or-flight" adrenaline to keep you going) to your hypothalamus (which helps regulate hormones), are stretched to the limit.

When you finally grab a sandwich, eating it in gulps because you feel so rushed and anxious, there's not much left to help the digestive system do its work. In addition to heartburn, bloating, and gas, you're contributing to your *leaky gut.*

OFF-TRACT 4: FEAR OF EXERCISE

If your idea of exercise is not using the remote control, digesting a meal can be difficult and create a whole host of digestive problems. Even a brief stroll will help nudge food down your gut, moving the digestive process along, step by step releasing enzymes that stimulate bowel activity. A sedentary lifestyle, on the other hand, helps make the digestive process sluggish. A study at the Minneapolis Veterans Affairs Medical Center found that exercise helped relieve the symptoms of constipation in elderly people. And the Mayo Clinic recommends exercise in treating constipation. In their study of 277 patients, they saw a 75 percent improvement rate when exercise and fiber intake were combined.

Without exercise, enzymes are sluggish. Hormones are sluggish. Bowels are sluggish. In short, everything but the toxins are sluggish. They are building up, and the *leaky gut* begins to flourish.

If your stress continues, if your lifestyle remains sedentary, if you eat a high-fat, sugary diet, you are helping create that *leaky gut*. This makes the role of Health Detective even more vital. By the time these toxic elements have built up enough to cause a *leaky gut*, you need more than a textbook to figure out what's wrong. Yeast infections, upper respiratory ailments, chronic fatigue, earaches, itchy eyes. The Health Detective (which now means you!) knows all these seemingly unrelated conditions can be closely connected to the *leaky gut*.

It might not need James Bond leaping out of planes, yet the *leaky gut* is still a villain to be reckoned with. But all is not lost. The *leaky gut* is a devious culprit, but it's not as smart as you. You are now in possession of vital information; you have been introduced to the tools you need to do something about the problem.

You can repair one of your body's "cracked" foundations—the *leaky gut*—and help prevent your symptoms from becoming full-fledged *bankruptcy* conditions. You can increase the odds for experiencing vitality, energy, and youthful vigor. And perhaps for the first time, you may be able to take a step to long-term good health. You can start making health deposits immediately and rid your Body Bank account of that *leaky gut* once and for all.

Remember Chris? I recently spoke to him on the phone. He and his family are living in a quiet home by a lake. He and his wife have their own business, an advertising agency. He's still working hard and enjoying every minute. And, oh yes, he's playing doubles in a local tennis tournament next week!

FOUNDATION REGIMEN
TO REPAIR AND RESTORE A *LEAKY GUT*

Add this Foundation Regimen to a basic multivitamin and mineral for vitality and well-being. (Refer back to Chapter 5.)

DIET (FOODS YOU SHOULD EAT AND THOSE YOU SHOULD AVOID)

- *Eat a healthy diet*, one rich in grains, vegetables, and quality low-fat protein, such as chicken and lean fish.
- *Limit high-fat products, dairy products, caffeine, sugar, alcohol, and artificial sweeteners.* These can irritate a vulnerable gut.
- *Eliminate any potential allergy-provoking foods*, such as cow's milk, wheat gluten (flour), barley, rye, oats, citrus foods, eggs, nuts, and corn.
- *Eat your fiber.* Fiber creates bulk to restore regularity and help the digestive system work more efficiently. In addition to fruits, vegetables, and grains, try psyllium husks or seeds (the main ingredient in popular over-the-counter fiber products). Start with $1/2$ teaspoon dissolved in water. You can increase slowly to 1 teaspoon daily, or 1 teaspoon twice a day. Add the water first, stir in the fiber, and drink quickly. You can also take your fiber in capsule form. *One crucial word of caution: Drink plenty of water with your fiber!*
- *Drink 8–12 glasses of bottled or filtered water* a day to help flush out your system and keep your insoluble fiber moving!
- *Avoid gas-producing foods* while you are cleaning your gut, including Brussels sprouts, onions, cauliflower, broccoli, and cantaloupe.

Do this entire program for two months, then cut the amounts in half and continue for one more month. Then discontinue the program. Two weeks after stopping the program, if you still have noticeable symptoms, repeat the entire program.

NUTRITIONAL SUPPLEMENTS

TAKE DAILY:

- *Pancreatic enzymes*, containing bile, can help eliminate excessive fullness, gas, and bloating after eating. Take as directed with food.
- *Powdered whey protein* with fructooligosaccharides (FOS) can help create a stable environment for restoring good bacteria. Stir 1 tablespoon in

¹/₂ cup water a half hour before a meal. Start slowly. As with all probiotics, the more you need it, the more your body might react to it at first, creating gassiness, bloat, and other discomfort. Give your body a chance to get accustomed to this health deposit. *If you are lactose intolerant, there is a plant fiber substitute (with FOS) you can take. Check with your health food store.*

- *L-Glutamine.* This amino acid helps heal and maintain the absorptive capacity of the intestinal walls. Take 500 mg on an empty stomach. *Discontinue after 2 months.*
- *N-Acetylglucosamine (NAG).* This amino acid helps protect the gut's mucusal walls. Take 500 mg on an empty stomach. *Discontinue after 2 months.*
- *B. bifidum.* This probiotic helps inhibit the overgrowth of bacteria and yeast in the large intestines. Follow directions on bottle.
- *L. acidophilus.* A good probiotic to take to help replace the good bacteria destroyed after a regimen of antibiotics or stress. Follow directions on bottle. You can also find *L. acidophilus* in "live culture" yogurt on your supermarket's refrigerated shelves. If you are allergic to dairy products, there are nondairy *acidophilus* substitutes available.

HERBS

⚠ *Cat's claw* will help cleanse and heal the gut by acting as a natural antioxidant and antiinflammatory. Also useful for the aches and pains and intestinal disturbances that can accompany a *leaky gut*. Follow directions on bottle or use tea bags purchased in health food stores.

⚠ *Please check Appendix C for further information.*

PROPER PROBIOTICS

These "good bacteria" can go far in helping to repair and restore a *leaky gut*. You can find probiotics in your health food store. Remember to start slowly and build up to full strength. (See Chapter 5 for more information on how to take probiotics.) There are several common types:

- *B. bifidum* works in the large intestine. A subspecies of biofidobacteria, this important probiotic helps produce B vitamins and keep infections at bay. It can be found in mother's breast milk.
- *L. acidophilus* is one of the most familiar probiotics. It helps produce the important digestive enzyme lactase, which helps digest milk and other dairy products. If you are lactose intolerant, it can be bought dairy-free. It has also been found to reduce blood cholesterol levels and the risk of certain forms of cancer. Yogurt is a good source of *L. acidophilus*, but make sure the packaging says "live cultures." Some yogurts in the supermarket have been overly pasteurized, losing the good, live bacteria.
- *L. bulgaricus* helps to condition the stool so it is more easily excreted.
- *Whey protein*, a milk-based product, enhances and restores a positive, conducive environment for the good bacteria to grow in the lower portion of your small intestines and colon. If you are lactose intolerant, you don't have to "weigh" the pros and cons of whey protein. There's a similar nondairy product available from plant fiber. It, too, creates a supportive, nurturing environment in your digestive system without the lactose challenge.
- *Transient* probiotics, such as *B. laterosporus* and *B. subtilis*, do not make the digestive tract their home. Rather, they are visitors who travel down the gut and provide "reinforcement" for the regular probiotic "troops." They, too, contribute to a strong gastrointestinal tract and overall good health.

Concentrated forms of these probiotics are available in health food stores.

But there's more to come—the secret's out. The *leaky gut* is not a villain that likes to work alone. It is not the only far-reaching condition that batters your body and undermines the healthful things you are currently doing—or creates an environment that opens the door to *bankruptcy*. There's another culprit, a silent partner-in-crime: the liver and a detoxification process that goes awry.

Read on.

Section IV

UNDERSTAND THE MYSTERIOUS COLLABORATOR

7

THE SILENT PARTNER-IN-CRIME: THE *TOXIC LIVER*

I never thought about having problems with my liver. I thought that was just for people who had way too many gin and tonics. But I was wrong. My liver had everything to do with my postnasal drip!
　　　—A 65-year-old investment banker and father of four who learned about healing from the inside

Janice had a favorite raincoat that she wore almost all the time. It was beige, big, and roomy—an all-weather security blanket. No, it wasn't a weight issue. Rather, Janice needed that raincoat to "hide" from the outside world, to be as invisible as possible. Janice was depressed; she felt as if her life were skittering out of control.

Her longtime boyfriend had recently broken up with her. Her parents were becoming more dependent, just as her teenaged son was becoming *too* independent. She'd been passed up for promotion at her telecommunications job. These facts alone would have made even the happiest of the Seven Dwarfs depressed, but as I learned over the weeks and months I got to know her, there was much more to Janice's woes.

She was not just emotionally in pain but physically as well. She had high cholesterol, with a total blood cholesterol level count of 274, which was dangerous for her fifty-five years. Janice had also had breast cancer five years before. She had had chemotherapy treatments and, although her cancer was in remission, it had left its traumatic mark.

119

Janice's disease had been replaced with a general malaise. Although she took many vitamins and tried to swim a couple of times a week at her gym, she was still sick; her joints ached. Not only were her cholesterol levels staggeringly high but she was tired all the time. The cholesterol medicine her doctor prescribed made her so nauseous and dizzy that she had stopped taking it.

Janice shuffled into my office on her first visit. I saw a person in pain, a person who looked as if her self-esteem was nil.

I began to examine Janice's present-day habits as well as her own past and her family's past. As always, I started looking for clues that would help me determine where Janice's troubles really lay and whether there were links among her high cholesterol, her aches and pains, and her fatigue. I asked Janice about her diet, if she drank a lot of coffee, and if her fatigue was ongoing from morning to late in the afternoon. I asked her about meals in her household when she was growing up, if she ate lots of meat, if the cupboards were traditionally stuffed with prepackaged snacks.

Janice's experience with chemotherapy caused me to consider the possibility of a *leaky gut*. I knew we'd have to deal with this disruptive foundation before we could even address any of her other concerns. (I also knew that helping repair her *leaky gut*, which can burden the liver, would benefit her total health as well, starting to clear up her other symptoms, too!)

There was more. Janice's high cholesterol could be an indication that her liver was not functioning up to par; a healthy liver, in most people, usually keeps cholesterol production in check. The chemotherapy she had had five years before had certainly been a burden on her body, creating an overwhelming load of toxins to filter. Her liver needed support. In fact, if Janice's liver had a voice, it would have said, "Help me! Heal me!"

The liver is an integral character in the breakdown of food. It produces bile, a substance necessary for fat metabolism, and stores it in the gallbladder, ready to be secreted, ready to break down food into its different components. It filters the by-products and waste products from digestion for release outside the body.

When I considered all Janice's stresses, the high cholesterol, the chemotherapy, the high-fat diet, I was led to consider the overburdened liver—and toxicity. I knew that if we didn't deal with the liver along with her possible *leaky gut,* Janice's symptoms might never go away.

But first I needed to help Janice's negative outlook. I knew that she had to begin to feel better about herself. She had to have the will, the strength, and the hope to succeed if she was to follow one of my Rescue Regimens. Positive attitudes are curative; they are a solid health deposit. A negative outlook on life, however, is just the opposite: a health withdrawal. Janice and I needed to talk more. . . .

We discussed her life, the positive things Janice had. She was free of cancer. She had a healthy son who still got good grades despite his teenage rebellion. She had a group of supportive friends who made her laugh. She might not have reached a higher rung on the corporate ladder, but she did get a raise and she liked the work she did. I tried to help Janice focus on these healthy, positive aspects of her life. I told her that since we were going to work together, I could help her understand what was going on in her body. I felt she would gain confidence once she saw how making sound, pertinent deposits to her Body Bank account could help her. And by helping her liver, she could very well lower her cholesterol, gain more energy, and begin to feel better than she had in a very long time.

These are the health deposits we discussed at that first, fateful meeting:

Silymarin, also known as milk thistle, was one of the first things I suggested Janice take with meals. This herb for the liver helps enhance bile production, which helps improve liver function. Various studies, from China to Scandinavia, have found that silymarin also helps liver regeneration. In a study done in a German hospital, alcoholics who suffered from cirrhosis of the liver survived longer if they took silymarin.

I suggested that Janice take Omega-3 fish oil because tests showed it increases HDL, the good cholesterol. I also told her to buy some dandelion tea at the health food store; it's an herbal tea that supports the liver and a wonderful calmative to sip before sleep. We worked together for several weeks, slowly making more and more healthy deposits while changing her diet to one that was low in fat and increasing her exercise to raise her HDL.

And then the miracle happened.

Janice followed my regimen to the letter. She really wanted to get better. In only two months (two months!), her cholesterol levels dropped from 274 to 180. Even better, 50 of those 180 points were HDL, the "good cholesterol" that keeps artery-clogging cholesterol (LDL) away.

Her physician was astonished. He had her tested twice; he couldn't believe that her numbers could drop so low without medication.

But I knew better. And Janice knows better now, too. We not only had to deal with her *leaky gut* foundation but also had to get to that *running in the red toxic liver*, its partner-in-crime and the primary source of her problems. By making the healthy deposits I outlined for her, Janice was able to help detoxify her overworked liver. The result? Many of her *bankruptcy* conditions actually disappeared!

Today, Janice not only is twenty pounds thinner but has more energy than she has ever had in her life. Her aches and pains have all but disappeared and, at one of our last sessions, she showed up in a fabulous, chic, form-fitting dress. Her baggy raincoat was nowhere in sight!

THE *TOXIC LIVER*: A BODY BANK FOUNDATION THAT NEEDS FIXING

If you were a scientist or a biologist, you would know that the liver is one of our most vital organs, a "security" you need to keep in a Body Bank's safety deposit box. You would know that:

- The liver is crucial in the life-sustaining digestive process, converting food into energy to be stored. It processes all foods, drugs, and medications.
- At the same time, the liver is a great filter, determining what is toxic and converting it, not into food but into nontoxic materials that can be excreted.
- The liver manufactures bile, triglycerides, and cholesterol to be transported and used by the body.
- The bile created in the liver (and stored in the gallbladder) helps break down fat. It restructures the fat molecules and lowers cholesterol so that fat-dissolving enzymes can break up the fat into smaller molecule packages.

LIVE-R AND LET LIVE-R

Did you know?
- Bile is created from used red blood cells.
- Bile gives stool its color.
- The liver is soft because none of its tissue has keratin (which makes skin tough) or fibers.
- A *toxic liver* can be caused by drugs, the environment, poisons, overeating, constipation, excessive fats in the diet, and excessive amounts of alcohol and caffeine. You can also be genetically programmed to have a liver that is a poor detoxifier.
- The liver is a miracle of regeneration. Tissue can be restored and repaired even after years of abuse. The only exception? Alcohol. The damage alcohol does can almost never be repaired.
- The liver can store only a limited amount of amino acids. Instead, it rebuilds the excess molecules, taking out the nitrogen and making glucose and fat. It uses the glucose to "feed" hungry cells. Excess fat is stored in adipose tissue (those ubiquitous "fat cells!").
- The liver is the most precise nutritionist in the universe. It offers purity through its three-in-one filtering, metabolic, and digestive role; portion control as it breaks down food and distributes it to cells; and cleansing, as it gets rid of toxic waste from the body—when it's running smoothly.

- The liver helps make those quick-dissolving enzymes and amino acids so necessary to the digestive process. This is one of the main reasons why the liver and the gut are so linked—and why a *leaky gut* usually means a *toxic liver*, too.
- There is no greater chemist than the liver. It does its job instinctively, methodically, every moment of your life. It is a filter system without equal, detoxifying the foods you eat so that your body can use them, so that you are not poisoned! It is also a perfect metabolizer and transporter, and one of the most important organs in your body. If the liver is overwhelmed, congested, or toxic, it can literally affect many systems in your body and every aspect of your life.
- The liver is intricately tied to the chemical processes that go on in your body. From estrogen and progesterone to insulin and glucose,

---

CRIMINALS AT WORK

Grade-A Health Detectives know the modus operandi of the *leaky gut* and the *toxic liver*. They know that they can usually be found together, with the *leaky gut* the "instigator," the mastermind who, as it does its damage, enlists the ultimately overburdened liver—which becomes the toxic partner-in-crime.

But, in my experience, each one can also stand alone. If you get help to the *leaky gut*, it can reduce the damage before the liver becomes involved.

The *toxic liver* can be created without the help of the *leaky gut* via external stimuli, something that is inhaled or handled. Coal miners, industrial factory workers, employees at chemical plants—these are all people who are at risk for a *toxic liver* because of their environment.

If you are not sure you have both a *leaky gut* and a *toxic liver*, I suggest you reread Chapters 6 and 7. See if the described symptoms sound familiar, and, if so, follow one or both of my Foundation Regimens accordingly.

Remember, the *leaky gut* and the *toxic liver* usually do work together and, chances are, if you have one, you'll have the other.

---

the hormones that your body needs to function are first converted into usable form in, yes, the liver.

- When the liver is off-kilter, the imbalance can affect not only your digestion but also your sinus elimination, your joints and muscles, your moods and emotions, and your menstrual cycle if you are a woman. Estrogen, so crucial to a woman's cycle, is metabolized into two substances, estrone and estradiol, which are then detoxified by the liver. The ultimate product is a nontoxic waste called estriol. But if the liver is overwhelmed and toxic, it cannot do its job. Estrogen can build up in the body, creating irregularity and a greater potential risk for breast cancer.

THE WINNING DETOX DANCE

The liver's main function is detoxification, a twofold biochemical process done in phases. In phase one, the molecules of undesirable food by-products are literally rearranged, thanks to the help of an enzyme called

DO YOU HAVE A *TOXIC LIVER?*

Look over these statements. If you agree with any of them, it's possible you have a *leaky gut* with a *toxic liver*, and you need to make some healthy deposits in your Body Bank account—as soon as possible.

- I love the fact that there's a coffee bar right across the street from my office. I can now get my caffeine "fix" anytime of the day I want!
- I drink too much alcohol.
- I smoke close to a pack of cigarettes every day.
- I'm a very allergic person. I just have to walk outside my door and I start to sneeze.
- My stomach always feels bloated. I can actually see it expanding after eating a meal.
- I can't stand to be around anyone wearing perfume. I can taste it in my throat.
- Sometimes I feel as if I were born with a cold.
- My skin is very dry and my nails keep breaking off.
- I always have this feeling of fullness, even when I haven't eaten for several hours.
- Nausea is my middle name. If I didn't know better, I'd think I was pregnant.
- I don't have regular bowel movements, and my stools are usually yellowish or have a green tint.
- I think I've been losing my hair. Lately, I've noticed I'm cleaning my hairbrush much more often.

cytochrome P450. This activated enzyme creates biochemical operations that start converting toxins, which are usually fat-soluble and (dangerously) stored in the body, into a more nontoxic, water-soluble form that can safely be excreted via the stool or urine. By the time phase one is completed, toxic substances are in an intermediate stage: not as toxic as before, but not yet completely safe.

In phase two, these intermediate-stage toxins are converted into the water-soluble nontoxic substances. Now they can easily be excreted by the body. In order for the transformation from fat-soluble toxic substances to water-soluble nontoxic substances to be completed in phase two, important nutrients are necessary, including various vitamins and minerals and certain amino acids, such as glutamine, cysteine, gluta-thione, taurine, and methionine.

Think of a healthy, functioning liver as a bank's investment adviser in phase two. Toxins are the loser stocks, he or she might suggest, such as eight-track stereo companies. They are made ready for elimination. But profitable, life-sustaining "stocks" that can be used by the body are stored or converted into energy. These are the winning stocks your banker will recommend, such as Disney and Microsoft. In other words, in phase two, the molecules that had been previously transformed are filtered and restructured, ready to be eliminated or used.

If this process goes awry because of bad investment advice, it can run your Body Bank portfolio into the red. *(If you feel your liver is very toxic, either because of your work or home environment or for medical reasons, it's imperative that you go slowly through the detox process.)*

WHEN THE DETOX DANCE LOSES ITS RHYTHM

A healthy liver instinctively goes into action as soon as food is ingested and toxins are introduced into the body, or when the body itself makes toxins during various biochemical activities (such as energy conver-sion and cell rejuvenation). Phase one and phase two occur without a hitch.

But when the liver is overwhelmed by toxins, when the amount it has to convert is more than it can handle, the detox dance falls apart. This can occur during illness; as a result of a poor diet; if you've con-sumed too much alcohol, drugs, or medication; or if you have a vita-min and mineral deficiency.

If the toxins cannot be properly transformed into their intermediate stage in phase one, the toxins remain in the system—the cytochrome P450 enzymes cannot do their job. The result is a dangerous by-product: those roaming free radical molecules that can damage the liver and put you at a greater risk of disease. This buildup of intermediate-stage toxins creates a whole host of symptoms and conditions, such as Jan-ice's aches and pains, her fatigue, and her high cholesterol levels. The *toxic liver* is not only created, but is flourishing.

TEST SIMPLE

There's a new cutting-edge diagnostic test, the Detoxification Profile, that can help you find out if you have a *toxic liver*, using only saliva after sipping caffeine and using a urine sample after swallowing an acetaminophen pill. It helps determine what you need to do to prevent a *toxic liver* from getting worse and where in the detoxification process you need to do it.

The way it works is easily demonstrated. Caffeine is almost completely detoxified during caffeine clearance, or phase one, of the detoxification process. If the caffeine is eliminated too slowly in saliva, it means that the cytochrome P450 enzymes, so critical in proper phase one detoxification, are not working as efficiently as they should. It means the liver is not effectively conducting phase one.

Acetaminophen is primarily detoxified during phase two: conversion of acetaminophen and salicyluric acid. In a healthy liver, it is broken down to identifiable substances in the urine. If the substances are broken down too slowly, it means the liver is inefficient during phase two. If the caffeine-saliva test results are fine, but the acetaminophen-urine results are poor, it can be dangerous. It means that the toxins cannot be properly eliminated by phase two—and the symptoms you already have may get worse.

This test is more comprehensive than other diagnostic tests, because it not only evaluates the major detoxification pathways but also pinpoints where—and what—nutritional support is needed.

A TATTERED "BILE" RIBBON: WHEN A LIVER BECOMES TOXIC

The liver is a highly sensitive organ, reacting to chemical imbalance very rapidly. Symptoms soon crop up, similar to symptoms of the *leaky gut*: fatigue, impaired digestion, sensitivity to odors, moodiness, and allergic reactions such as a stuffed nose or a dry throat. This battered liver can seriously hamper your healing progress; if it is not treated, it can ultimately lead to such ubiquitous *bankruptcy* conditions as rheumatoid arthritis, Alzheimer's disease, chronic fatigue syndrome, depression,

---

BANK S-TELLARS

*And in man or woman a clean, strong, firm-fibred body is more beautiful
than the most beautiful face.*   —Walt Whitman,
                                        "I Sing the Body Electric"

---

intolerable premenstrual syndrome, and fibromyalgia. Here are some of
the withdrawals that can create a *toxic liver*:

- A toxic environment may be directly linked to the creation of a
  toxic liver. We are exposed to foreign substances, from pesticides to
  industrial chemicals, from food additives to pollution, from mercury in the makeup we use to lead in our pipes, almost every day.
  These toxins enter our body and overburden our liver. Some
  1995–1996 U.S. statistics:
  2.4 billion pounds of industrial chemicals are released into the air
  every year.
  Each nuclear reactor makes 20–30 tons of waste every year. Each ton
  can have more than 100 million curies, a radioactive measurement.
  Every year, 240,000,000 tons of hazardous waste are dumped in
  landfills.
- Taking acetaminophen while consuming alcohol can hasten liver
  toxicity. A study in the *New England Journal of Medicine* has found
  that taking too many acetaminophen tablets, especially while
  drinking, can cause liver damage. And, of course, too much alcohol is directly linked to cirrhosis of the liver, an abnormal change
  in living liver tissue.
- Eating a diet that's too low in calories can be as toxic to the liver as
  a high-fat one. One study found that obesity and a high-fat diet overburden the liver with fats that need more and more bile to be broken down, ultimately causing liver injury. And Dr. Jeffrey Bland, one
  of the pioneers of research in this field, has found that fasting
  (a onetime cure for a *toxic liver*) can actually add to liver toxicity. Important nutrients are not taken into the body, especially the important amino acid glutathione, essential for phase two detoxification.
  This nutrient deficiency also creates a deficiency in enzyme activity,
  which means that toxins can build up, creating those hostile free

WITH ADELE'S COMPLEMENTS!

If there are only two concepts you remember after reading this book, make them the *leaky gut* and the *toxic liver*. I cannot tell you how many clients have vastly improved their health by following regimens that helped their gut and their liver. Not only has their digestion been enhanced but so have their endocrine system, their immunity, and their nervous system. They now have renewed vigor and a sense of well-being—some for the first time in their lives.

Make the choice. Grab on to life. Apply the lessons learned from these two concepts and you'll be taking the first big steps on the road to healthy living. It may feel confusing when you first start. You might feel overwhelmed. But please be patient. It will all come together soon. It doesn't take a great deal of time. It just takes commitment. It takes faith.

Do it! I'm right here with you!

radicals and delivering them throughout the body. Without proper nutrients, especially antioxidants, these free radicals attack and challenge the immune system. A vicious cycle is born.

- Antibiotics may hurt not only the gut but the liver as well. A *leaky gut*, harmed by antibiotics, provides the trigger for an overload of toxins in the digestive tract and throughout the body. The liver becomes overwhelmed; it cannot do its detoxification job properly.

- Stress affects every organ in our body, slowly depleting our resources and damaging our liver. When we are under psychological or physical stress, our bodies demand more of a "defense system." The adrenaline that is released during stressful times activates the body's metabolic processes, many of which originate in the liver. While the liver is trying to manufacture and release its stores of needed hormones, our cells are still clamoring for more oxygen to "feed" our immunity warriors and keep them strong. The result is great oxidative stress throughout our body. This physiological stress, in turn, makes us vulnerable to attack from the roaming free radicals created by an overloaded and overworked *toxic liver*.

A BOUNCED CHECK: IS IT MENOPAUSE
OR IS IT MY LIVER?

I have always believed that menopause should be a natural process, not a condition. In menopause, estrogen and progesterone production is decreased by the ovaries. This drop increases the risk of cardiovascular disease and osteoporosis. It can also create symptoms such as intermittent flushing and mood swings.

However, flushing can also be the result of an overtaxed, overburdened liver and you might not be going through menopause at all. Some clues are:

- Is your flushing accompanied by very dry skin and nails?
- Do your periods continue to be regular?
- Do odors and perfume scents make you nauseous?
- Does your flushing come after having an alcoholic drink?
- Do you also feel bloated, nauseous, and constipated?

If you answered yes to any of these questions, it's possible that your liver is overburdened and creating your flushing, not the decrease in hormones that occurs during menopause.

If these symptoms don't pertain to you, it is possible that you are going through menopause. Here are some suggestions to help make the passage more comfortable:

REMEMBER
⚠ *Please check Appendix C for further information.*

VITAMINS, MINERALS, AND OTHER NUTRITIONAL SUPPLEMENTS
⚠ *Vitamin E.* Helps reduce menopausal symptoms, especially hot flashes. Up to double. Take 400 mg.
- *Pantothenic acid.* Helps reduce the stress that accompanies menopause. Up to 250 mg.
- *Gamma-oryzonal.* An amino acid that helps reduce flushing. Take as directed on an empty stomach. *Discontinue use after 2 months.*
- *Chaste tree berry.* Helps relieve the symptoms of menopause by balancing both estrogen and progesterone hormonal function. Take capsules as directed.

- **We might compound the problem by trying to relieve our stress in less than healthy ways; drinking and eating too much also overburden a liver, damaging it further.**

Some of these withdrawals from the Body Bank are obvious; others are more subtle. Without first addressing that *toxic liver*, you might find yourself like Janice when she first came to see me—miserable, frightened, and wondering what she was doing wrong.

TOXIC SIGNS

Like Janice, you might not know your liver is toxic or overburdened. If your lifestyle is unhealthy, you might have a clue, but here are some signs that would make any Health Detective suspect a *toxic liver*:

- Extreme fatigue
- An overall weakness
- Edema, or swelling of your limbs
- Shortness of breath, as if you were having an anxiety attack
- Impaired digestion, anything from bloating and belching to gassiness
- Sensitivity to odors
- Moodiness and irritability, leading to depression and mental confusion
- Early-onset menopausal-type symptoms: hot flashes, extreme mood swings, and disorientation
- Constipation
- Hair loss
- Bodily aches and pains
- Small growths on the eyelids called celesiums
- Flulike symptoms, including a stuffy nose and a clogged throat, sneezing, and coughing
- The beginnings of many *bankruptcy* conditions, such as osteoarthritis or cardiovascular problems

If you believe you have a *toxic liver*, it's time to switch from withdrawals to healthy deposits, and make your Body Bank account strong.

SPECIAL TREATS FOR THE *TOXIC LIVER*

Just like leaving a job you cannot stand or saying good-bye to a bad marriage or changing careers in midstream, you *can* change a *toxic liver* into a healthy one. You can have control over your destiny, your bank account—and your health.

Here are some insiders' tips:

LIVER GIVERS 1: THE GALLBLADDER CONNECTION

Yes, the liver produces bile and cholesterol, but like all "factories," it needs to store its inventory. That's where the gallbladder comes in. This tiny, rounded organ near the stomach stores the liver's bile and cholesterol mixture that is necessary for the breakdown of fat. When you eat, the liver calls for supplies. The gallbladder sends its bile to the small intestines, where the digestive process is already in the works. When your liver is healthy, the bile juices keep the cholesterol from solidifying. But if you eat a high-fat diet, the overworked liver produces too much cholesterol, which overwhelms the bile. The result is crystallized cholesterol, or gallstones, and high cholesterol levels.

But fatty foods are not the only culprit. If your liver is already toxic, overloaded and overworked, it might not produce enough bile to dissolve the cholesterol. A too low-fat diet can also damage the bile-cholesterol balance. Without fat, the liver is "silent." It doesn't need bile to dissolve fat, so it doesn't call for supplies from the gallbladder. Consequently, the inert, still cholesterol in the underused gallbladder has a chance to solidify, also creating gallstones and high cholesterol levels.

LIVER GIVERS 2: THE CABBAGE PATCH

Cabbage is a liver's best friend. It contains glutamine, one of the most important amino acids needed for phase two detoxifying. But eat it steamed; raw cabbage might be too hard to digest in sensitive gastrointestinal tracts, at least in the beginning. And if you have a history of digestive problems, hold off until your gut is healed.

LIVER GIVERS 3: THE LEMON SQUEEZE

Lemon is known for its "breakdown" properties, or *catabolism.* I recommend lemon juice often, as do many of my colleagues, because lemon juice seems to help eliminate waste matter from the body. You'll know it's working when your sinuses begin draining. Keep a box of tissues handy! Here's the health deposit recipe:

Squeeze ¼ lemon into a cup of warm water. Drink one or two times a day to start. The sicker you are, the slower you should start. If you've been suffering from a *toxic liver* for a long time and your symptoms are severe, start with the same ¼ lemon in a cup of warm water once a day. Gradually build up to ¼ lemon twice a day, then ½ lemon once, then twice daily. (If you take large amounts too soon, you can be dealing with excessive detoxification "drainage.")

Beware this excess detoxification drainage: I remember looking forward to spending a sunny afternoon at the zoo with my grandchild, Charlotte. Before leaving to pick her up, I'd taken my first whole lemon with water at one time; I'd been feeling congested and I wanted to see if I could encourage drainage. After only about a half hour of saying hello to the animals, I felt as if I was coming down with the worst head cold. You know the kind, when you wish you could detach your head and throw it away. I had to blow my nose continually. I felt miserable—and heartbroken. I was sniffling, sneezing, my eyes were watering, I was a mess! I quickly went through the whole box of tissues I'd tucked under my arm. Suddenly, just like that, the faucet was turned off, everything stopped. My symptoms disappeared; it was as if it had never happened. But the afternoon was ruined. I had already taken Charlotte home because my detoxification "drainage" had just been too much.

So don't do too much too soon. Go slow! Otherwise, you too might find yourself ruining a good time at the movies, a meal with a group of friends, a romantic interlude, or, like me, a delightful afternoon at the zoo with my grandchild.

LIVER GIVERS 4: HERBAL MAGIC

Herbs can help detoxify and support your liver, but you must go slowly and knowledgeably. Some studies have found that certain herbs, such as *Crotalaria, Symphytum* (comfrey), and *Heliotropium* (heliotrope), can actually cause toxicity in the liver—but this doesn't have to frighten you. You just have to remember not to take herbs for long periods of time and to choose them wisely. Generally, herbs should be taken for a period of three to four weeks. Rest for one week, then repeat if necessary, unless otherwise directed. Here are some tried-and-true healthy deposits that can heal and nurture the liver. You can purchase these herbs as capsules or as packaged tea at your health food store. Follow the directions on the label.

- *Silymarin*, or milk thistle, serves as a tonic to help the liver perform its job. *(Do not take silymarin if you are pregnant.)*

FOUNDATION REGIMEN
TO CLEANSE AND STRENGTHEN A *TOXIC LIVER*

Start the Foundation Regimen to Repair and Restore a *Leaky Gut*, if indicated. It will most likely be needed as well. Do both regimens at the same time.

ON AN ONGOING BASIS:

DIET—FOODS YOU SHOULD EAT AND THOSE YOU SHOULD AVOID

- Good nutrition is crucial because it supports and nourishes the detoxification process, just as a high-fat, sugary diet hinders it. The best diet for your liver is one that combines *low-fat protein, fresh fruit, fresh vegetables,* and *complex carbohydrates.*
- Add foods that are *rich in amino acids*, such as lean protein, mixed grains, and seeds.
- *Eat lots of green, leafy vegetables.* They are high in vitamin K, which has been found to be deficient in people with liver problems. *(Warning: If you are on blood thinners, stay consistent with the amount of foods rich in vitamin K you consume. If you already eat a lot of vitamin K foods, don't stop. If you'd don't, avoid overloading on vitamin K–rich foods.)*
- And because the liver is so sensitive, it's best to *limit or omit* food and drink that is likely to contain toxins or potential food allergens, including *alcohol, caffeine,* and *processed foods.*
- *Avoid raw meat* (such as steak tartar), *raw fish* (such as sushi), *and raw eggs* (which are sometimes used in Caesar salads). They can contribute potential parasites to further harm your liver.
- *Do the "lemon squeeze"* to help drainage. Use $1/4$ to $1/2$ a lemon squeezed into warm water before meals several times a day.

Do this entire program for two months. After two months, cut the amounts in half and continue for another two weeks. Then discontinue the program. Repeat the entire program if you still have noticeable symptoms.

VITAMINS, MINERALS, AND OTHER NUTRITIONAL SUPPLEMENTS

Follow the Basic Health Regimen for Vitality and Well-Being, adding the following one at a time, every third day (take them in any order you want, but remember to go slowly: the more toxic your liver, the more chance of a reaction):

△ *Please check Appendix C for further information.*

TAKE DAILY:

- *Basic Health Multivitamin and Mineral.*
- *Vitamin C* is an important antioxidant, needed to help destroy free radical buildup. It also helps support the liver, which can become overtaxed in times of stress. Take 2000–4000 mg. The buffered C is gentler on your stomach.
- ⚠ *Inositol*, a vitamin-like substance, helps prevent fat buildup in the liver. Take 500 mg before going to sleep.
- ⚠ *Choline*, a vitamin-like substance, helps fat and carbohydrate metabolism and general liver function. Take 300–700 mg.
- *L-Methionine*, an amino acid, helps in the breakdown of fat and helps prevent fat buildup in the liver. Take 500 mg on an empty stomach. *Discontinue after 2 months.*
- ⚠ *L-Cysteine*, an amino acid, helps prevent fat buildup in the liver. It is also an important component of liver detoxification. Take 500 mg on an empty stomach. *Discontinue after 2 months.*
- *L-Taurine*, an amino acid, is important for the production of bile. Take 500 mg on an empty stomach. *Discontinue after 2 months.*
- *L-Carnitine*, an amino acid–like substance in structure, helps prevent the buildup of fat in the liver and increases fat metabolism. Take 250–500 mg on an empty stomach.
- *Digestive enzymes with bile* help aid the breakdown process and the detoxification process. Take at every meal as directed.

HERBS

- *Silymarin, or milk thistle,* helps strengthen the liver and prevents free radical damage while acting as an antioxidant. Take as directed.
- *Ginkgo biloba* is a strong antioxidant that helps increase circulation and provide energy. It also helps the liver function more efficiently. Take as directed.
- *Dandelion root tea* helps purify the liver and increase bile production. Drink 1–2 cups daily.
- ⚠ *Alfalfa* helps cleanse the liver. It comes in capsules, as a tea, or as a liquid to be added to water. Take as directed.

- *Dandelion root* helps cleanse the liver of its toxic elements and increase bile production.
- *Ginkgo biloba* is a strong antioxidant that helps the liver function more efficiently. It also helps provide energy and increase circulation.

LIVER GIVERS 5: WATER, WATER EVERYWHERE

If I have one word for you, it's *water*. Drink as much as you can—between ten and twelve glasses of filtered or spring-certified bottled water every day. Water helps prevent dehydration and aids elimination, whereas constipation hampers liver function. This is a fast, easy, health deposit that begins working with the first sip!

THE DYSFUNCTIONAL COUPLE

If you have a *toxic liver*, chances are that your gut is not in prime shape, either—although they can occur separately. However, the two usually work in tandem, and if your lifestyle is one consumed with alcohol, caffeine, sugar, starch, and high fat, both the gut and the liver could be off-kilter. "The chicken or the egg" debate is not important here. The fact that one affects the other, and both affect the entire body, is. (Remember my raspy throat and my need to do the *lemon squeeze*!)

The liver and the gut make up your foundation. A *leaky gut* and a *toxic liver* are conditions you can't afford to keep if you're determined to be well. Understanding how they work—and how to balance them—are two very crucial steps on the path to healing from within.

Together, they create conditions with their own set of symptoms—clues that let you know you are *running in the red*. Unless they are recognized, the conditions repaired, and your health restored, the symptoms resulting from this impaired foundation will lead to other conditions: the *bankruptcy* states that you anguish over, suffer from, and deal with day after day—the bronchitis, the acne, the depression, the high cholesterol, the irritable bowel syndrome, and more. But relief is at hand. You'll find insights, knowledge, and remedies described in the very next section of *Healing from the Inside*. The rest of the steps to optimal health and long-term vitality are coming up.

Section V

PREVENT CRIME IN YOUR NEIGHBORHOOD— KEEP YOUR BODY SAFE AND STRONG

8

Achieving Long-Term Health: How to Use Healing from the Inside

I knew I had something wrong with me. I even knew what it was, but I couldn't get rid of it. My condition just got worse—and I got more and more confused. I was ready to take care of myself, but I just didn't know where to start—until now.
— A 38-year-old elementary school teacher who'd recently come to me troubled by an ear infection

"Where do I begin?"

"There are hundreds of remedies out there, from herbs I can't pronounce to nutritional supplements that promise the world. Which is the one for me?"

"I need to know what to take—and what won't do a thing."

"How can I prevent conditions from taking root?"

"How can I maintain good health as I get older?"

"How do I know something will help? How much do I take, anyway?"

"I want a remedy—but I need a step-by-step plan to get me going."

"Help!"

These are all statements from my clients—people from all walks of life who have come to me either through referrals from physicians and friends or because they just weren't getting better and were looking for a new approach.

I've worked with thousands of people troubled by different ailments, many with symptoms just like yours. I can say, even without meeting you, as I have said to my clients, that it would be to your advantage to determine if your gut or your liver might be *running in the red,* undermining your good health.

Now that you are beginning to understand the basic concept of the Body Bank, as well as how to work as a Health Detective, we can go on to your specific symptoms—the aches and pains, the mental distraction, and the more serious conditions that affect your well-being and quality of life.

The remaining chapters in this book are devoted to just that: the illnesses that cause you pain and the remedies to help relieve them. You can get back to a place where depression is replaced with hope, where pain is replaced with strength, where fatigue and lethargy are replaced with energy and a zest for life.

Together, we can work to turn your *running in the red* account around by stopping those sabotaging withdrawals and adding healthy deposits. Together we can strive to make your Body Bank a strong, brilliant, and gleaming structure.

To that end, I've made the fifth section as comprehensive and easy to follow as possible. Here's how.

KEEP YOUR BODY BANK SECURE

The next eight chapters are divided by *bankruptcy* conditions—and the *running in the red* symptoms that can lead to specific *bankruptcies*—from gastrointestinal to respiratory problems, from allergies to muscle, joint, and skeletal conditions. You only have to turn to the chapter you feel addresses your ailment to discover some important Health Detective clues and Rescue Regimens that may help.

To make things even easier, each chapter is set up in exactly the same way, in the same format and the same order.

- You'll always find an illuminating, sometimes surprising, sometimes inspiring, story from my own practice to help you understand how the Health Detective uncovers clues and finds links that lead to the particular chapter's *bankruptcy.*
- You'll find a brief quiz to get you thinking in the right direction and a short group of statements that describe symptoms related to this chapter's *bankruptcy.*
- A quiz is only as good as the information it ultimately unfolds.

A BODY BANK REMINDER:
UNIVERSAL SOLDIERS

Just like a good night's sleep and a hearty laugh, there are specific remedies that will help turn many *bankruptcy* conditions into healthy Body Bank accounts. For details, review Sections One and Two. You'll find the lowdown on some basic remedies, including homeopathy, probiotics, and exercise, that constitute healthy deposits to your Body Bank account.

Just to recap, here are a few of those basics that *will* get you on the road to feeling better. They'll help reduce the stress that lowers immunity and makes you vulnerable to all kinds of conditions. A study in the *Annual Review of Psychology* found that such negative factors as stress, depression, and repression negatively influence immune function on both a cellular *and* a hormonal level.

- *Acupuncture.* Many traditional physicians are beginning to recognize the power of acupuncture to help ease the pain of everything from migraines to lower back pain and PMS. In fact, acupuncture is so popular in America today that we pay approximately $500 million for services from licensed, experienced acupuncturists.
- *Meditation and relaxation.* We have spent millions, tried everything from pills to counting sheep, but the fact is that focused relaxation does reduce stress. Whether your calming tool is audiotapes, biofeedback, self-hypnosis, or meditation, you can feel better when you stop the world, get off, and take a relaxation break. In fact, one study in India found that when patients suffering from epilepsy performed yoga meditation, they improved considerably within six months.
- *Hands-on therapy.* Massage is so potent a stress and emotional pain reducer that some health insurance companies, such as Oxford, now reimburse patients who go to qualified, licensed massage therapists. In fact, when massage is combined with essential oils as in aromatherapy, it can reduce pain and anxiety, as well as eliminate water retention and toxins.

Every *bankruptcy* chapter provides vital *health-links* that will be invaluable as you do your own Health Detective work.
- Each chapter contains my Preventive Regimens to help keep your specific *running in the red* symptoms from becoming that full-fledged *bankruptcy*. Use these regimens in conjunction with my Foundation

Regimens for *leaky gut* or *toxic liver* (both of which can be underlying many of your symptoms), if applicable. If you're not sure of your gut or liver's involvement, reread Sections III and IV to see if you should do one or both of my Foundation Regimens as well.

- The final section of each chapter details some of the more common *bankruptcy* conditions, in alphabetical order. Simply look up your condition and you'll find some facts, some *health-links,* and some Rescue Regimens to add to your Preventive Regimens.

Here's an example of how to keep your body safe and strong by learning to read the signals:

Perhaps you've been watching your cholesterol climb. You turn to Chapter 10, "Heart and Circulatory Bankruptcies." You start your Health Detective work, taking the quiz and reading how problems with your eyes and your ears can connect to symptoms in other organs, in other systems of the body.

If the symptoms sound like those you are experiencing and you have uncovered the *health-links* that indicate you are in line for this *bankruptcy,* begin the Preventive Regimens for keeping your heart strong and your circulation vibrant. *Along with* these Preventive Regimens, also see if your symptoms indicate that you should *simultaneously* follow the Foundation Regimens for a *leaky gut* and a *toxic liver.*

If your symptoms do not go away or if you are experiencing a full-fledged *bankruptcy* of high cholesterol, you turn to "High Cholesterol," listed under "H," read about it, then add the Rescue Regimen for high cholesterol to your Preventive Regimen for keeping your heart strong and your circulation vibrant.

Everyone can benefit from the Basic Health Regimen, and, if you have symptoms, the Foundation Regimens and the Preventive Regimens. You should see some improvement within three weeks of starting the Regimens. A sense of well-being and improved health should be apparent within two months. Remember: healing from the inside out takes time, but the rewards will be lasting.

DON'T BE THE SWELLED HEAD!

Whenever any of my clients need to lose weight, I always tell them to beware of the Fathead—that psychological saboteur that can rear its ugly head. Even when you're controlling the blood sugar that causes physiological cravings, eating all the right foods at the right time, and exercising at least three times a week, the Fathead can be ready, willing, and able to hurt your best efforts. The reasons are universal—a combination of psychological underpinnings, habit, and stress.

When you have a condition that has caused you pain and grief your entire life, and you begin to take care of it by making healthy deposits, you'd think you'd keep going on the straight and narrow. After all, your aches and pains have begun to fade. Your quality of life has vastly improved. You smile more. But suddenly, you forget a supplement here, a vitamin there, because you are feeling so good. You eat a few more fatty desserts than you should. You stop going to the gym. Your healthy deposits have turned into those fierce withdrawals and, before you know it, you don't have much energy. You don't feel well at all. You have the equivalent of what I call the Fathead from my 5-Day Miracle Diet: the Swelled Head.

Physicians call this noncompliance, a situation that occurs when a patient begins to feel so good that he or she tosses out that high blood pressure medicine, that antidepressant, that insulin, causing the illness to come back.

It's no different with complementary therapies. If you stop the Rescue Regimen too soon, your condition can return.

No one wants to be the Swelled Head. Remember how terrific you feel? It's called lifestyle, and it doesn't mean giving up that scrumptious dessert at your daughter's wedding or that fabulous, lazy weekend in the Caribbean. It just means moderation in all things. That's what the Greeks said, and they were around for quite a few millennia. As far as I know, not one of them was ever accused of having the Swelled Head.

RECONDITIONING:
THE RULES BEHIND THE REGIMENS

My Rescue Regimens have always been an exhilarating part of my work. They are the "drawing room" conclusion in an Agatha Christie yarn, the final chapter in a suspenseful mystery. Think of it: Make these healthy deposits (some of which may surprise you) and you can begin doing wonderful things for your Body Bank account. Continue making these healthy deposits and your symptoms might not only soon improve but should provide substantial returns on your initial investment!

But as with most things in life, these Rescue Regimens can be safer and more effective if you follow some basic rules. Think of them as the ambience that makes for a great mystery, the texture and atmosphere that brings things alive. And, above all, use them!

The Golden Rule: Always Consult a Health Professional Before You Begin Any Regimen

The first is one you have heard before, from me and from countless others. It's simple and easy to remember. But the message is vital, an important reminder that can make all the difference in your well-being.

Although many of my clients have used these regimens with much success, everyone is different and can react differently with different remedies. The regimens are to introduce you to the concepts and remedies that may help restore your body to vital health. For optimal results, the programs may need to be tailored to your specific situation, taking into account any predisposition to vitamin, mineral, or herbal sensitivity.

The Golden Rule Sequel: Never Stop Taking a Medication Prescribed by Your Physician Until He or She Instructs You to Do So

These remedies should not be used to replace your medical care without the advice of a trained health professional. In correcting imbalances within your body, you may come to a time when you won't need as high a dose of blood pressure medication or as much insulin as you are currently taking—if you'll even need it at all. But always listen to your health practitioner or doctor. Use my remedies and healthy deposit suggestions in conjunction with proper diagnostic tests and your practitioner's sound advice—with a not-impossible goal of tossing away those pills, those inhalers, and those feelings of hopelessness and pain.

Appendix C of this book gives a detailed, alphabetized accounting of the various remedies available. You'll find brief descriptions and usage, all at a glance. And most important, you'll find a list of possible contraindications for each supplement, as indicated. These are the

WITH ADELE'S COMPLEMENTS!

It's a simple phrase—two words that are easy and quick. But they have tremendous power—if you heed them. The next time you have the choice between a bag of greasy potato chips and an apple, between a fresh, crisp salad and a prepackaged, prefried burger, a yoga class and a trip to the crowded mall, a bottle of sparkling water and a sugary soda, think of these two words. Make them your motto for life. They'll help keep you on track, vital and strong:

CHOOSE HEALTH!

conditions that might cause a specific remedy to harm rather than heal. It's best to go over this material with your doctor or health practitioner if you are currently taking or about to take any medication. *(If there are possible contraindications for a particular supplement, you'll see the warning symbol △ right next to it in every regimen. Please pay attention to it!)*

THE RULING CLASS

Last, but not least, there is a practical Body Bank lesson for you to learn. If you've done your Health Detective homework and you've discovered you need to do my Foundation Regimens for a *leaky gut* and a *toxic liver,* begin these three weeks *before* starting any of the Preventive Regimens.

Always continue the Basic multivitamin and mineral; this is an ongoing ingredient in all programs for long-term health and vitality.

Always begin with the smallest dosage first in the ranges suggested and see if it helps. If not, increase the dosage slowly, over two weeks, until you reach one that works and is still within the suggested guidelines.

And remember to start slowly, trying one supplement at a time. If you have any adverse reactions, discontinue and start a different supplement. (See Chapter 5 for information about taking vitamins, minerals, nutritional supplements, and herbs.)

These guidelines are not meant to scare you away from achieving a healthy Body Bank account. Rather, they are meant to demonstrate that complementary therapies need to be taken seriously, just as you

would traditional prescriptions. The big difference is that these remedies heal by treating the *body as a whole*, from within, not just specific
symptoms. These remedies replenish and restore.

They can be good for you.

Use them well and you will be treated well.

Your Body Bank account will thank you for the rest of your days, by
helping you to heal from the inside out.

9

GASTROINTESTINAL BANKRUPTCIES

I tried every medicine out there. I not only got second opinions, but third and fourth ones, too. No luck. I thought I was stuck with irritable bowel syndrome for life—until I learned that by eliminating some foods and adding supplements, I could keep it at bay!

—A 28-year-old mother of two and a client who had just started my Rescue Regimen

Joyce knew she was in trouble when she had to run out of her seat just as the dinosaurs were about to attack on the movie screen. She mumbled to her husband to watch the kids as she stumbled out to the aisle, step-ping over toes and grimacing. She spent the rest of the movie in the women's room, hunched over in agony, unable to leave the stall.

Joyce was scared. She'd had a severe pain in her stomach for the past four months and had been to two gastroenterologists who hadn't been able to find anything. She had tests for Crohn's disease, for ul-cers, for colitis. She had both an upper and a lower GI series. Nothing. But lately her cramps had been getting worse. She had lost her brother to pancreatic cancer and was terrified that it could be happening to her. She'd noticed in the past few weeks that her stools had changed, one of the possible warning signs for cancer. Joyce couldn't take being ill for so long without having answers to what was causing her pain.

The incident at the movies was the last straw. She had to do some-thing. She had two young children who were in grade school, she had a part-time job, and she wanted to enjoy whatever free time she had with her family. When Joyce told her family physician what had happened, he diagnosed her condition as irritable bowel syndrome, a condition that had no specific cure. He prescribed prednisone, a corticosteroid drug, to help reduce the inflammation in her gut.

The pain subsided, but only slightly. Plus she now had the added symptoms associated with any corticosteroid drug. In Joyce's case, the side effects included bloating, weight gain, and mood swings. In addition, she was suffering from vaginitis and skin irritation.

Joyce started snapping at her children; she became distant to her husband. She quit her job because she was not well enough to sit at her desk. She stayed home, watching afternoon TV, leaving only for car pools and household errands.

Finally, disgusted with her life, her constant illness, and her terror of the future, she decided to try something different. "Irritable bowel syndrome is ruining my life," Joyce said to me that first day. She looked miserable, something I could easily understand. An illness that lasts for months, infringing on your life, is a cruel twist of fate, especially when the condition is so vague, so ambiguous. There was no cure, no relief in sight—or so Joyce believed. And stress over this hopelessness was a major withdrawal in itself.

THE CASE OF THE CRUEL CRAMP: SOLVED

We began our Health Detective work, discussing Joyce's family life, her diet, and lifestyle, and discovering a whole host of clues along the way.

In the same way detectives know to look for fingerprints when a crime has been committed, I knew that we had to first look at Joyce's foundation. Almost every gastrointestinal condition begins with a *leaky gut* that has to be repaired before any health deposits can be made. To that end, I put her on my Foundation Regimen for a *leaky gut* while we continued our Health Detective work in the weeks to come.

Because irritable bowel syndrome is associated with food intolerance, I also suggested in that first visit that she stop eating cheese and other milk products. She had told me that these were the foods she loved best, frequently eating cottage cheese and ice cream, thinking

---

BANK S-TELLARS

You don't have to believe my fortune cookie, but still . . . *"Nature, time, and patience are the three greatest physicians."*

---

that these soft foods would ease her symptoms. Although Joyce didn't want to give up her favorite foods, she wanted more to be free of pain; she agreed. It helped, but only slightly.

The following week, we tried a diet of less fat, since high-fat foods can be very difficult to digest. And once again, it helped—up to a point. Worse, Joyce was beginning to feel deprived. Not only did she have pain but eliminating the food she enjoyed had brought only minor relief. Even trying to establish an eating schedule to help regulate her digestive enzymes was to no avail.

Unfortunately, my Foundation Regimen didn't seem to be doing much good, either. Joyce still had debilitating cramps and pain associated with irritable bowel syndrome. I knew that something wasn't right, something was eluding us. At our next session, Joyce and I talked about the things she loved to do. "Travel. I love to travel! But, with the kids, my illness, I haven't been anywhere since my husband and I went on a cruise down the Nile on our vacation."

Travel. The Nile. Egypt. Exotic locales—a new reason why Joyce's symptoms might not have been responding well to treatment came to mind. I suggested she make an appointment with a parasitologist to be sure that parasites had not lodged in her gut, parasites that she could have picked up on her trip to the Middle East.

It was a relief to find out Joyce did indeed have an amoeba in her gut, one that was overriding the healthy deposits she was making. The parasite had to be gotten rid of before any regimen would work. Her healing had to begin from within. The parasitologist put Joyce on very powerful antibiotics, wiping out the amoeba along with much of her good flora.

We restarted her regimens and finally could see an improvement. Joyce was no longer fighting an uphill battle; she no longer had the parasite handicap, and my Foundation Regimen for the *leaky gut* could do its work. I immediately put her on the highest level of the regimen to help restore the damage that the parasites, the antibiotics, and even the prednisone had done to her gut.

We also began a program to diminish yeast—another opportunistic invader—which can easily overwhelm and take advantage of a gut that is challenged. Joyce soon reported an improvement in some of her other conditions. Both her vaginitis and her skin rashes responded when she eliminated sugary, high-starch foods and fermented products, such as vinegar, from her diet.

Within a few months Joyce's determination and patience had paid off. Her irritable bowel syndrome seemed to disappear. She no longer had to see a movie twice to catch the whole thing.

DO YOU HAVE GASTROINTESTINAL *RUNNING IN THE RED* SYMPTOMS?

Joyce knew that she had a problem with her gut when she came to see me, but perhaps you're not sure. Maybe your overall lethargy, ill health, and pain seem so consuming that you don't know which part of your body to link the symptoms to. To help find the links in your own Health Detective work, look over the following statements. If some of them ring true, they could very well be warning symptoms of gastrointestinal distress—symptoms that need healthy deposits to prevent an actual *bankruptcy*.

- I remember my mother's painful "attacks" after a rich, heavy meal. Now I know she had gallstones—and it runs in the family.
- I drink water from the tap. Why not? It wouldn't be running through my pipes if it wasn't safe, right?
- It seems as if I have a case of flatulence whenever I'm in public. In fact, I'd say I'm always gassy, and if it's not flatulence, it's burping.
- As soon as I finish eating, even if it's just a slice of turkey and some veggies, I get cramps.
- Sometimes I don't even try to eat until 2:00 in the afternoon. I'd rather avoid the foods than chance the discomfort.
- I get incredible anxiety from all the stress in my life. My stomach sends me messages by producing so much acid that I have to pay attention.
- Because of my chronic bronchitis, I take a lot of antibiotics almost every winter, wrecking havoc in my stomach.

- I feel nauseous if I wait too long to have lunch. If I don't eat by 1:00 at the very latest, forget it. My stomach hurts all afternoon.

Adele's Body Bank Disclosure

A good Health Detective knows that you don't necessarily have to live with the pain of gastrointestinal symptoms. You don't have to accept that gassy, bloated, or nauseous feeling as the norm. Nor do you have to experience the incapacitating pain that Joyce once felt. Discover and learn how to read the signs. Start taking action to uncover the mystery behind your symptoms. Determine some of the withdrawals you have been making, and decide to exchange them for healthy deposits. Here are some major clues to help you identify possible gastrointestinal problems that could be *running* you *in the red.*

GUT RUT 1: OVERLY SENSITIVE STOMACH

You might not have to look any further than a *leaky gut* for the source of your gastrointestinal symptoms, especially if you have a sensitive stomach. Do your nerves seem to materialize as butterflies in your stomach? Are you prone to gas or heartburn? Do some foods seem especially tough on your system, making digestion difficult? Does a "bug" always seem to land in your stomach first, before hitting your respiratory tract, your lymph nodes, or any other system in your body? If any of these sound familiar, you could have a sensitive stomach and be in line to collect future problems in your gastrointestinal tract.

The best protection against oversensitivity is a hard shell. In this case, that means a strong, impenetrable gut, which in this fast-paced, seemingly insensitive world sometimes has to be built and strengthened. In my practice, clients who have sensitive digestive systems almost always need the Foundation Regimen for a *leaky gut.* Both this regimen and the Basic Health Regimen or the Multivitamin and Mineral Supplement should be in place for approximately two weeks before going on to the Preventive Regimen for the gastrointestinal tract.

GUT RUT 2: BREAKING UP IS HARD TO DO

I call them "tough digesters," the foods that make eating hard to do. These are the foods that people with sensitive stomachs can find difficult to digest, adding to their gastrointestinal woes.

CONSTIPATION COMPANION

The key word here is *diet*—and you don't have to look through too many keyholes or lift up too many rugs to find the villain. A low-fiber diet, rich in fat, can make even the most diligent, once-a-day person constipated. Combine this diet with a lack of exercise and you could have a gut that's sluggish, filled with undigested food particles, and overwhelmed by toxins seeping out into the bloodstream.

But there are other clues to unearth as well, and these enter the psychological realm. Perhaps you were overly toilet trained and the "potty" brings anxiety. If that's too Freudian for you, there's always the "t-factor"— time. When stress and an impossible schedule keep you running from morning until night, there's literally no time to go to the bathroom.

More clues: the aluminum salts in antacids, as well as such drugs as antihistamines, antidepressants, diuretics, and high blood pressure medications, can cause constipation. A *toxic liver* can cause constipation. It's a link that bile production is hampered because bile, normally produced in a healthy liver, softens the stool.

Unfortunately, laxatives not only create an overdependence but can increase irritation of the intestinal walls, creating poorer conditions and making the constipation worse.

The older population complains a lot about constipation, as evidenced by studies that show they spend a great deal of money on laxatives. They should, instead, spend a great deal of time educating themselves in the facts that moderate exercise, a high-fiber diet, and plenty of water can prevent this condition in the first place. In fact, a study in the *Journal of the American Geriatric Society* found that fiber increased stool frequency in a group of elderly outpatients whose only complaint was chronic constipation.

Constipation can also be a symptom of a more serious condition. A good Health Detective knows that he or she might be dealing with a *toxic liver*—one that is overburdened and cannot help produce normal stool. If you think that's a possibility, do the Foundation Regimen for a *toxic liver* before doing any of the Rescue Regimens.

The first on the list is *lactose,* the sugar in milk and other dairy products. Lactose needs the enzyme lactase for digestion. People who live with sensitive guts often don't have enough lactase in their system.

Consequently, the lactose in milk doesn't get broken down properly and the individual suffers such miseries as cramps, diarrhea, and gas. If you experience any of these symptoms after drinking a glass of milk, you could be lactose intolerant.

The second tough food is *gluten*, which can be found in wheat, oats, barley, and rye. It can be highly reactive in certain people and cause digestive distress. In a study done in Cambridge, England, 60 percent of gastrointestinal patients had worse symptoms after eating foods containing wheat gluten. Although gluten is easily avoided when it comes to bread, bran, and cereals, keep in mind that gluten is also used as a food preservative. Check your labels and avoid the offending products if you experience any symptoms.

There are other foods considered potentially allergic to the gut. People who suffer from irritable bowel syndrome may have reactions to corn, citrus fruit, onions, potatoes, coffee, eggs, and foods containing the sugar substitute sorbitol.

If you suspect that foods are causing your discomfort, try an elimination diet. That is, eliminate all the potential tough digesters and the gut allergy foods for one week. If you feel remarkably better, put one of the foods back in your diet. Observe, listen to your body, wait and watch. If you still feel good after one week, try adding a second food. Slowly add a food every week. If you have any reaction, you should be able to discover which food is the culprit and avoid it.

GUT RUT 3: STRESSING STRESS

Stress and the stomach have been linked as long as people have taken pen to paper to describe their feelings: "a knot in the stomach," "that gnawing feeling," "butterflies in the stomach." That anxious, nervous feeling that comes from unrelenting stress can go directly to your gut, impacting on your digestive process and causing distress, from ulcers to colitis, from heartburn to diarrhea.

Stress can be a hefty gastrointestinal withdrawal from your Body Bank, especially if you have a sensitive stomach. It can create excess acid in the gut and cause stomach upset. In fact, one of the major culprits in irritable bowel syndrome can be stress. Try one of the "Universal Soldiers" of a healthy life to help reduce stress: a massage, guided imagery, a walk in the park.

GUT RUT 4: THE ACID TEST

Hydrochloric acid, or HCl, is secreted by the stomach to help break down the food you eat. Too much or too little HCl interferes with the digestive process, creating gastrointestinal symptoms such as heartburn, stomach cramps, and gastric ulcers.

Too little acid production can be the result of growing older or lack of exercise. Too much can be the result of stress; overuse of aspirin and over-the-counter nonsteroid antiinflammatory medication, such as ibuprofen; overeating; even wearing too tight a belt!

Take this "acid test" to see if you are suffering from too little or too much HCl: When you start to feel discomfort after eating, swallow a tablespoon of lemon juice or apple cider vinegar. If the pain subsides, you probably have too little stomach acid. If the pain increases, you should suspect that you have an excess of HCl.

GUT RUT 5: LOOK OUT! IT'S THAT POOR DIET AGAIN

You've heard it so many times you're probably sick of it. But some clichés are just that because they are wise and true. And although "eat a healthy diet" doesn't have the same poetic cadence as "a rolling stone gathers no moss," it is still as wise and true. A high-fat diet, low in fiber and fresh vegetables and fruits, is a major culprit in many gastrointestinal disorders. Not only can a too soft and too rich diet create an inefficient digestive system, it can help bring on such conditions as hemorrhoids, constipation, and heartburn. In addition, the wrong foods will not supply the right ingredients to heal within.

You can start changing your "food blues" now by substituting low fat for high fat, such as olive oil for butter, and adding fresh fruits and vegetables to your diet for fiber and a nutritional boost.

GUT RUT 6: EXERCISE YOUR BODY, NOT JUST YOUR MIND

Getting an aerobic workout several times a week does more than tone your muscles, strengthen your cardiovascular system, and help you lose weight. It also helps your gastrointestinal tract. If your idea of exercise is hailing a cab, it's possible that your lack of motion has helped create such gastrointestinal symptoms as heartburn, nausea, and constipation— if you don't already have a full-blown *bankruptcy* condition. A sedentary lifestyle hinders the secretion of digestive enzymes, so vital to the

PREVENTIVE REGIMEN
FOR STRENGTHENING AND REVITALIZING
YOUR GASTROINTESTINAL TRACT

If antibiotics or stomach upsets have been a frequent part of your life, restore your system with this program.

Be sure to start slowly, introducing supplements gradually, because people with these gut conditions are generally sensitive and can be reactive. The Foundation Regimens for a *leaky gut* and/or *toxic liver* are usually indicated before beginning this regimen, because gastrointestinal problems have these underlying conditions. Do both Foundation Regimens, if you have recognized a need for them in your reading of Chapters 6 and 7, for 3 weeks, then add this Preventive Regimen.

ON AN ONGOING BASIS:

DIET
- Take *water-soluble fiber*—psyllium seed husks or pectin—every day. Mix 1 teaspoon with a glass of water.
- *Drink* at least 8 glasses of bottled or filtered water every day.
- *Eat* at least 5 servings of fruit and/or vegetables every day. Avoid raw fruit and vegetables if your symptoms point to Crohn's disease or colitis.
- *Increase your dietary fiber* by switching from white flour, white rice, and other refined starches to fiber-rich whole-grain foods.

⚠ *Please check Appendix C for further information.*

VITAMINS, MINERALS, AND OTHER NUTRITIONAL SUPPLEMENTS
TAKE DAILY:
- *Basic Multivitamin and Mineral Supplement* (p. 92).
- *B complex.* Take 50 mg. Maintains a healthy gastrointestinal tract. Necessary for proper nutrient metabolism and absorption. Up to double.
- *Vitamin B_{12}.* Helps digestion and enhances nutrient absorption. Take 500 mcg.
- *Vitamin C.* Take 500 mg.

- *Fish oil.* This Omega-3 essential fatty acid helps ease inflammation of the gut. Take 2 capsules.
- ⚠ *Multienzyme with pancreatin and bromelain.* Assists in breakdown of food and helps ease inflammation. Take as directed with each meal.
- *L-Taurine.* A key component in bile. Necessary for fat digestion and absorption of fat-soluble vitamins. Take 500 mg on an empty stomach. *Discontinue after 2 months.*
- ⚠ *L-Glutamine.* An amino acid that helps heal an inflamed, irritated gut lining. Take 500 mg on an empty stomach. *Discontinue after 2 months.*
- ⚠ *Choline.* A vitamin-like substance that helps fat breakdown and enhances fat and cholesterol absorption. Take 500 mg.
- ⚠ *Inositol.* A vitamin-like substance important in fat metabolism and in maintaining proper cholesterol levels. It can make you pleasantly drowsy. Take 500 mg before going to sleep.
- *Calcium citrate.* Helps to calm a nervous stomach. Take 1000 mg in split doses.
- *Magnesium citrate.* Helps to balance calcium. Take 500 mg in split doses.
- *Flaxseed oil.* Repairs and protects intestinal lining. Take 2 capsules.

HERBS

- *Aloe vera juice.* Helps support the intestinal mucosal walls. Drink twice daily as directed.
- ⚠ *Alfalfa.* Contains vitamin K, which is needed to maintain proper intestinal flora. Take liquid or capsules as directed.
- *Garlic capsules.* Aid digestion and help destroy toxins that could harm the digestive system. Take one with each meal. Use only yeast-free capsules.

proper breakdown of foods. Physical activity also helps nudge waste down the large intestines. Even a simple thirty-minute walk four times a week can help ease constipation.

Colitis does not have to remain a debilitating condition. Neither does an ulcer. If you experience any of these "gut ruts," add the Preventive Regimen for gastrointestinal problems to the Foundation Regimen for a *leaky gut* after two weeks.

There's still no reason to give up, even if your withdrawals have created a *bankruptcy.* Look up your condition in the following pages. Explore its links in the Health Detective work. And consider starting the Rescue Regimen (in addition to my other regimens) for your specific condition. By healing from the inside out, you can help yourself more than you know—it just takes knowledge, insight, and desire. You can start to take charge now!

CROHN'S DISEASE

JUST THE FACTS, PLEASE . . . THE MYSTERY EXPOSED.
It's no wonder you feel discomfort. Crohn's disease is the pain you feel as a result of irritating ulcers in your small intestine that eventually scar, thicken, and cause blockage. The inflammation, open sores (ulcers), and scarring occur deep in the mucosal walls, especially in the lower portion of the small intestines called the ileum. (This is why the disease is sometimes called *ileitis.*)

THE EVIDENCE . . . EXHIBITS A TO Z.
Crohn's disease might be the result of an immune system that turns against itself. The inflammation of the small intestine, the first sign of Crohn's disease, is truly an attack—as if your own antibodies had turned against you. Since stress can help suppress an immune system and an antibiotic regime can destroy the "foot soldiers" of the immune system (the good bacteria that gobble up germs), it's wise to put some stress-reducing healthy deposits into your Body Bank. Another withdrawal with a wallop? Smoking. More smokers than nonsmokers get Crohn's disease. Another reason to quit to add to the long, long list.

GRADE-A DETECTIVE WORK.
A nutrient deficiency may be a link to Crohn's disease. A study of forty-seven patients with Crohn's disease in an American hospital found that they had deficiencies in essential fatty acids. Another hospital study, this one in Japan, found that a malabsorption of vitamins B_1, B_2, B_6, and folic acid occurred in patients with Crohn's disease. Research has also found that food additives can play a role in Crohn's disease, especially silica, a substance added to toothpaste and some supplements, and carrageenan, a thickening agent made from seaweed that is used in ice cream and other diary products. Finally, watch the water you drink! A parasite called *Giardia*, which lives in certain streams and mountain springs, has been found to cause Crohn's disease–like symptoms.

"DID I REALLY EAT THE WHOLE THING?"

Heartburn doesn't have anything to do with the heart. Rather, call it the "overindulgent disease." In heartburn, stomach acids reflux (or flow back) into the esophagus through the lower esophageal sphincter (LES). This stomach acid doesn't belong in the esophagus and it results in a burning feeling. A LES that opens too much means that gravity can't keep it closed. This is usually the case with too much food in the stomach, obesity, or pregnancy.

But you don't always have to be overweight to get heartburn. You just have to have poor food habits. If you eat a lot of pasta with garlic sauce, chocolate, chocolate, and more chocolate, you're going to feel the reflux. Garlic, onions, and, yes, chocolate, among other foods, relax the LES too much, allowing acid to travel back up.

To help alleviate the symptoms of heartburn, try calcium carbonate instead of antacids. It works in a similar way, without the large amounts of aluminum and sodium.

Drink plenty of bottled or filtered water. It could help dilute an overly acidic stomach.

Finally, try a soothing cup of green tea; it provides alkalinity to soothe your symptoms.

RESCUE REGIMEN
FOR CROHN'S DISEASE

Follow Preventive Regimen for gastrointestinal problems for two weeks. Then add this Rescue Regimen.

If you see △, check Appendix C for further information.

TIPS

- Crohn's disease means that the digestive system is usually very reactive. *You must go slowly,* starting one supplement at a time and making sure you have no adverse reactions before starting another one.
- An *elimination diet* is critical to determine any possible food allergies. (See page 208 for details.)
- Follow the Foundation Regimen for a *leaky gut* for three weeks before starting this Rescue Regimen.

VITAMINS, MINERALS, AND OTHER NUTRITIONAL SUPPLEMENTS
TAKE DAILY:

- *B complex.* Take an additional dose of 100 mg.
- *Fish oil Omega-3 capsules.* Act as an antiinflammatory. Take two capsules.
- *N-Acetylglucosamine (NAG).* An amino acid–like substance that helps protect the mucosal wall of the intestines. Take 500 mg on an empty stomach.

HERBS

- *Silymarin, or milk thistle.* Helps support liver function. Take 70 mg twice daily.
- *Echinacea.* Helps to reduce infection. Take as directed.

COLITIS

JUST THE FACTS, PLEASE . . . THE MYSTERY EXPOSED.
An inflammation of the intestines, colitis causes tiny ulcers, sores, and tears in the mucosal walls. Its symptoms include bloody stools and/or bouts of severe diarrhea. It is similar to Crohn's disease, with one major difference: colitis attacks the large intestine only.

THE EVIDENCE . . . EXHIBITS A TO Z.
Stress is a major cause of this condition. Considering that this is one of the most common conditions people get affecting the large intestine, it could be more evidence of how rampant stress is in today's world!

KEEPING YOUR CONDITION "BEHIND BARS"
RESCUE REGIMEN FOR COLITIS

Follow Preventive Regimen for gastrointestinal problems for two weeks. Then add this Rescue Regimen.

If you see △, check Appendix C for further information.

VITAMINS, MINERALS, AND OTHER NUTRITIONAL SUPPLEMENTS
TAKE DAILY:
△ *Vitamin E.* d-alpha tocopheral 400 IU.
- *Pantothenic acid.* A B vitamin that helps repair damage caused by stress on the colon walls. Take 200 mg three times a day.
- *Multi–amino acid complex.* Helps repair and restore the gut. Take one a day on an empty stomach.
- *Proteolytic enzymes.* Will help break down fat in the intestines. Take as directed with meals.

HERBS
- *Red clover.* A flower that helps soothe an inflamed colon. Take as directed on bottle or as a tea.
- *Fenugreek.* Seeds that help moisten the mucosal walls of the intestines and calm inflammation. Take as directed.

AD NAUSEAM: A HEALTH DETECTIVE QUIZ

There you are, sitting on a bus or plane, or maybe you're at a party, and suddenly you feel ill, as if you're going to throw up. Again. These feelings of nausea are affecting your quality of life.

The first thought that comes to mind is a stomach virus. But maybe you should think instead about a food allergy. Nausea is a common symptom of a sensitivity to dairy products, wheat, or other foods. This reaction itself may be traced back to a *leaky gut* and a *toxic liver*, where nutrients aren't properly metabolized and the breakdown of food is incomplete.

Before you can determine the cause of your nausea, you must rule out certain other conditions by using various diagnostic tests, accompanied by some clever detective work:

- Do you have a fever? (If yes, you could have the flu.)
- Do you normally feel nauseous after eating very fatty foods? And, speaking of fats, is your diet filled with them? (If you've answered yes to both questions, you could have gallstones or an ulcer.)
- Does your nausea come with extreme thirst and a need to urinate? (If yes, you could be diabetic.)
- Have you been exposed to mononucleosis? (If yes, that could be your problem, especially if you've been kissed!)
- Do you take a lot of medication, followed by countless cups of coffee? (If yes, you may have a *toxic liver*—one of the reasons people get nauseous.)

In short, there are almost as many conditions that create nausea as there are symptoms. But one thing is certain: your body is telling you something. You are making too many withdrawals from your Body Bank and you must start with those healthy deposits. (Unless, of course, you're a woman and the good news is that you might be pregnant!) Here are some hints I give my patients:

- *Start reducing all caffeinated beverages,* including coffee, tea, and carbonated soda. Too much caffeine can make you feel nauseous (as well as harm your gastrointestinal tract!).
- *Avoid smoking.* Cigarettes can irritate the esophagus and the stomach.
- *Try not to eat right before going to sleep.* Give your food time to digest.
- *Eat a sensible diet.* Too many fried and fatty foods will make anyone nauseous. (Remember those commercials where a chubby man in pajamas sat on his bed wailing, "I can't believe I ate the whole thing!")
- *Say good-bye to artificial sweeteners.* They create toxic overload and can create allergic reactions, such as nausea. Ditto MSG (monosodium glutamate).
- *Try an elimination diet* to see if your nausea is a result of a food allergy or a tough digester. (See page 208 for details.)

GRADE-A DETECTIVE WORK.

Symptoms of colitis have been found in people who have taken such antibiotics as amoxicillin, clindamycin, penicillin, tetracycline, and trimethoprim. Once these drugs were discontinued, the colitis disappeared. Other research has found colitis-like symptoms in salmonella poisoning. Once the bout of food poisoning passed, so did the colitis.

DUODENAL AND GASTRIC ULCERS

JUST THE FACTS, PLEASE . . . THE MYSTERY EXPOSED.

It conjures up images of Type A, cigar-smoking workaholics chomping on antacids while barking and yelling at their subordinates. But in reality, an ulcer is a serious condition in which perforations tear the mucosal wall of the gut. Whether gastric (in the stomach) or duodenal (in the intestine), the symptoms remain the same, ranging from an upset stomach to a burning pain.

THE EVIDENCE . . . EXHIBITS A TO Z.

There are many reasons stomach acid builds up in the system, one of the culprits that create an ulcer. If you wait too many hours before eating something, your digestive enzymes are all ready to "chow down" and there's nothing to dissolve. The acid builds. Chewing gum also builds up acid. There you are, chewing and chewing and never swallowing. What's a digestive juice to think?

Stomach acid is also genetic. You can inherit too much acidity from one or both of your parents. Did you inherit a Type A personality by watching your overachieving parents work endless hours always trying to get ahead of the next guy? Did you inherit the idea that taking a break or having some fun is somehow wrong?

GRADE-A DETECTIVE WORK.

Ulcers are not simply a result of acid buildup. They can also occur when you take too much aspirin, steroids, or other antiinflammatory medications, such as ibuprofen.

The newest evidence shows that an ulcer may even be caused by

KEEPING YOUR CONDITION "BEHIND BARS"
RESCUE REGIMEN FOR DUODENAL AND GASTRIC ULCERS

Follow Preventive Regimen for gastrointestinal problems for two weeks. Then add this Rescue Regimen.

If you see △, check Appendix C for further information.

ON AN ONGOING BASIS:
DIET
- *Avoid coffee, alcohol, milk, carbonated or hot drinks, ibuprofen, animal fats, and chocolate.* These can all irritate the gut, causing more pain and more perforations in the mucosal lining.
- *Eat small meals frequently.* This helps cut down on excess stomach acid.
- *Fresh cabbage juice* is chock-full of glutamine, an amino acid that helps promote the growth of mucus on intestinal walls.
- *A banana* a day may help keep the acid away. Bananas stimulate the production of mucus on stomach and intestinal walls. Researchers in Australia found that bananas reduced the incidence of ulcers by 75 percent in animals.

VITAMINS, MINERALS, AND OTHER NUTRITIONAL SUPPLEMENTS
TAKE DAILY:
- *Bromelain.* An enzyme that helps soothe an inflamed gut. Use the chewable kind. Take as directed.

HERBS
- *Licorice.* Must be the deglycyrrhizinated form to prevent raising blood pressure. Reduces the pain of an ulcer. Take as directed.
- △ *Bilberry.* Helps increase gastric mucus secretion, coating the stomach. Take as directed.
- *Alfalfa.* Provides vitamin K, a necessary component for blood clotting. Take as directed.

FLAT-OUT FLATULENCE

Believe it or not, gas is a normal part of the digestive process. But there can be too much of a good thing. When air enters your stomach, it's expelled via a belch. Eating too quickly, drinking something too cold, chewing gum—all these might end in an "excuse me" and a belch.

Flatulence is air expelled from the rectum. It can be the result of the high-fiber foods you eat, such as beans and vegetables, which are only partially digested in the small intestines. Bacteria go to work on these "tough-skinned" high-fiber foods, breaking them down even more in a process called fermentation, which produces gas.

You can also have flatulence if you drink milk and you have a lactose intolerance. Fatty foods are also hard to break down, especially if a *leaky gut* is already in place. All these produce an uncomfortable feeling and flatulence.

If flatulence is making you flush with embarrassment, here are some hints:

- Avoid fermented food, such as cheese, vinegar, and alcohol.
- Use over-the-counter natural enzymes before eating beans and other high-fiber foods for "extra ammunition." They really work!

Flatulence can be nothing but "classical gas," but it can be a symptom of other conditions: colitis, Crohn's disease, or irritable bowel syndrome. Check with your health practitioner if your flatulence continues on a daily basis and try the Preventive and Rescue Regimens for gastrointestinal problems as well as the Foundation Regimens for a *leaky gut* and a *toxic liver*.

---

bacteria, *Helicobacter pylori*. Studies have found *Helicobacter pylori* present in 92 percent of all people with duodenal ulcers and in 73 percent of all people with gastric ulcers.

GALLBLADDER DISEASE

JUST THE FACTS, PLEASE . . . THE MYSTERY EXPOSED.
You can have gallstones your whole life and never know it. These crystal-like deposits simply float around in the gallbladder, where bile, manufactured by the liver, is stored. Bile itself is made up of cholesterol and bile juices; it is crucial for breaking down fat. When you consistently

---

BANK S-TELLARS

To eat is human
To digest divine.   —Mark Twain

---

eat fatty foods, the liver produces more cholesterol than bile acids. An imbalance is created. Cholesterol builds up in the gallbladder; the juices cannot cope; the cholesterol cannot be dissolved. This extra cholesterol can become crystallized gallstones. And if these stones happen to float into the ducts that connect the gallbladder to the liver and the small intestines, watch out! You can feel terrible nausea and intense pain.

THE EVIDENCE . . . EXHIBITS A TO Z.
If you are a woman over forty, you are more likely to get gallstones than a man of the same age. Because of the likelihood of a high-fat diet, an overweight person is more susceptible to gallstones, too.

However, a diet too low in fat can also contribute to gallstones. Since there's less need for gallbladder activity when there's little fat to digest, the liver doesn't need to store as much bile. Consequently, cholesterol has a greater chance to solidify and form crystals. (See Section IV for the link between gallstones and a *toxic liver*.)

GRADE-A DETECTIVE WORK.
Over 1 million people get gallstones every year, thanks in part to a high-fat diet. In fact, a study done on animals found that saturated fats increased the amount of gallstones, but monounsaturated fats, such as safflower oil, had no effect. The result? Get the fat you need from your diet via olive, safflower, or canola oil, not butter!

KEEPING YOUR CONDITION "BEHIND BARS"
RESCUE REGIMEN FOR
GALLBLADDER DISEASE

Follow Preventive Regimen for gastrointestinal problems for two weeks. Then add this Rescue Regimen.

If you see △, check Appendix C for further information.

TIP
- The gallbladder and the liver are closely linked. If you have gallstones, chances are your liver may be overburdened as well. Do the Foundation Regimen for a *toxic liver* for 2–3 weeks before starting this Rescue Regimen.

ON AN ONGOING BASIS:
DIET
- *Drink lots of filtered or bottled water every day.* It helps liquefy bile.

VITAMINS, MINERALS, AND OTHER NUTRITIONAL SUPPLEMENTS
TAKE DAILY:
- *Vitamin C.* Take an additional 1000 mg.
- △ *Vitamin E.* d-alpha tocopheral 400 mg.
- *L-Methionine.* An amino acid that helps to prevent fat buildup in the liver; helps break down the fat. Take 250 mg on an empty stomach. *Discontinue use after two months.*

HIATAL HERNIA

JUST THE FACTS, PLEASE . . . THE MYSTERY EXPOSED.
You might have a hernia and not even realize it. If you have persistent heartburn, difficulty swallowing, a bloated feeling after you've eaten, or shortness of breath, you might have a hiatal hernia—in which a portion of the stomach pushes out and over the diaphragm.

THE EVIDENCE . . . EXHIBITS A TO Z.

Approximately 80 percent of all hernias are *inguinal* hernias, in which a section of the intestines or the bladder pushes out into the groin; they should not be confused with hiatal hernias. Hernias are more common in overweight people. In general, hernias are more uncomfortable than life-threatening.

GRADE-A DETECTIVE WORK.

Some clues that make you vulnerable to hiatal hernias:
- How fast you eat
- How much you challenge your digestive system by overloading on too much food too quickly
- How often you recline while eating
- How often you lie down right after eating

KEEPING YOUR CONDITION "BEHIND BARS"
RESCUE REGIMEN FOR HIATAL HERNIA

Follow Preventive Regimen for gastrointestinal problems for two weeks. Then add this Rescue Regimen.

If you see △, check Appendix C for further information.

TIP
- *Do not lie down* for at least two hours after a meal. Your symptoms of heartburn and digestive discomfort can worsen.

VITAMINS, MINERALS, AND OTHER NUTRITIONAL SUPPLEMENTS
TAKE DAILY:
- *Proteolytic enzymes plus pancreatin.* Helps in the breakdown of fat. Take as directed with meals.
- *Papaya enzymes.* Rich in proteolytic enzymes. Take as needed when heartburn pain strikes or before meals for two to eight days.

IRRITABLE BOWEL SYNDROME

JUST THE FACTS, PLEASE . . . THE MYSTERY EXPOSED.

The muscle between the small and large intestines must work properly in order for waste to move on out. But in irritable bowel syndrome (IBS), the smooth muscle in the colon spasms. Think angry and you will have a fairly accurate picture of your digestive tract if you have IBS. Your symptoms most likely include bloating, gas, stomach cramps, depression, excess mucus in the stool, and diarrhea or constipation. Once you've gone to the bathroom, you'll feel better, but not for long. The pain, unfortunately, will come back.

THE EVIDENCE . . . EXHIBITS A TO Z.

You cannot imagine how many people who suffer from IBS have a *leaky gut,* caused by parasites that moved in a long time ago. The intestines have a hard time pushing food along, resulting in stomach pain and spasms that are followed by either a bout of diarrhea or constipation. Although IBS is more chronic than other gastrointestinal disorders, it does no permanent damage to the intestines.

GRADE-A DETECTIVE WORK.

A study in the *Journal of the American Dietetic Association* found that most IBS patients have diets that are too low in calories, iron, and calcium. Another study has found that lactase activity is reduced in IBS patients. Both studies point to the possibility of lactose intolerance—one of those "tough digesters" and a very real contributor to IBS.

Another clue: it's been found that most people have twice the amount of anaerobes (bacteria that don't need air) in their gut, which make for healthy digestion. But those who suffer from irritable bowel syndrome have many more aerobes (bacteria that need air) in their stool. This makes an ideal environment for a *leaky gut,* creating an imbalanced digestive system and gastrointestinal distress such as pain, cramps, and bloating.

A BOUNCED CHECK: HEMORRHOIDS

There's a reason why secretaries, bus drivers, psychologists, taxi drivers, and even judges suffer from hemorrhoids: they sit a lot. This puts pressure on the muscles in the abdomen; gravity pulls the weight down and veins in the anus and rectum become weak.

Heredity, too, is a factor. If one or both of your parents had hemorrhoids, you might have inherited their weak veins. Did your mother have varicose veins? This shows a predisposition to veins that "give in" to pressure. Hemorrhoids can also be a link to circulatory problems. For this reason, you should always check with your physician or health practitioner if you develop hemorrhoids.

Anything that strains the gastrointestinal tract can also cause hemorrhoids: constipation, coughing, bending too much, or sneezing.

Diet, too, plays a crucial role. Research gathered by *American Family Physician* found that insoluble dietary fiber, such as psyllium seeds, was effective in treating and preventing hemorrhoids. A low-fiber diet, on the other hand, leads to constipation, which in turn leads to straining and hemorrhoids. Add a lifestyle with a "never drink water" withdrawal and you don't need a bank statement to know that *bankruptcy* is ready to happen.

WITH ADELE'S COMPLEMENTS!

Remember, nobody's perfect—and you don't have to be, either. You might be feeling a bit overwhelmed by all the choices you have, all the regimens you have at your fingertips. You don't have to do everything all at once. Go slowly. See how you feel. One supplement at a time. One regimen at a time. Health deposits, added one by one, accumulate and gain strength over time.

Healing from the Inside is ultimately about the bigger picture: you. Your life. Your choices. Your decisions.

And remember, I'm always here, inside the pages of this book, someone you can turn to again and again. I want you to be healthy. And even more, I want *you* to *want* to be healthy.

KEEPING YOUR CONDITION "BEHIND BARS"
RESCUE REGIMEN FOR
IRRITABLE BOWEL SYNDROME

Follow Preventive Regimen for gastrointestinal problems for two weeks. Then add this Rescue Regimen.

If you see △, check Appendix C for further information.

TIPS

- Do the Foundation Regimens for a *leaky gut* and a *toxic liver* simultaneously for three weeks before starting this Rescue Regimen. These are almost always linked to irritable bowel syndrome. (See Chapter 6 and 7 for more information on a *leaky gut* and a *toxic liver*.)
- Get tested for possible parasites. They could be the underlying cause of a *leaky gut*.

ON AN ONGOING BASIS:
DIET

- *Avoid milk and dairy products.* If you are lactose intolerant, they can make your symptoms worse. You can also try over-the-counter lactase-containing pills or lactose-free products.
- *Start an elimination diet* to see if there are any "tough digesters" or allergies in your IBS connection. (See page 208 for details.)

VITAMINS, MINERALS, AND OTHER NUTRITIONAL SUPPLEMENTS
TAKE DAILY:

- △ *Calcium.* Take an additional 500 mg.
- *Magnesium.* Take an additional 500 mg if well tolerated.
- *Multi–amino acid complex.* Aids in healing intestinal lining. Take one on an empty stomach.

HERBS

- *Peppermint.* Helps reduce gassiness, bloating, and stomach pain. Take the enteric-coated capsules only; other forms can cause heartburn. Take as directed.

You are just starting to explore this new way of looking at yourself. You are just beginning to have a better understanding of how to keep gastrointestinal problems from getting worse and how to help heal *running in the red* symptoms that have become *bankruptcy* conditions. Most of all, the message is that you don't have to suffer continuously from your gastrointestinal upsets. You don't have to live with cramps, heartburn, pain, or spasms. You can do something about your "sensitive stomach." You can choose health!

Now that we've taken a "bite" out of the gastrointestinal system, let's go on to matters of the heart.

10

HEART AND CIRCULATORY BANKRUPTCIES

Before I chose health, I was on a path to a heart attack. Today, my heart is healthy—and I feel better than I did when I was forty! Keep those deposits coming! —A 70-year-old retired female schoolteacher who first came to see me eleven years ago and who still keeps in touch

David had a passion for pasta smothered with tomato sauce, which had been simmering on the stove for hours. He'd lovingly chop the onions, the tomatoes, and the garlic, stirring them in a recipe that had been in his family for generations. He'd add a loaf of just-warmed bread, then enjoy some biscotti and a cup of espresso for dessert. As he told me when he'd first come to my office, "I'd be ready to go up to heaven right now."

Unfortunately, David had a *bankruptcy* condition, which meant curtailing his delicious Italian dinners. He had just gone to his doctor for a physical, something he'd been putting off for years. As part of his examination he'd been tested for cholesterol, and his levels were way too high—over 325. His triglyceride levels were even worse—they hovered in the 800 range. Bad withdrawal news for anyone, but especially for a middle-aged, overweight man whose own father had died of a heart attack years before.

David was a housepainter by trade, one of the most reliable in the business. He'd single-handedly put new coats of paint on many of the houses in my neighborhood. People liked him. He never overcharged and was always ready with a quick smile and a jaunty step. He appeared to be in the best of health. I knew he was approaching sixty, but he looked like a man ten years younger.

So I was extremely surprised when he came to me, not to solicit work but as a client. He felt trapped, convinced that he was on his way to a heart attack, with no way to avoid it. Unfortunately, a heart attack wasn't out of the realm of possibility. I knew David's numbers were dangerously high—doubly so because there was a history of heart problems in the family. He was active, yes, but it was backbreaking labor he did, not healthy deposits such as walking, swimming, or any other aerobic exercise that would allow him to reach his target heart rate zone.

David was overwhelmed, worried. He didn't know where to start. A widower for the past two years, he had many responsibilities he had to handle alone. There was the painting business to keep up, a son in college, and a granddaughter he wanted to be around to see get married. His doctor insisted he lose weight and begin an exercise program immediately, but he was immobilized. He wrung his hands. "What do I do first?"

The first step is always the hardest: making the commitment to do something about your health. David had already made that first big step by coming to see me. He was ready for the second: some serious Health Detective work to determine the links to his problem.

THE CASE OF THE HOUSEPAINTER WITH A HEART: SOLVED

When it comes to potential heart problems, diet is one of the first things to consider. Our Health Detective work was no exception. We began exploring the foods David ate on a regular basis—the famous tomato sauce, the pasta he ate almost every day, the whole loaf of bread, spread with real butter, that he polished off in one meal. These dinners were followed by breakfasts, lunches, and snacks that always contained some kind of caffeinated beverage, from coffee and espresso to cola. David had been a vegetarian since he'd come over from the "old country." He ate cheeses, cooked and fried vegetables, starches, and occasionally indulged in delicious Italian pastries.

David knew what he had to do. It was one of the first healthy deposits I suggested for him: cutting out the fat and passing on the butter, the mayonnaise, and the large amount of oil he used in his sauce. He switched to low-fat or nonfat cheese. But his cholesterol levels didn't drop significantly; neither did his triglycerides.

He added some exercise the following week, a brisk thirty-minute walk every other day. For two full months, David faithfully followed his new diet and exercise regimen. But although his "good" cholesterol (HDL) increased slightly, his "bad" LDL cholesterol remained at dangerously high levels. His triglycerides also dipped a bit, thanks to the seven pounds he had taken off on his new regimen. But his numbers had not improved enough. David's cardiologist even put him on cholesterol-reducing medication; that, too, did not reduce his numbers enough.

Something wasn't right. The healthy deposits he was making to his Body Bank should have significantly decreased his cholesterol and triglyceride levels. Even more telling, David developed some seemingly unrelated symptoms. He started to feel such overwhelming exhaustion that he cut back his painting jobs; he also complained that he felt totally disoriented.

These symptoms told me to look beyond David's diet. The signs could be associated with a *toxic liver*. His liver, while trying to process cholesterol, was also dealing with the toxicity of the paints he used every day, not to mention the cholesterol medication he'd started to take. An overburdened liver might not be up to processing cholesterol adequately. The result? Higher levels.

But there was more. The diabetes in David's family got me to thinking that although he was not yet diabetic himself, he might have hyperinsulinemia—a different carbohydrate metabolic malfunction that could be a warning for late-onset diabetes. I sent him to his physician for a glucose tolerance test (GTT) with corresponding insulin levels. The test came back positive. It was not that he didn't have enough insulin but, rather, that he produced too much. In addition, his cells were insulin-sensitive, or resistant to allowing the insulin to bring glucose past their walls. The end result was excess glucose or high blood sugar—with the glucose stored as fat (or fat that remains in the bloodstream, causing high cholesterol levels).

This situation is often referred to as syndrome X, which is presently being studied and researched as an explanation for very high, stubborn cholesterol and triglyceride levels. David could stop eating fat from now until forever and his cholesterol levels would remain high. It was the carbohydrates that could be causing his problems, the carbohydrates and his reactions to them that made his cells insulin sensitive. His vegetarian meals with their high percentages of starch, combined with a *toxic liver*, made it a wonder his levels went down at all!

We were making headway in resolving David's health mystery, but there was one more connection that could prove dangerous to David's health if it was not addressed. Homocysteine is a by-product produced in the body from the breakdown of protein. (See Chapter 4 for more on this *health-link*.) An excess of homocysteine has also been linked to heart problems. How do you get an excess of this substance? From drinking too much coffee, for one thing, and David drank espresso all day long. Another contributing withdrawal could be David's vegetarian diet, which was deficient in vitamin B_{12}. Low levels of B_{12} are linked to high levels of homocysteine in the body.

David began my Foundation Regimen for a *toxic liver*. I also added a vitamin B_{12} supplement and suggested that he gradually switch from espresso to decaf coffee, hoping he would eventually consider the switch to herbal tea. And although it was difficult at first, David chose health and banished his nightly pasta and bread (except for special occasions). David's situation flies in the face of nearly every case that has been made over the past ten years for eating a high complex-carbohydrate diet. Because of his metabolic error, a high carbohydrate diet was detrimental to his health.

The benefits far outweighed any regrets David might have had. Within two months, his energy had been restored. He was no longer exhausted; his thinking was sharp and clear. David had lost weight and looked and felt younger than he had in a long time. The best news was that his cholesterol and triglyceride levels both dropped so dramatically that he was able to trade in the cholesterol medication for a diet high in low-fat protein and low in carbohydrates.

David no longer lives in the shadow of a possible heart attack. He feels strong and ready to dance at his granddaughter's wedding when the time comes.

DO YOU HAVE *RUNNING IN THE RED* HEART OR CIRCULATORY SYMPTOMS?

David's case was unusual. The majority of people with high cholesterol will do well with a high-carbohydrate, low-fat diet. But not all. Some share David's disorder; they too may wind up with high cholesterol. Like David, they might have a possible *running in the red, toxic liver* that is becoming a full-fledged *bankruptcy* condition.

For David, the numbers were there in black and white. But with healthy deposits, he could now prevent his cholesterol levels from getting out of hand. He understood that as far as his cholesterol was concerned, he could not follow mainstream dietary advice. In addition to his low-fat diet, he had to eat a low-carbohydrate diet to lower his cholesterol. He was finally starting the process of healing from the inside out.

Perhaps you are at a crossroads—the place David was before he received his *bankruptcy* "notice." Maybe you're not sure what your problem is. Maybe you suspect you have problems with your heart, but your different symptoms confuse you. You've checked with your physician and you've taken the usual screening tests. So far nothing shows. But what about the future? What can you do now to prevent your *running in the red* symptoms from becoming a heart and circulatory *bankruptcy*?

To help you in your own Health Detective work, look over the following statements. If any of them ring true, you could very well have one of the common heart or circulatory conditions I'll be going over in this chapter.

- I could still rock 'n' roll with the best of them at weddings. It's the chest pains I feel *after* a twirl around the dance floor that make me feel old—and cautious.
- I get shortness of breath from just going up the one flight of stairs from my living room to the bedroom!

- My hands and fingers are always cold. I just tell them "cold hands and warm heart." I wonder whether I have a circulatory problem.
- Salad is for rabbits, unless you add cold cuts, cheese, croutons, and eggs.
- My child is not doing well in school, but she won't tell me what's wrong. Talk about worry—and stress!
- Show me the beef, preferably rare, and I'll eat it even seven days a week.
- I haven't weighed myself in years, but every time I put on a suit or pants from the year before, they're too tight to wear. Maybe I should change dry cleaners?
- I *love* carbohydrates. Pasta, cereal, bagels, rolls, bread, white rice, and fruit make up the bulk of my diet.

These situations all seem to point to the same thing, something we all know makes for a healthy heart: eat low-fat foods, rich in green, leafy vegetables; exercise regularly; and learn how to manage the stress in your life without overindulging or pulling out your hair.

In fact, most of the risk factors for coronary heart disease are withdrawals that we can change to health deposits—habits that, by choosing health, can turn your liability into an asset. These include everything from cigarette smoking to a sedentary lifestyle, obesity to high blood pressure.

But there are some more subtle withdrawals that, as David discovered, can create heart and circulatory *running in the red* symptoms—signs that, if not recognized or heeded, can lead to a full-fledged *bankruptcy*.

THE HEART OF THE MATTER 1: HOMOCYSTEINE AND YOU

It's the word on everyone's lips, a new link to heart disease that can affect many people: homocysteine. Actually, Dr. Kilmer McCully, a Harvard pathologist, found this new trigger back in 1969, but most experts did not pay attention to him. The scientific community shunned him, preferring to stick with cholesterol as the root of heart trouble.

But today Dr. McCully's theories are being examined in a new light, and high homocysteine levels should soon take their place—along with high cholesterol, high blood pressure, and smoking—as a major risk factor for atherosclerosis and other heart conditions. The ongoing

Physician's Health Study at Harvard, which continues to follow 271 men throughout their lives, has found that 95 percent of those participants who had had heart attacks also had high levels of homocysteine. A 1997 study in the *New England Journal of Medicine* found that high homocysteine levels were as much a risk of heart disease as smoking or high cholesterol.

Homocysteine is an amino acid that results from the breakdown of another amino acid, methionine, which is found in animal protein, such as meat, eggs, and dairy products. Your body uses homocysteine, but only a small amount; it can be toxic in high quantities and needs to be properly converted in order to prevent its damaging effects. Too much, and homocysteine levels in the blood build up, resulting in weakened artery walls, the buildup of plaque—and heart disease.

But this link appears to be broken with three B vitamins: vitamin B_{12}, vitamin B_6, and folic acid. Homocysteine and other waste by-products of normal metabolism are detoxified by a process called methylation—which needs the proper amounts of vitamin B_{12} and folic acid to work efficiently. Vitamin B_6 converts homocysteine to cysteine, a nontoxic, harmless amino acid.

Doing the Basic Health Regimen (see Chapter 5) will ensure you are getting the necessary amounts of these vitamins and, if you already have symptoms of heart disease, the Preventive Regimen for Strengthening and Revitalizing Your Heart and Your Circulation (page 182) will help give your body the extra support it needs.

To further ensure that you are getting enough of these B vitamins, make sure you eat a diet rich in fresh vegetables, fruit, and small to moderate amounts of lean protein. These foods include broccoli, spinach, fish, and chicken.

THE HEART OF THE MATTER 2: SYNDROME X

No, this is not a villain for a new generation of *Star Trek* watchers. Syndrome X is all about, in a word, carbohydrates. Most people think that the fat in our blood (made up of triglycerides and cholesterol) comes from dietary fat, and for most people it does. It was eating fat that thickened our artery walls with cholesterol deposits, that raised our blood pressure, that made our poor heart work much too hard. But the newest studies show that it is, for some, the carbohydrates they eat as well. Physicians call this phenomenon Type IV hyperlipidemia.

Basically, a person who has syndrome X is reactive to carbohydrates, leading to excessive insulin secretion. The liver will send insulin—the hormone that processes sugar—to facilitate moving the glucose from the bloodstream into the cells. But the cells become resistant; they won't "eat"; they will not let the glucose in. The liver sends out more insulin, still trying to process the carbohydrates (grains, potatoes, bread, corn, peas, fruits, and, of course, desserts). The result is an over-production of insulin and the potential for high blood sugar and long-term weight gain, among other conditions.

As with David, a low-fat diet won't be all that's needed to ease your heart problems if you have syndrome X. Research at the Heart Disease Prevention Clinic in Minneapolis found that people who were hyper-insulinemic and followed a low-fat diet lowered their cholesterol by only 5 percent.

Other research, done in Northern Ireland in 1990, found that hyperinsulinemia was a definite link in such diseases as high choles-terol and atherosclerosis. If you cut out fats and still can't get your levels down, then you may well have hyperinsulinemia.

If you crave your carbs and can't live without that bagel or that banana, if you eat more than three pieces of fruit a day, if your choles-terol is high and you don't know why, if you have always been a "yo-yo" dieter, you could be dealing with syndrome X. I recommend strip-ping the carbs from your diet as well as reducing the fat. (See page 181 for the details on stripping the carbs.)

THE HEART OF THE MATTER 3: A COENZYME RELATIONSHIP
Many people consider it a miracle supplement, especially in Japan, where millions of people swear by it. It is coenzyme Q10, and it's been used to combat the effects of aging, strengthen the heart and circula-tory system, soothe the intestines, help prevent ulcers, treat mental ill-ness, and even ease the side effects of chemotherapy!

And there are studies that back up most of these claims. At the University of Texas, people who had congestive heart failure and took coenzyme Q10 had over a 75 percent chance of survival after three years; those who did not take the enzyme had only a 25 percent chance of survival. Further studies, in Texas as well as in Japan, found that coenzyme Q10 may help control hypertension.

Coenzyme Q10 is actually a vitamin-like substance that exists in the body, but the amount decreases as you get older. It is a powerful anti-oxidant that is very similar in action to vitamin E.

A study at the University of Pittsburgh and the Pittsburgh Cancer Institute has found that coenzyme Q10 and vitamin E work well together. Not only does the vitamin E protect coenzyme Q10, but coenzyme Q10 protects the antioxidant properties of vitamin E!

THE HEART OF THE MATTER 4: FANCY FLAVONOIDS

When your mother told you to eat your vegetables, she knew what she was talking about! Fruits and vegetables contain not only valuable vitamins and minerals but also flavonoids—vitamin-like substances that act as powerful antioxidants. Eating your five servings of fruits and vegetables a day, as well as other plant foods, can help ensure that you are getting your bioflavonoids, some of which include quercetin, rutin, and hesperidin. You might even notice that your vitamin C supplement contains bioflavonoids, giving you a double healthy deposit.

A study at the National Institute of Public Health and Environment Protection in the Netherlands found that the chances of heart complications were considerably reduced in elderly men if they ate foods with flavonoids every day. These men got their flavonoid dose from apples, tea, and onions. But you can also find it in all plant foods, in the white "peel" of citrus fruits, berries, apricots, grapes, lemons, oranges, prunes, peppers, and the herbal tree extracts ginkgo biloba and pycnogenol.

THE HEART OF THE MATTER 5: A FISHY STORY

Yes, fish oil can protect your heart, helping to prevent the buildup of plaque and to lower triglyceride levels. Here's some evidence that "tips the scales" in favor in fish oil:

As reported in the *Journal of the American Medical Association*, a study of over 300 patients in Washington who had had heart attacks found that Omega-3 fish oils reduced their risk of another attack. Another study, this one reported by the *Annals of Nutrition and Metabolism*, reported that Omega-3 fish oils significantly helped heal the hearts of patients who had had sudden attacks.

TURN A BOUNCED CHECK INTO A
DEPOSIT SLIP: "STRIPPING THE CARBS"

Edema is swelling, pure and simple. Fluid builds up in the face or limbs and leads to bloating. It is a symptom rather than an actual *bankruptcy*. Edema symptoms are best treated with a healthy diet deposit. Stay away from caffeine, alcohol, salt, fried foods, and highly allergic foods such as dairy products and wheat.

Edema's roots can be found in allergies; problems with protein absorption in the gut; vitamin deficiencies, especially B; heart failure; or syndrome X (hyperinsulinemia), especially if you have stubborn high cholesterol and triglyceride levels that just won't budge. You may want to investigate whether you have hyperinsulinemia by taking a glucose tolerance test with corresponding insulin levels. Or perhaps you'd prefer to simplify things by trying to keep your blood sugar controlled by eating the following way. Stabilized blood sugar eliminates the cravings for carbohydrates.

STRIPPING YOUR CARBS

1. Eat a bread at breakfast, along with a protein. This could be an egg-white vegetable omelet on a piece of toast.
2. Eat only low-fat protein and vegetables at lunch. Use olive oil sparingly. No rolls!
3. Stick to low-fat protein and nonstarchy vegetables at dinner, having only carbohydrates at dinner every other day, if desired. Even though the current index says otherwise, limit such highly glycemic (and too easily converted) starches as pasta, bagels, popcorn, white flour, and white rolls. Opt for winter squash, beans, lentils, or whole-grain rice in limited portions.
4. Eliminate fruit for one week; then you may have one fruit right before dinner, if desired.
5. Stabilize your blood sugar by eating veggie snacks every two hours between meals—and eat meals on time at reasonable hours. You'll find that you won't crave carbohydrates and are more easily able to reduce consumption of them.

This program is designed to minimize insulin reactions.

PREVENTIVE REGIMEN
FOR STRENGTHENING AND REVITALIZING
YOUR HEART AND YOUR CIRCULATION

If heart problems live within your family tree, follow this Preventive Regimen for your healing deposit.

Be sure to start slowly, introducing supplements gradually. The Foundation Regimens for a *leaky gut* and/or *toxic liver* are almost always indicated. Do both Foundation Regimens, for three weeks, if applicable, then add this Preventive Regimen.

ON AN ONGOING BASIS:
- Don't forget to incorporate *exercise* into your life. Oxygen is pumped faster through your body; your circulation improves; your heart strengthens.
- A *healthy diet*, low in fat and high in fiber, fresh fruits, and vegetables, does more than provide important vitamins, minerals, and other nutrients. It can also help you lose weight, which lowers cholesterol levels, reduces high blood pressure, and produces less strain on your heart.
- *Managing stress* is an important component of heart health. Try to reduce your stress load and improve your coping skills with yoga, massage, meditation, or deep relaxation tapes.

If you see △, please check Appendix C for further information.

VITAMINS, MINERALS, AND OTHER NUTRITIONAL SUPPLEMENTS
TAKE DAILY, IN ADDITION TO A HIGH POTENCY VITAMIN-MINERAL SUPPLEMENT:
- *Folic acid*. A B vitamin that aids in proper conversion of homocysteine. Take 400 mcg.
- △ *Vitamin E*. A powerful antioxidant. Helps circulation and to prevent plaque accumulation in arterial walls by preventing oxidation of LDL cholesterol. Take 400–600 IU.
- *Vitamin B$_{12}$*. Aids in proper conversion of homocysteine. Take 500 mcg.
- *Vitamin B$_6$*. Aids in proper conversion of homocysteine. Take 100 mg.
- *Vitamin C with bioflavonoids*. Helps protect arterial walls. Take 1000 mg twice daily.
- *Coenzyme Q10*. A vitamin-like substance that helps strengthen the heart, lower cholesterol, and helps reduce high blood pressure. Take 100 mg.

- *Selenium.* A powerful antioxidant that helps keep your heart healthy. Take 100 mcg.
- *Fish oil.* Helps to prevent blood clotting and lower cholesterol. Take 2 capsules.
- *Lecithin granules.* A lipid that helps prevent cardiovascular disease and the buildup of plaque. Helps eliminate cholesterol from the body. Sprinkle 1 tablespoon on food or mixed in a glass of water.
- *L-Taurine.* An amino acid that helps stabilize heartbeat. Take 250 mg on an empty stomach. *Discontinue use after 2 months.*
- *L-Carnitine.* An amino acid–like substance that helps stabilize heartbeat. Take 250 mg daily on an empty stomach. *Discontinue after 2 months.*
- *Digestive enzymes with bromelain.* Helps body process fats. Take as directed with each meal.
- *Calcium.* Helps to maintain healthy cardiac muscle function. Take 1000 mg split dose.
- *Magnesium.* Reduces spasms while supporting tone of muscles. Take 500 mg.
- *Flaxseed oil.* Reduces risk for hardening of arteries. Take 2 capsules.

HERBS
- *Garlic.* Helps prevent the oxidation of cholesterol. Take 2 capsules.
- ⚠ *Cayenne.* Helps maintain a healthy heart and strengthens circulation. Take in capsule form as directed.
- *Hawthorn berries.* Helps dilate blood vessels and strengthen the heart. Also helps decrease cholesterol levels. Take in capsule form as directed.

As these "Heart of the Matter" insights show, our understanding of what really causes and prevents heart disease is changing every day. But by understanding your body and applying your Health Detective work, you can certainly be on the way to a healthier heart.

ANGINA

JUST THE FACTS, PLEASE . . . THE MYSTERY EXPOSED.
"This is not a heart attack." Repeat. "This is not a heart attack." Angina is your heart's way of telling you it's not getting enough oxygen, either

KEEPING YOUR CONDITION "BEHIND BARS"
RESCUE REGIMEN FOR ANGINA

Follow Preventive Regimen for heart problems for two weeks. Then add this Rescue Regimen.

If you see △, check Appendix C for further information.

VITAMINS, MINERALS, AND OTHER NUTRITIONAL SUPPLEMENTS
TAKE DAILY:
△ *Vitamin E.* Add 200 IU.
- *L-Carnitine.* Add 250 mg on empty stomach. *Discontinue after 2 months.*
- *N-Acetylcysteine (NAC).* This amino acid–like substance is a strong antioxidant. It helps break down fats before they can clog artery walls. Take 500 mg on an empty stomach. *Discontinue after 2 months.*

HERBS
- *Pycnogenol.* Pine bark extract. An antioxidant, helps strengthen and restore the heart muscle and the circulatory system. Take 50–100 mg in capsule form.
- *Ginger.* Enhances circulation. Take in capsule form as directed or chew one or two fresh slivers every day.

because the coronary arteries that lead to the heart are blocked or because of overexertion. Whatever the reason, consider this a warning.

THE EVIDENCE . . . EXHIBITS A TO Z.
If you suffer from angina, you are not alone: 3 million Americans experience angina, mostly men over thirty. After sixty-five, angina doesn't differentiate between the sexes. The same risk factors for heart attack apply here: high blood pressure, obesity, smoking, high cholesterol, diabetes, and hyperinsulinemia. The most common prescription drug given for angina is nitroglycerin. It dilates the coronary arteries so that oxygen can enter the heart, and it relieves the pain. Although nitro-

glycerin may stop an attack, it can happen again—unless you make changes in your present lifestyle.

GRADE-A DETECTIVE WORK.
Angina by itself is not serious, but it can lead to arrhythmia and an actual heart attack. Clogged coronary arteries mean that you most likely have another, and more serious, *bankruptcy* condition: atherosclerosis.

ARRHYTHMIA

JUST THE FACTS, PLEASE . . . THE MYSTERY EXPOSED.
Better than a five-piece band, better than a drummer, better than a clock, your heart is one of the most exquisitely kept machines ever created. But even hearts sometimes wind down. They might skip a beat. They might add a beat. They might change tempo. Any heartbeat irregularities or palpitations are called arrhythmia and, although usually not dangerous, it is a condition not to be ignored.

THE EVIDENCE . . . EXHIBITS A TO Z.
The sinus node is the conductor that sends out electrical impulses to keep the heart pumping at a steady beat. But sometimes the sinus node gets out of whack or artery walls get clogged with cholesterol and blood flow can't keep up the tempo. However, sometimes an arrhythmia is just arrhythmia—a simple misfire that occurs from too much caffeine, a reaction to an antihistamine, or stress.

GRADE-A DETECTIVE WORK.
Arrhythmia usually causes no harm. Once the stressful situation passes, the offending medicine is eliminated, or the coffee is finished, the arrhythmia goes away. Serious arrhythmia occurs in the upper chambers of the heart. In this case, it can be a sinus node that has gone off-key. This is usually when a pacemaker steps in. Ventricular fibrillation—a fast, furious, and disorganized arrhythmia occurring in the ventricles—is the number-one cause of sudden death in the United States. If you have an attack of arrhythmia, you should see your physician to determine if medical attention is necessary.

A BOUNCED CHECK: ATHEROSCLEROSIS

Call this the grandfather of all cardiovascular conditions, the most common and the most dangerous if not treated. It's a cumulative disease, building up over years, but with patience and some healthy deposits, clogged arteries can be cleansed and a sluggish heart can pump like new.

Atherosclerosis is, literally, the hardening of the arteries. After years of abusive withdrawals, from too much fat to too little salad, the arteries become inflamed; the walls become clogged with a buildup of cholesterol and fatty deposits. Eventually, this debris calcifies and hardens into a plaque that can stop life-sustaining blood from passing through. The result? A heart attack or a stroke.

Atherosclerosis damage can be an inherited trait; you might have inherited a vulnerability for LDL (bad) cholesterol buildup. Artery walls can also be hurt by the carbon monoxide in smoke, unrelenting stress, and high blood pressure.

But healthy deposits, from beginning an exercise program to cutting back on fats, can stop atherosclerosis and even reverse it:

- Start eating five servings of fresh fruits and vegetables a day.
- Eat fish at least three times a week.
- Begin an exercise program: walking, dancing, jogging—whatever you like to do!
- Try to de-stress with massages, quiet time, or a walk in the country.
- Start the Preventive Regimen for heart problems. Two weeks later, slowly increase your bioflavonoids and vitamin C to a total of 3000 mg.

KEEPING YOUR CONDITION "BEHIND BARS"
RESCUE REGIMEN FOR ARRHYTHMIA

Follow Preventive Regimen for heart problems for two weeks. Then add this Rescue Regimen.

If you see △, check Appendix C for further information.

ON AN ONGOING BASIS:
DIET
- Eat the 5-Day Miracle Diet way to have good blood-sugar levels.

Crashing blood sugar may cause rapid heartbeat; this program helps stabilize your blood-sugar levels. Have a breakfast of a starch and protein within a half hour of getting up. Eat a "hard chew" vegetable or fruit snack within two hours and every two hours before lunch. This can be carrots, green beans, or an apple. Eat a lunch of protein and veggies no later than 1:00. Eat a "hard chew" snack or a "soft chew" snack (an orange or cantaloupe) every three hours after lunch. Eat a dinner of protein and veggies and starch. Limit pasta to every other night only. Do not eat after dinner.

VITAMINS, MINERALS, AND OTHER NUTRITIONAL SUPPLEMENTS
TAKE DAILY:
- *Magnesium.* Add 300 mg.
- *L-Taurine.* Add 500–600 mg on an empty stomach. *Discontinue after two months.*

HIGH CHOLESTEROL

JUST THE FACTS, PLEASE . . . THE MYSTERY EXPOSED.
Cholesterol is a natural fatty substance manufactured within our own bodies. In small doses, it helps aid in many of our most basic body functions, including cell growth, nerve insulation, and hormone production. Unfortunately, there can be too much of a good thing, especially when it comes to cholesterol. Not only does the liver manufacture exactly what we need, but we also ingest cholesterol in the foods we eat, from meat and eggs to butter, including the saturated fats found in margarine and certain vegetable oils.

In short, we get too much. Lipoproteins—sort of a "shopping cart" containing fat and protein produced in the liver—carry this heavy load of cholesterol around in our body, most of it low-density lipoprotein (LDL), or "bad" cholesterol. Once our body takes what it needs, the LDL is left in our bloodstream, still floating around. Eventually, it clings to our artery walls, clogging passageways and attracting blood clots. That's why it's called "bad" cholesterol.

A RAY OF HOPE FOR RAYNAUD'S SYNDROME

This circulatory *bankruptcy* is far from the heart. Named after the French physician who first discovered it (Maurice Raynaud, 1834–1881), this condition results in the constriction of blood in the fingers and sometimes the toes.

At first, the numbness and poor circulation seem a reaction to cold; the fingers turn white or very red. They start to tingle.

Raynaud's syndrome is usually the result of smoking, a major withdrawal. It has also been diagnosed in people with arteriosclerosis or angina, as well as those who are taking beta-blockers to lower their blood pressure or ergot-based medications to ease their migraine headaches.

Any deposit that returns circulation to the fingers is a good one.

- Stop smoking!
- Massage and bodywork are important in Raynaud's syndrome.
- Avoid caffeine and decongestants.
- Try the Preventive Regimen for the heart and circulation to relieve symptoms.
- Increase your vitamin E to double the amount on the Preventive Regimen to help improve circulation. (Read about its contraindications in Appendix C.)
- Increase your coenzyme Q10 to double the amount on the Basic Health Regimen. It helps improve oxygenation to the mucosal linings.
- Take dimethylglycine (DMG), an amino acid that helps improve oxygenation to tissue. Take as directed on an empty stomach.

But where there is bad, there is always good. Enter high-density lipoproteins (HDL), the scrubbing bubbles that carry LDL cholesterol back to the liver for processing and eventual elimination. HDL helps to keep the arteries clear. That's why it's called "good" cholesterol.

The risk of heart disease comes with the ratio of LDL to HDL cholesterol you have in your body. If you have a sufficient amount of HDL cholesterol to combat the LDL, your risk of heart disease is much less. That's why knowing the amount of LDL cholesterol in relation to your HDL can be more important than *total* cholesterol numbers.

DIFFERENT STROKES

A stroke is very similar to a heart attack, except that it occurs in the brain rather than in the heart muscles or the coronary arteries. Strokes might seem to come on abruptly, but there are warning signs, called transient ischemic attacks, or TIAs for short. These mini-strokes last for moments or up to half an hour. You might black out. You might shake. Although you come out of a TIA intact, know that you are at risk.

The best remedy for stroke is the one for heart disease. Eat right, exercise regularly, learn how to manage stress effectively, and do my Preventive Regimen for the heart. Healthy deposits all.

THE EVIDENCE . . . EXHIBITS A TO Z.

One of the obvious risk factors for high cholesterol is obesity, a situation you can address. But you don't have to be overweight to have high cholesterol, especially if you're eating all those saturated fats and trans-fatty acids.

A more subtle risk factor is a *toxic liver*, overburdened from a lifetime of assault. Working its detox job in double time, it is not efficient and not functioning up to par. Since cholesterol is manufactured in the liver, congestion and toxicity can upset the lipoprotein (shopping) cart.

Another issue with high LDL cholesterol is lack of exercise, another risk factor that you can change! The good news is that studies have found that HDL is raised with every turn, step, or jog you take. If your idea of exercise is looking for the remote control, chances are your HDL levels could use a jump start.

GRADE-A DETECTIVE WORK.

High cholesterol is a warning, announcing what it may cause later, such as atherosclerosis, heart disease, stroke. These are frightening conditions that may be prevented by making some healthy deposits now. For example, a study done at the University of Kentucky found that eating even just 1 cup of cooked beans a day will appreciably lower blood cholesterol—by 10 percent. And other studies found that over the long term, eating beans gives HDL cholesterol levels a 17 percent edge over LDL.

Homocysteine, an amino acid derived from the breakdown of animal protein, has been found to contribute to high cholesterol when it accumulates in the bloodstream. If you are eating too much animal protein and not getting enough vitamins B_{12}, B_6, and folic acid—watch out! Your homocysteine may not be converted properly, possibly resulting in a buildup of plaque on the artery walls.

KEEPING YOUR CONDITION "BEHIND BARS"
RESCUE REGIMEN FOR HIGH CHOLESTEROL

Follow Preventive Regimen for heart problems for two weeks. Then add this Rescue Regimen.

If you see △, check Appendix C for further information.

TIPS
- Follow the Foundation Regimen for a *toxic liver* 2–3 weeks before starting this program. High cholesterol may be a sign of an overburdened, overwhelmed liver.

ON AN ONGOING BASIS:
DIET
- Try my "stripping the carbs" program (see page 181) if you feel you have a "carbohydrate sensitivity" and may suffer from hyperinsulinemia.

VITAMINS, MINERALS, AND OTHER NUTRITIONAL SUPPLEMENTS
TAKE DAILY:
- *Folic acid.* Add 400 mcg.
- △ *Vitamin E.* Add 200 IU.
- *L-Carnitine.* Add 250 mg on an empty stomach.
- △ *Inositol Hexanicotinate.* Helps to reduce cholesterol levels. Take 250 mg. If well tolerated increase to 250 mg three times a day.
- *Psyllium husk.* A fiber that helps reduce cholesterol levels. Take in capsule form before meals or powder as directed, both with a full glass of water.

HYPERTENSION

JUST THE FACTS, PLEASE . . . THE MYSTERY EXPOSED.

It's called the silent killer—and for good reasons. High blood pressure (or hypertension) usually has no obvious symptoms. In fact, half the people who have hypertension don't even know it. But left unchecked, hypertension can lead to a heart attack or a stroke, or sudden death. The good news is that checking your blood pressure today is as easy as taking your temperature. You can buy kits in drugstores for self-monitoring, you can take a fifteen-minute break from your busy routine and have it checked by a nurse in your doctor's office, or you can take advantage of blood pressure testing days at hospitals, at work, and in your community.

Blood pressure is exactly what it sounds like: the force of the blood whooshing through the arteries. If pressure is too high, the blood hits the walls with tremendous force, making them vulnerable to injury.

THE EVIDENCE . . . EXHIBITS A TO Z.

There are 40 million Americans with hypertension. It is the most common heart condition and also one of the most dangerous. It is the main cause of stroke and one of the major causes of heart attack. But hypertension is also one of the easiest conditions to control.

If you have hypertension, it is crucial that you see your physician as soon as possible. He or she can give you medication to help lower your blood pressure. But don't use your medication as an excuse *not* to change bad habits. Choose health! By consistently making some healthy deposits, you might see your numbers drop so low that you will be able to come off the medication (under a doctor's supervision, of course).

First and foremost, lose weight! For every two pounds you lose, you also lose one millimeter of mercury off those blood pressure numbers.

Regular exercise has also been found to reduce blood pressure. Walking is a safe, easy exercise to try if you haven't gotten out of a car or off of a couch for a while. All you need is a pair of walking shoes and you're ready to go.

STALKING THE WILD . . . CELERY

Did you know that if you eat a stalk of celery every day, you may be able to help lower your blood pressure? Celery oil helps dilate the muscles that regulate blood pressure. In fact, one laboratory study found that rats who ate four stalks of celery a day decreased their blood pressure by 13 percent.

GRADE-A DETECTIVE WORK.

Believe it or not, although we know that the predisposition for hypertension can be inherited, the mystery as to *why* people actually do get it remains 95 percent unsolved.

The other 5 percent of cases can be the result of kidney disease or tumors that cause the adrenal glands to secrete too much of the hormones that raise blood pressure levels. This 5 percent can also be the result of exposure to environmental toxicity. Heavy metals, such as the cadmium found in paint and the lead contamination in drinking water, have been found to cause hypertension. Studies of people with high blood pressure found that they had cadmium levels three to four times higher than that of the general population.

Your heart is the "pulse" of your life's energy, vitality, and strength. Because of your heart and the rest of your circulatory system, you are able to distribute nutrients to hungry cells. You are able to ensure that rich, healthy blood is pumped through your arteries and veins.

KEEPING YOUR CONDITION "BEHIND BARS"
RESCUE REGIMEN FOR HYPERTENSION

Follow Preventive Regimen for heart problems for two weeks. Then add this Rescue Regimen.

If you see △, check Appendix C for further information.

TIP
- Have your physician check for hyperinsulinemia if your good attempts to reduce weight, cholesterol, and blood pressure fail,

especially if there is late-onset diabetes in the family. The test determines insulin levels. It should not involve only fasting. An accurate diagnostic test is one that checks insulin during glucose tolerance test over the course of several hours.

ON AN ONGOING BASIS:
DIET
- If you have hyperinsulinemia, try my "stripping the carbs" program (see page 181) to help reduce your carbohydrate reactions.

VITAMINS, MINERALS, AND OTHER NUTRITIONAL SUPPLEMENTS
TAKE DAILY:
△ *Calcium.* Add 200 mg.
△ *Magnesium.* Add 400 mg.
- *Coenzyme Q10.* Add 100 mg.

You now have some insight into the care for this life-sustaining heart, as well as a better sense of how Health Detective work is involved. You are becoming more aware of some of the heart and circulatory withdrawals you might have made in the past, and the healthy deposits you can start to make right now to make a *real* difference. The choice is yours. I hope you choose health! Your heart will thank you for years to come.

But there are still several more health mysteries to solve. Allergy *bankruptcies* are next.

WITH ADELE'S COMPLEMENTS!

Don't despair if, at first, it seems as if your condition is getting worse. You have to remember that your body has been in a state of withdrawal for years. Then, suddenly, here you are, putting healthy deposit after healthy deposit into your Body Bank. Give your body time to stabilize, to grow accustomed to this new improved state. This "waiting period" is especially true for deposits you make for the sake of your *leaky gut* and your *toxic liver*. Since they have the biggest impact on your health, they will feel your new "wellness" the most.

Patience is more than a virtue. It is necessary—and rewarding!

11

ALLERGY BANKRUPTCIES

I thought it was normal to get headaches, to be cranky a lot, to be tired almost all the day. Who would have thought what I really had was an allergy!
—A 32-year-old secretary, mother of two, and happy former client

Suzanne knew she was allergic. That wasn't the problem. It was the impact the allergies were having on her life.

She had had asthma and allergies ever since she was a child. She remembered her mother carefully listening to the pollen counts on the radio every morning before she was allowed to go outside. And those birthday parties where all her friends had ice cream and cake and she had to eat lemon ice.

Suzanne's mother took her to specialist after specialist. Nothing showed up—until she went to an allergist. Patch tests showed that she was allergic to just about everything: dust, pollen, dander, penicillin, and items from all four major food groups, from milk and eggs to broccoli and radishes.

She tried to make peace with her allergies, staying away from the foods that irritated her skin and made her mouth blister. She avoided picnics in the spring and the great outdoors in general. As much as she wanted to have a dog like her friends, she learned to make do with a goldfish and a turtle. Her mother kept the house spotlessly clean and Suzanne slept on hypoallergenic sheets and pillows.

Her allergic reactions continued throughout her childhood. By the time she was a teenager, she would develop instant, painful mouth sores as soon as she ate most uncooked fruits or vegetables. Her diet became so aggravatingly limited that she began to form a really unhealthy menu

---

A BOUNCED CHECK:
A COMMON CHILDHOOD AILMENT

Although it sounds scary, otitis media is the technical name for ear infection, the plague of many a parent and child. Antibiotics are usually
given to stop the pain. Unfortunately, studies have found that, with a
regimen of tetracycline or any other antibiotic, ear infections will come
back within the month.

Most ear infections have been linked to food allergies. In an amazing 86 to 93 percent of children who suffer from chronic ear infections,
those who have stopped eating the culprit food or inhaling the environmental villains have had their ear infections clear up, never to return.

A smart Health Detective knows to look at the gut if your child gets
recurring earaches. Both food allergies and frequent, recent antibiotic
regimens have been linked to a vulnerable gastrointestinal tract, one
that provides fertile soil for a *leaky gut*. Here are some hints to help
take the ache out of an ear:

- My Foundation Regimen for a *leaky gut* is designed for *adults only*! It
  can help earache symptoms clear up; however, check with your
  health practitioner about adapting it for growing children.
- The longer a baby is breast-fed, the less likely the chance of ear
  infection.
- Mullein oil, used by Native Americans for centuries, is a natural ear
  drop that can ease the pain of otitis media. Heat it gently and put
  one to two drops in your child's ear. You can find mullein oil in most
  health food stores.
- Eliminate milk products. They create mucus and may trigger allergic
  reactions.

---

consisting of nothing but high-sugar foods. Sugar was one of the few
things that did not cause her painful symptoms.

As Suzanne grew older and went out into the world, it became in-
creasingly difficult for her to keep her allergies in check. She couldn't
travel during college breaks; she requested a single room, just in case
she might be assigned a roommate who wore perfume.

When Suzanne reached adulthood, she had more than adjusted to
her allergies; she had accepted them as a way of life. The sneezing, the

---

BANK S-TELLARS

'Tis in ourselves that we are thus or thus. Our bodies are gardens, to the which our wills are gardeners.

—William Shakespeare, *Othello*, Act I, Scene 3

---

red, teary eyes, the skin rashes, the mouth sores, the dry throat—these were all symptoms she felt on an almost daily basis.

One night over dinner at a Chinese restaurant, she inadvertently ate some shrimp. She felt as if her throat were closing; she couldn't breathe. Her friends, who'd eaten the same shrimp dish without any problem, immediately rushed her to an emergency room—a place that, unfortunately, Suzanne knew far too well.

Throughout the allergy-induced dramas of her days, Suzanne had continued to go to an allergist. "I'm allergic to everything," she told me the first time she'd come to my office. "Healthy things, too. Apples. Carrots. Cantaloupe. String beans."

Her emotional distress was surpassed only by her physical pain: red, watery, swollen eyes, sores in her mouth, diarrhea, stomach pain, blotchy skin, a constant cough, sneezing, and a nonstop runny nose. In short, Suzanne's symptoms were devastating and with her constantly. Her husband suggested she see a psychologist, just to help her adjust to the impact these limitations were having on her life.

This was the Suzanne I met at our first meeting: fearful, angry, and depressed, forced to live a life that was eroding any possibility of joy.

THE MYSTERY OF THE CARROT JUICE AND THE PEELER: SOLVED

As always, Suzanne and I began with the basics: the Health Detective work that would help us determine the withdrawals behind her debilitating symptoms and provide clues as to what healthy deposits would have the most impact.

The fact that Suzanne had a severe allergy *bankruptcy* was obvious;

we had to find out why her symptoms were getting worse and if there were any underlying conditions that were, literally, destroying her life.

Considering the incredible amount of sugary foods she'd been eating, I knew we had to suspect an excess of yeast as a contributing factor and, if it was, we could then look at the possibility of a *leaky gut.* But that alone wasn't enough. Suzanne was the exception to the "always eat a healthy diet" rule; fresh produce triggered those hateful sores in her mouth. Even more frustrating was the fact that not all veggies and fruits produced this particular allergic reaction, and not all the time. Suzanne found that she could actually eat a little bit of produce, at least for a while. She was able to put up with the watery eyes and scratchy throat that inevitably followed. But eventually, if she continued to eat the offending veggie, the sores would come out.

Food allergies are peculiar things, almost conditions with a will of their own. Sometimes they appear as a sudden assault, a jolt of symptoms immediately after eating the "toxic" food. Sometimes they are days or months in the making, slowly building to a threshold point where symptoms, seemingly out of the blue, begin. (See Section III on the *leaky gut* for more details.) And, as you'll see later in this chapter, sometimes allergies occur from eating too much of a specific food. The body begins to resist the food it is addicted to, with more intense allergic reactions a few hours after eating it. Perversely, this allergic reaction makes you actually crave *more* of the food.

Why this allergy to fruits and vegetables? Had Suzanne gone over her threshold with so many fruits and vegetables?

We had to probe further. I asked Suzanne what she fed her two young children. The first thing that popped into her mind was carrot juice. "It's the one healthy treat they love," she told me. She made two quarts of it herself several times a week. Making fresh carrot juice meant handling carrots. Even though she didn't dare drink any carrot juice herself, the chopping, the peeling, the washing, the *touching* of them affected her ability to eat carrots—something she had been able to tolerate until recently without developing sores. Suzanne was so sensitive that this overload of carrots now made her react to almost every other kind of produce. She had crossed her threshold.

But there were more questions to ask and answers to discover. The *leaky gut* and its *toxic liver* companion became more important as Suzanne and I continued. She had recurring yeast infections. She had taken a great many painkillers and decongestants, including acetaminophen, in a futile attempt to treat her symptoms. She ate very little real food for fear of getting an allergic reaction, causing a deficiency of the nutrients that would have supported her body. Suzanne had subjected her gut to withdrawals from her Body Bank that had weakened her liver at the same time, which was now overworking, trying to keep up with its job to detoxify. "I can't eat fresh fruit and vegetables. I can't drink milk. I can't eat wheat. I live on rice, homemade chicken broth, and lots and lots of cookies!" Suzanne's multivitamin and mineral supplement, which she took diligently every day, was not a big enough healthy deposit to affect so much withdrawal activity.

When she told me that her father, a naval officer, traveled to many exotic places over the years, I asked about parasites. I knew it was possible to pass parasites from one to another through the handling of food. And, if left unchecked, they continue to flourish through the years. Although Suzanne didn't know about herself, she knew that her father had been diagnosed with parasites many years before. She was surprised at my asking about it; parasite problems had never been discussed in her family or with any of the specialists she had seen.

We decided that Suzanne should go to a parasitologist for testing, just in case this was an underlying withdrawal. Nothing was found; perhaps the strong, frequent antibiotics she had taken as a child had taken care of any parasites that she might have harbored. In any case, the antibiotics themselves had been a tremendous withdrawal on her vulnerable gut.

I then suggested she begin the Foundation Regimen for a *leaky gut* and carry it to the highest dosages; over the next few weeks, we added the Foundation Regimen for a *toxic liver*. We immediately began making other deposits to ease Suzanne's symptoms. The first one? Asking her husband to make the carrot juice. Within weeks, her most acute symptoms started to lessen. Her internal healing had begun.

As Suzanne's gut and liver became stronger, we were able to try an elimination diet to determine exactly what she was allergic to; the results were surprising. Now that her foundations were healing, she had fewer reactions. Although she still had to stay away from carrots and milk, she could tolerate other fresh vegetables and fruits—in ever-increasing amounts—without developing painful sores in her mouth. She'd even been able to visit her mother's house in the woods for the first time in years at the height of the allergy season.

When I asked her on our most recent visit how she was feeling about the changes she was experiencing, Suzanne barely paused before saying, "I haven't been to an emergency room in six months and that's a wonderful, wonderful thing!"

DO YOU HAVE *RUNNING IN THE RED* ALLERGY SYMPTOMS?

Perhaps your symptoms aren't as dramatic as Suzanne's, but you too might be suffering from an allergy in the guise of a migraine headache, a skin rash, or a stuffed-up nose. Whether your allergy symptom is related to the environment, to the dust, air pollution, pollen, or perfume you breathe in, or to the foods you eat, your Body Bank account is reacting by sending out symptom withdrawals. Take charge of your account. You can start making healthy deposits right now.

The first step? Determining if you have *running in the red* symptoms of allergy. See if any of the statements below pertain to you and your condition. If you answer yes to any of them, your Health Detective radar should go up.

- Every morning, it's cereal and milk, milk and cereal. Even on weekends, except for an occasional brunch with friends.
- When I have a headache—and I get a lot of them—I immediately take acetaminophen, not realizing that I could be setting the stage for more allergic reactions.
- When others' thoughts turn to love in the spring, mine turn to anxiety and depression: it's only a matter of time before I start sneezing . . . and sneezing.
- I was what they call a colicky baby. I remember my mother telling me that she couldn't breast-feed me and I had to drink formula made with soymilk.
- I get aches and pains in my joints that come and go. I never know when my body's going to hurt—at work, relaxing at home, or even walking down the street.

- Sometimes my heart starts racing after I've eaten a meal—or sometimes I sweat for no reason at all.
- I was so happy when yeast infection medication became an over-the-counter purchase. I was tired of having to call my gynecologist all the time for a prescription.
- I love antiquing, but I had to stop. Every time I'd walk into a shop, I'd start to sneeze and my nose would run as soon as I checked out the first jam-packed room.
- I have one glass of wine almost every night with dinner. I really need to relax!
- I just have to see a cat purring down the street and my eyes start to water and burn.
- Whenever I go to the movies or the theater, I keep my fingers crossed that someone with perfume or cologne won't sit next to me. It never fails: my throat tightens up, I start to cough, and it ruins the show for me.

The aches and pains of arthritis; the cramps and gas of irritable bowel; the sneezy, scratchy, stuffed-up signs of respiratory ailments. The surprise is not that allergies can be responsible for your seemingly unconnected symptoms like aches and pains, but that you can make enough health deposits to stop or minimize such allergic reactiveness. Here's some Health Detective information to help you discover any allergic reaction propensity you might have, so that you can identify the healthy deposits for your Body Bank account.

REACTION RETRACTION 1: A CONFUSED IMMUNE SYSTEM

It sounds simple: When you have an allergic reaction to something that others find harmless—say, eating whole-wheat bread or scratching your dog's belly—your immune system is not acting correctly. But why?

For the answer, think *Star Wars*, with those heroes of your inner galaxy, the antibodies. When a foreign substance enters your body, either through your mouth, your nose, or your pores, its molecules (called antigens) are sniffed out by those brave antibodies, the immunoglobulins, or Igs for short. The immunoglobulin-G (IgG) team are the fierce heroes responsible for literally eating up those antigens, be they preservatives, foreign substances such as dust particles, or bacteria that entered via an open cut. The immunoglobulin-A (IgA) team operates in a smaller area, but they are just as deadly, effective in neutralizing potentially contagious germs found in mucus and spit.

Normally, these antibodies do their job and your body silently applauds. But enter the antibody immunoglobulin-E (IgE), which is primarily responsible for allergies. The IgE antibodies are found at low levels in everyone else's serum, but allergic people have high levels of IgE. These antibodies want to be heroes, but they don't have the skill; the team fumbles and gets confused. The foreign cells that the IgE antibodies try to destroy are not necessarily harmful to people—these are dust mites, fish, pollen, and fur. But the IgE antibodies get so excited that they literally become inflamed and slather these seemingly nontoxic cells with chemicals. If you have high levels of the IgE antibody, you'll get a fast allergic reaction. If you suspect you have an allergy, take your pulse right after you either eat, touch, or inhale a suspect allergen. The IgE reaction is so fast that your pulse rate will immediately be increased.

In susceptible people, the chemicals that IgE antibodies spew on the offenders cause allergic symptoms ranging from sneezing and coughing to, in very severe cases, asthma and anaphylactic shock (where the throat begins to tighten and close up).

REACTION RETRACTION 2: WE ARE APPROACHING THE THRESHOLD . . .
REPEAT, WE ARE APPROACHING THE THRESHOLD
Most people who suffer from allergies are so used to their condition that they don't even realize something different is happening. This is especially true for intermittent allergies, or those that come and go. For example, you can have a full-fledged attack after eating one strawberry one day in your life, yet in another situation, when you've had a good night's sleep and you feel wonderfully relaxed, the strawberries can be eaten and there's no problem.

Since there are many contributing factors to an allergic reaction, it's good to understand the role the reaction threshold plays. There you are, unknowingly breathing in dust mites in your living room, your office, your bedroom. Here you are, happily eating your eggs scrambled, fried, and boiled. Suddenly, an allergy attack comes on. You start to wheeze and sneeze; your throat feels like sandpaper; you develop mouth sores. But this reaction is not as sudden as you might think. Your body knew better. When you first began to eat or inhale the allergy-provoking material, your IgE antibodies were silent. But as you ate more eggs or breathed in more dust, your IgE antibodies went on alert, still quiet. Then, when your threshold was reached—the point at which the trigger substance finally begins to bother you—those antibodies went into action, spewing their chemicals at the antigens and causing your allergic symptoms.

REACTION RETRACTION 3: FOOD ADDICTION

Your body is not without a sense of irony. Allergic reactions do not have to be just to strange, exotic foods. Allergies can occur with common foods you eat all the time. In fact, people who regularly eat thirty or fewer types of food are more predisposed to allergies than those who eat a variety of earth's bounty.

Call this an addiction allergy. An allergy doesn't have to come out as a rash or a hacking cough. A reaction can be that bolt of energy you feel after eating a certain food. It feels good, so you want to eat or drink more. Maybe you love orange juice. You adore orange juice—in fact, you're addicted to orange juice. For some people, the rush is from the sugar; for others it's the allergic jolt. Yes, orange juice can be addictive, but it might be an allergy that gives you that "zap" of energy that, several hours later, becomes a pounding headache, usually when you're ready for more juice. A splitting headache and what do you do? Reach for two aspirins and swallow them with a glass of orange juice. The headache disappears or, rather, is masked. In fact, a study in the *British Medical Journal* found that taking aspirin before ingesting an allergen enables you to drink or eat more of the offending item. Thus, unwittingly, you can possibly drink even more orange juice because of the aspirin you took with it.

But a few hours later, the headache is back and you're ready for your next "fix." And so begins a cycle of addiction and allergic reactions that soon blend together until you can't differentiate the two. As with Suzanne and her carrots, your body simply overloads on a particular food or drink, setting the scene for you to react to an ever-increasing number of other foods.

REACTION RETRACTION 4: THE TIES THAT BIND

Sometimes you can't help it. Your father or mother had the excessive IgE antibody encoded in his or her genes and you were unlucky enough to inherit this particular withdrawal. Research has also found a

---

A BOUNCED CHECK:
FOOD ALLERGIES AND FISTFIGHTS

Food allergies can cause more than an upset stomach or overwhelming fatigue. They can be so intense that they create violent behavior. Research done on children found that just a small amount of a food allergen was responsible for angry outbursts, signs of hyperactivity, irritability, and disorientation.

The foods most likely to cause behavioral allergic reactions are eggs, sugar, oats, wheat, corn, chocolate, milk, tomatoes, grapes, oranges, apples, and soy products.

---

connection between mothers who smoke and infants who develop allergies when they are born. (Yet another reason to quit smoking if you haven't yet done so!)

More mother and child news: A study at St. Mary's Hospital on the Isle of Wight found that a family history of allergic reactions makes you—and your siblings—susceptible to such reactions. In this case, it was a peanut allergy that was in the family. In your case, it could be chocolate or shellfish or carrots.

REACTION RETRACTION 5: THERE IT GOES AGAIN . . . THE *LEAKY GUT*

If you get a lot of yeast infections, you should suspect an excessive population of yeast residing in your body, which can lead to a *leaky gut*. It's something you might have inherited from your mother. In this case, it's not in the genes but in your surroundings: a birth canal too rich in yeast. But you do not have to panic. A small yeast population shouldn't be "something new to worry about." It's only when you continually make withdrawals, feeding and supporting that yeast population, that problems arise.

Excess yeast is a prime foundation erosion and a prime contributor to dysbiosis and the eventual *leaky gut*. (See Section III.) Add an overburdened liver (see Section IV), trying to cope with the toxins, and you have a situation that can only get worse unless you begin to make some healthy deposits and repair your *leaky gut* and your *toxic liver*.

PREVENTIVE REGIMEN
TO HELP AVOID ALLERGIC REACTIONS

Reduce your tendency to allergic sensitivities by following this program.

Be sure to start slowly, introducing supplements gradually, to help prevent any possible reactions. The Foundation Regimens for a *leaky gut* and a *toxic liver* are almost always indicated. Do both Foundation Regimens for three weeks, if applicable, then *add* this Preventive Regimen.

TIPS
- This regimen, as with all the regimens in this book, is meant for adults. See your health practitioner for a program designed for children. Remember that children share the same foundations as adults. They, too, may not have to suffer from allergies. Ask your health practitioner to adjust the Foundation Regimens for a *leaky gut* and/or *toxic liver* for growing children.

ON AN ONGOING BASIS:

DIET
- *Avoid sugar.* It can raise your blood sugar levels too fast, then drop them too quickly. It can increase stressful anxiety, which in turn increases allergic reactions.
- *Avoid foods that are potentially reactive, such as wheat, eggs, and milk products.*

If you see △, please check Appendix C for further information.

VITAMINS, MINERALS, AND OTHER NUTRITIONAL SUPPLEMENTS
TAKE DAILY:
- *High-potency multivitamin-mineral supplement.*
- *Vitamin C.* Involved with inflammatory response. Helps your body fight off allergy-producing substances. Add 2000–3000 mg. Divide the dosage into several equal amounts. Use the buffered form for easier digestion.
- *B complex.* Necessary for proper digestion of nutrients and important to help reduce the allergic reactions of anxiety, depression, and fatigue. Add 100 mg.

- *Pantothenic acid.* A B vitamin that supports your adrenal glands in times of stress. Take 250 mg.
- *Quercetin.* A bioflavonoid that enhances immune function. Take 500–1000 mg.
- ⚠ *Multidigestive enzyme with bromelain and HCl.* Enhances digestion. Bromelain acts as an antiinflammatory and enhances quercetin activity. Take as directed before each meal.
- *Calcium.* For stress reduction. Take 800–1000 mg.
- *Magnesium.* Necessary to maintain calcium balance. Take 400–500 mg.
- *Flaxseed oil capsules.* Aids in reducing inflammatory reactions. Take 2 capsules.

HERBS

- *Vervain tea* has a calming effect. Drink as directed on box.
- *Tea tree oil.* May help soothe and cool allergic reactions on skin. Apply topically as directed.

Do you think that tickle in your throat is something to live with? Your burning eyes? The overwhelming fatigue or feelings of depression? Even if you suffer from these symptoms only as something that comes along with spring cleaning, it's important to know that you don't have to accept them. You can take care of yourself—now. Research has shown that the *leaky gut* and the *toxic liver* burden the body by increasing the toxic load, very often resulting in allergic reactions. If these two conditions remain uncorrected, allergic reactions may also remain, no matter what healthy deposits you make. Therefore, you probably need to begin my Foundation Regimens for a *toxic liver* and a *leaky gut* before starting my Preventive Regimen for allergies.

And even if your symptoms have become a full-fledged allergy *bankruptcy,* there's no need to accept it with resignation. You can fight it and choose health—with the Rescue Regimens. Here's the scoop on some of the more common allergies.

A FOOD ALLERGY BALANCE SHEET

Here are some of the most common foods that cause allergies—and substitutes that can still taste delicious without that bitter aftertaste.

LIABILITIES	ASSETS
Gluten flour (found in wheat products)	Gluten-free breads, pastas, and cereals; rice, potatoes
Shellfish	Deepwater fish
Peanuts	Walnuts
Chocolate	Carob
Strawberries	Blueberries
Additives and preservatives	Organic, free-range foods

FOOD ALLERGIES

JUST THE FACTS, PLEASE . . . THE MYSTERY UNFOLDS.

If a reaction begins right after eating a certain food, it's easy to pinpoint the possibility of a food allergy, especially if it happens again after eating the same food another time. But threshold, stress-triggered, and addictive allergies are harder to determine. (See the "Reaction Retractions," pages 200–203.)

THE EVIDENCE . . . EXHIBITS A TO Z.

Histamines, formed by certain bacteria in food, can create the same allergic symptoms as the actual food. They are also found inside your body, in skin (or mast) cells. When your skin is irritated, the histamines are triggered into action, creating such symptoms as headaches, hives, and watery eyes. Antihistamines help destroy these unleashed histamines, but they can also make you extremely drowsy. Since they don't help get rid of your underlying problems, you're forced to take them again and again. Sulfites trigger histamine destruction. If you get a headache when you drink wine, it's possible that you have an allergy to the sulfites used as a preservative.

GRADE-A DETECTIVE WORK.

It's true that food allergies are prevalent, but there are people who think they are allergic to everything—while, in reality, they are not allergic at all. In fact, only about 2 percent of Americans suffer from actual food allergies. Others simply have food intolerances. (See Chapter 9.) There are certain foods that are not digested properly, either as a result of improper enzyme action during the digestion process, a *leaky gut* or a *toxic liver*, or a hormonal imbalance. (See Chapter 15 on endocrine bankruptcies.)

KEEPING YOUR CONDITION "BEHIND BARS"
RESCUE REGIMEN FOR FOOD ALLERGIES

Follow Preventive Regimen for allergy problems for two weeks. Then add this Rescue Regimen.

If you see △, please check Appendix C for further information.

ON AN ONGOING BASIS:

DIET

- Do an *elimination diet* to help reduce allergic stress and identify offending foods. (See page 208.)
- *Avoid food preservatives* and *food chemicals* whenever possible. They can be highly reactive.
- *Have an ELISA* (Enzyme-Linked ImmunoSorbent Assay) test done to determine food allergies.
- *Eliminate those foods that cause allergic reactions* until you have been able to make a substantial number of deposits via the *toxic liver* and *leaky gut* Foundation Regimens.

VITAMINS, MINERALS, AND OTHER NUTRITIONAL SUPPLEMENTS
TAKE DAILY:

- *Pantothenic acid.* Take additional 250–750 mg. Divide dose into several equal amounts.
- *Vitamin C.* Take additional 1000 mg.

THE "ELIMINATION DIET" FOR FOOD ALLERGIES

Allergies usually don't occur overnight. They develop over time, as you eat a specific food day in and day out, until you reach your threshold and you become intolerant: you get an allergic reaction. In order to find out who the culprit is, an elimination diet will help you in your Health Detective work. Although I've mentioned it before, this diet is so important in determining your allergies, it bears repeating:

The most common food allergies include reactions to foods containing gluten, such as wheat, barley, oats, and rye, milk and dairy products, shellfish, chocolate, nuts, beef, eggs, strawberries, and the "nightshade" vegetables (such as potatoes, tomatoes, eggplant, and peppers).

Remove all foods you suspect from your diet for two weeks, gradually introducing one potential allergen at a time. If there is no reaction within two weeks after eating whole-wheat bread, for example, add another suspect. Maybe the next food you add is strawberries. Again, let's say you have no reaction for two full weeks. Perhaps you try eggs next. During the second week, you get a scratchy throat and an upset stomach. Eggs could very well be your allergen. Remove them from your diet for a few days and see if the symptoms clear up—and if they start up again after you eat one egg.

Keep going until you've separated "the wheat from the chaff" and can identify your food allergies. Avoid these foods as much as possible.

ENVIRONMENTAL ALLERGIES

JUST THE FACTS, PLEASE . . . THE MYSTERY EXPOSED.

In the same way certain foods can cause allergies, so can environmental pollutants. Pollen (think hay fever in the spring and summer), dust, mold in basements and bathrooms, pet dander, and dust mites can all cause the headaches, sniffling, stuffiness, red eyes, and "I just feel plain horrible" symptoms of allergy in those who are susceptible.

THE EVIDENCE . . . EXHIBITS A TO Z.

The wife of one of my clients had a cat. Unfortunately, my client was allergic to her cat's dander. His reaction was almost immediate: burning, smarting eyes, blotchy skin, and a nose that wouldn't stop running. His allergic reactions were so bad, in fact, that the couple had to seek counseling to deal with the tensions this situation created. I don't suggest you have to do anything as drastic, but you can determine your allergy withdrawals in your house in the same way you do an elimination diet with your food. Remove all potentially offending cleansers, polishes, and waxes. Seal up your medicine cabinet. Give your perfumes and aftershaves to a neighbor for safekeeping. Introduce each product back into the house one at a time. If you get a reaction, you'll immediately know which pollutants are irritating you.

GRADE-A DETECTIVE WORK.
If you suffer from pollen in the spring and fall, you are not alone. More than 20 million people suffer from hay fever, including 90 percent of allergy-afflicted children. Symptoms include red, irritated eyes, runny nose, scratchy throat, and sneezing. If these sound familiar, they should. They are similar to the symptoms of a common cold or flu. How to tell the difference? When you have an allergic reaction to pollen, the mucus from a runny nose (that never seems to stop!) is almost clear. It is thin and watery. If you have a cold and a stuffed-up nose, your mucus will be thick and yellow or green.

KEEPING YOUR CONDITION "BEHIND BARS"
RESCUE REGIMEN FOR ENVIRONMENTAL ALLERGIES

Follow Preventive Regimen for allergy problems for two weeks. Then add this Rescue Regimen.

If you see △, check Appendix C for further information.

VITAMINS, MINERALS, AND OTHER NUTRITIONAL SUPPLEMENTS
TAKE DAILY:
- *Vitamin C.* Add 1000 mg.
- *Pantothenic acid.* Add 250–750 mg. Divide dose into several equal amounts.

SKIN ALLERGIES

JUST THE FACTS, PLEASE . . . THE MYSTERY EXPOSED.
Skin rashes are usually more embarrassing than life-threatening. The skin, a first line of defense from invading toxins, usually shows the aftermath of battle as rashes, eczema, hives, or blotches. The skin is also susceptible to allergies. Its cells are particularly vulnerable to histamines, from outside pollutants or from within the body itself. The result is inflammation and red, patchy skin.

THE EVIDENCE . . . EXHIBITS A TO Z.
Contact dermatitis is exactly what it sounds like: touching or using something that causes an allergic skin reaction. This includes perfumes, shampoos, bubble baths, aftershave cream and cologne, makeup, rubber, certain atopical ointments, metal, and poison ivy. Its rashes, redness, hives, and blotchiness usually go away in a few days after you remove the offending material. Atopic dermatitis, on the other hand, is chronic. You most likely develop it first as a baby; this is usually a clue that you are allergic, like the rest of the family. Its symptoms include rashes and red, irritated skin in the crook of the elbows and behind the knees.

GRADE-A DETECTIVE WORK.
Maybe you've revisited the "scene of the health crime" over and over again—to no avail. Maybe you need to look a little closer—at latex. Yes, this wonderful synthetic material will hold your stomach in, stretch with you with each jumping jack, and make you feel slinky at a party. But it can also be causing your skin rash, your hives, your blotchy face. Studies have found that if you have allergies to fruit containing proteins that are the same ones as found in the rubber tree, it's very possible that you might be allergic to latex, too, which is made from the sap of the rubber tree.

BANK S-TELLARS

Give me health and a day and I will make the pomp of emperors ridiculous.
—Ralph Waldo Emerson

KEEPING YOUR CONDITION "BEHIND BARS"
RESCUE REGIMEN FOR SKIN ALLERGIES

Follow Preventive Regimen for allergy problems for two weeks. Then add this Rescue Regimen.

If you see △, please check Appendix C for further information.

VITAMINS, MINERALS, AND OTHER NUTRITIONAL SUPPLEMENTS
TAKE DAILY:
△ *Vitamin E.* Important for immune function. Take 200 IU.
△ *Zinc lozenge.* Low levels have been linked to skin allergies. Helps heal and prevent acne and other skin irritations by enhancing immune function. Take 25 mg.
• *L-Lysine.* An amino acid that helps antibody formation. Heals skin and helps in forming collagen. Take as directed on an empty stomach. *Discontinue after 2 months.*

You don't have to let allergies get the best of you. You can gain control of your life—and your good health—right now. You can start by making any one of the healthy deposits explored in this chapter into your Body Bank account. Allergies can be a bothersome *bankruptcy,* but stopping your withdrawals now, repairing and rebuilding your *leaky gut* and your *toxic liver* foundation, and helping to prevent future problems with the Preventive and Rescue Regimens can help you begin to smell the roses and glow with good health.

Now, for more empowering information, let us go into the mind.

12

PSYCHOLOGICAL AND STRESS-RELATED BANKRUPTCIES

I was so depressed I couldn't get out of bed. I was tired and wired at the same time. I tried medication, but it didn't work. Nothing worked—until I changed my diet. —A 40-year-old journalist and father

It started about a week before her birthday. Doris was turning sixty-nine, not a milestone birthday, but as Doris herself would later say, "Every birthday is important!"

She didn't think so at the time. When her friends mentioned her birthday, she shrugged it off. She didn't need to celebrate. Since her husband had died eight years before, she didn't like to think about birthdays. They were just markers of time.

Although Doris didn't admit it to anyone, there was one person she was counting on to remember her special day: her daughter. Sondra lived two hours away in another state—too far to see each other all the time, but close enough to get together on special occasions.

Doris missed Sondra; she wanted to see her on her birthday, even though she'd never voice it. She had learned early on not to make waves, to be a "good girl" and to put other people's needs in front of her own.

Sondra called a few days before the big day. Mother and daughter chatted on the phone for a few minutes, then Sondra mentioned her mom's birthday. She told her that the family really wanted to celebrate it with her, but they had an important business dinner the same night. Could they celebrate the next night at some wonderful restaurant and make it a long weekend? "You'll come back up here and spend a couple of days."

Doris was pleased that Sondra wanted to spend some time with her. She told herself it didn't matter if they celebrated on the actual day or not. Big deal. Birthdays were for kids, anyway.

But something happened after that phone call. It was a subtle change—nothing that Doris's friends could see, so slight that even Sondra, if she wasn't distracted with her own family, might not catch. Doris, always a sound sleeper, started to have insomnia.

The first night she couldn't sleep was the night of the phone call; it continuously got worse. It got so bad that when Doris did see Sondra after her birthday, she only stayed overnight. She couldn't sleep and she was worried that someone would see the lamp on in the guest room in the wee hours of the morning; she didn't want anyone to ask questions. She herself didn't know the answers.

Doris was understandably exhausted, but the problem went beyond a lack of sleep. Always a well-groomed woman, Doris suddenly became sloppy. She stopped dyeing her hair; she wore the same clothes for days. She lost her appetite and dropped weight she didn't need to lose.

And still she couldn't sleep. Doris began to dread nighttime. She hated going into her bedroom and looking at her bed. She knew she couldn't sleep, so what was the point? More times than not, she woke up late in the afternoon on her living room couch. She felt drowsy all the time; she was disoriented. To compensate for her lack of energy, Doris began to eat sweets and drink lots of coffee. As time went on, she found herself craving them both. Sometimes Doris would go through an entire box of cookies without even realizing it; she'd start to panic if she didn't have something sweet in the house.

Doris was getting scared—and scattered. Even Sondra was beginning to notice. She'd come for a visit and was appalled at the way Doris was living. She insisted her mother seek some help.

Doris agreed; she was secretly pleased that her daughter cared so much about her.

It was around this time that I began seeing her. Doris had started seeing a psychologist; the doctor was a colleague of mine and she referred Doris to me. She didn't like the way Doris was eating and thought that I might be able to help her chronic insomnia.

I saw a sad, scared woman that first day. But in the vulnerable smile she gave me as she entered my office, I also saw someone who wanted help, who wanted to be well.

THE CASE OF THE MOTHER-DAUGHTER CONVERSATION: SOLVED

We began our Health Detective journey the way I always do—with questions. About Doris's eating habits, her daily routines, her family history. Doris knew she was depressed; her biggest symptom was lack of sleep.

I knew that her poor diet, the sugar, and the caffeine helped contribute to that symptom. But I also knew that it wasn't the true root of her problem. We talked about the vicious cycle that made her depression so insidious. Doris's insomnia both exhausted and undermined her every move. This listlessness and neediness made her reach out for a sugary snack and coffee-rich beverages. The snacks in turn gave her a quick "hit" and an equally quick drop. Her blood-sugar levels swung out of control, giving her more sleepless nights and a depression that got worse and worse.

The situation became a roller-coaster ride, a walk up the down escalator. The more Doris's blood sugar dropped, the more she craved foods that would quickly lift her up. The more she craved, the more she ate.

But trigger foods were only part of the story. Doris's poor diet meant that she wasn't getting enough calcium, which can also contribute to insomnia. In addition, without eating green, leafy vegetables and fresh fish, Doris wasn't getting her fair share of magnesium. Double trouble: magnesium deficiency has been linked to irritability and anxiety. The cycle continued, without a deposit being made to Doris's Body Bank in quite a while.

Although I wanted to immediately recommend some healthy deposits, I knew there was something else, something that might stop Doris from making progress, that might spiral her back into a depression as she started to feel better.

Over the next few sessions, we began to talk about family, about our hopes for our children. And since Doris had made some healthy

BANK S-TELLARS

Be not afraid of life. Believe that life is worth living, and your belief will help create the fact.   —Henry James

deposits, she was finally getting some sleep. She was able to think more clearly, to examine her life and what was going on emotionally.

She was ready to explore some of her very sensitive feelings—how, rational or not, it pained Doris to think that her daughter's business engagement was more important than she. Once Doris was able to release her anger, she could look at the feelings beneath the anger. She began to make tremendous inroads in her therapy and she began to make more and more healthy deposits for her body and soul. Her depression began to lift; she began to sleep better.

One of her biggest deposits was that she was able to speak to Sondra about her feelings. Her daughter had been shocked, totally unaware of her mother's sensitivity. She hadn't even realized the impact of what she had done. They vowed to spend more time together to talk.

DO YOU HAVE *RUNNING IN THE RED* PSYCHOLOGICAL OR STRESS-RELATED SYMPTOMS?

Maybe the reasons for your depression are more obvious than Doris's—a change of season or loss of a loved one. Or maybe your symptoms are just like hers. Perhaps you, too, have anger and hurt hiding beneath a slew of withdrawals. Whatever you are dealing with in life—the hurt, the disappointment, the anxiety, the loneliness—they will be more intense if you are low in blood sugar, a major withdrawal. Life feels more manageable when your chemistry is in balance.

Read on and take the following quiz. If you agree with any of these statements—as far from a psychological problem as they may appear—it is possible that your Body Bank account is showing the strain of too many withdrawals.

- I'll be reading a book or a report and suddenly it seems like a foreign language. I have to read the same sentence over and over to make any sense of it.
- I can't sleep at night. My mind goes over and over the same things—all the anxious thoughts I have about my boss, my husband, my child, my life!
- I'm obsessed with my health. Even when I have a checkup and I feel great, I don't trust the results.
- Everything is a chore. Even a simple thing like going to the drugstore or the dry cleaners, or even making a sandwich, becomes an all-day affair.
- I never take the time to cook for myself. Dinner is usually anything that's easy.
- I've had a major change in my life recently. It was actually something very positive: a promotion. But I just learned that I have to relocate to another state.
- I can never sit still. I'm always tapping my fingers or shaking my leg.
- I never have breakfast in the morning. It's enough just to try to get out on time.
- I love chocolate, but whenever I eat a piece, my throat gets scratchy and my nose starts to run. Even though I know it's not wonderful for me, I can't seem to turn it down.

The brain is amazingly complex. The microscopic chemical actions and reactions that occur within its surface layers tell us how and what to feel, how and what to think, how and what to move. In short, the brain contains the essence of who and what we are. It's no wonder that even the smallest, most seemingly inconsequential "glitch" in our body will affect the brain and, consequently, our very being.

Here is some food for thought on these "glitches," some possible withdrawals you need to understand for successful Health Detective work.

DEPRESSION EXPRESSION 1: FAMILY MATTERS

Emotional illness is one of the most debated conditions. Which came first, the chicken or the egg? Heredity or environment? Over 11 million people suffer from some form of depressive condition, and yet we still don't have the answers why. Studies have found that 50 percent of

---

HE WHO LAUGHS LAST

Laughter really is the best medicine. There is actually a laughing meditation that has three steps: stretching, laughing, and silence. It has
been found to help people look at things a little bit differently, to feel a
little bit lighter, a little bit more accepting.

---

all people who end up with depression had at least one depressed parent. Yet depressive conditions can be triggered by a stressful situation.
You can feel depressed and no one else in your family ever suffered.
On the other hand, some health practitioners consider depression a
contagious illness. If your spouse is depressed, for example, there's a
good chance you'll become depressed, too.

DEPRESSION EXPRESSION 2: CALLING ALL NEUROTRANSMITTERS!

Messages to and from our brain to the rest of our body are accessed
by neurotransmitters—electrochemical dispatchers that are infinitely
more efficient than our most progressive post office, with one exception. They are more sensitive to the "weather." Rain, sleet, and snow
might not keep away our mail, but any deviance in our body's chemical imbalance, any hint of an account that's *running in the red,* and
watch out. Messages get waylaid, mistaken. Neurotransmitters that
affect our mood include serotonin, dopamine, and norepinephrine.
You're probably thinking what Doris thought when I told her these
names: "Great. Now I can pass a fill-in-the-blank test on the brain.
What does it mean?"

In a word, everything. In fact, they are part of a major solution to
our psychological mystery. These particular neurotransmitters are very
much affected by food. Yes, food—the nutrients, the supplements, the
vitamins and minerals we put into our body. Any nutritional deficiency, food allergy, or malabsorption problem may push the envelope
a little too far. You might wind up with a full-blown psychological and
stress-related *bankruptcy.*

DEPRESSION EXPRESSION 3: AS THE WORLD CHURNS

Call stress the trigger, the bolt of lightning, the crash of thunder, that
plummets you down the depression path. Whether it be from a traumatic

---

WITH ADELE'S COMPLEMENTS!

You don't have to "beat yourself up" when you feel depressed or anxious. It's not your fault. You are no less terrible or better than the next person. You're a human being. There is a reason why you're depressed, and chances are, it has nothing to do with your net worth. It has to do with things you're not even aware of: a poor diet, low blood sugar, a lack of nutrients, unresolved emotional conflicts.

So stand tall. Cast off the weights you've been holding all this time. Take a deep breath. Congratulations! You've just started to take control of your mind and body. Slowly, gradually, you can begin to change.

---

event in your life, a daily erosion of tension, a sedentary lifestyle, even recent surgery, stress affects your physical body and, ultimately, your emotional state. In fact, research shows that 80 percent of all physical conditions, from backaches to heart problems, may be caused initially by stress.

When you are under stress, your entire body heeds the call. Adrenaline is secreted from the adrenal glands, which is a call to arms for the body to prep up for "fight or flight." This red alert means that fat, protein, and carbohydrates are metabolized faster, which in turn results in amino acid, magnesium, and phosphorus excretion. The body loses its ability to absorb nutrients efficiently; it can't keep up with the body's accelerated, fast-paced need.

Adding insulting stress to injury, the pituitary gland releases cortisone and cortisol, which suppress the immune system. Your blood pressure rises, your heart pumps faster, and your digestion slows; fats and sugar are released from storage.

In short, it's no mystery that stress changes the very texture, the very nature, of your body. If it is an ongoing situation, this powerful withdrawal can do some serious damage, not the least of which is the creation of a full-fledged psychological *bankruptcy*.

DEPRESSION EXPRESSION 4: LOW-BLOOD-SUGAR BLUES
I've long been an advocate of good blood sugar. It's a state that many of you may not have experienced in your life. It's the place where your blood sugar is in balance, not too high and not too low. This balance

provides lasting energy, a wonderful feeling of physical and psychological well-being. When you eat too many sugar-laden foods or simple carbohydrates, the release of sugar is the high you first experience. Your body responds with a rush of insulin to take care of the sugar. Unfortunately, these foods deliver too much glucose too fast. Too much glucose and your blood sugar shoots up, sending an emergency call for insulin. This excess insulin causes the fast crash down after the high. Your body craves more sugar and starch, more reactive foods to help bring you back up.

Glucose is one of the major foods for the brain, and the brain cannot store it. The result? As soon as you have low blood sugar, you can also have altered brain activity: disorientation, forgetfulness, anxiety, and depression.

DEPRESSION EXPRESSION 5: THE MAGNESIUM MAGNATE

Call it a sane brain food. Magnesium, the mineral so vital for metabolic function, is also a component of mental health. Researchers at the Albert Einstein College of Medicine have found a deficiency in magnesium in people suffering from depression, anxiety, and psychotic hallucinations. Other studies have found that when mental patients do not respond well to medication, there's usually a magnesium deficiency lurking in the background. The result? Nervousness and a body that cannot rest.

You'll find a healthy dose of magnesium in green leafy vegetables, nuts, fish, seeds, and wheat germ. (Both magnesium and calcium are important components of the Basic Health Regimen. See Chapter 5 for details.)

If you are feeling hopeless and helpless, out of control with either food or alcohol, overwhelmingly exhausted or completely wired, these "depression expressions" may not appear to be connected. But that is because you have not yet identified the impact that food and nutrients can have on your emotional well-being.

I'm not saying that everything you are is what you eat; there are legitimate and very real reasons for psychological pain. But I am saying that impairments and depletions caused by toxins in your body can play a role in your emotional problems. Indeed, the slightest imbalance in your digestive tract—stress, low blood sugar, and more—can throw off your body's vital biochemical processes. This environment

PREVENTIVE REGIMEN
FOR PROMOTING EMOTIONAL WELL-BEING
AND REDUCING STRESS

This regimen is designed for those who tend to store their daily stress.

Be sure to start slowly, introducing supplements gradually, to help prevent any possible reactions. The Foundation Regimens for a *leaky gut* and *toxic liver* are almost always indicated. Do both Foundation Regimens for three weeks, if applicable, then add this Preventive Regimen.

TIP
- Do some form of stress-reducing therapy to help your body and mind cope better with life's vicissitudes. Meditate, go for a walk, get counseling, keep a journal, or use your own relaxation technique.

ON AN ONGOING BASIS:

DIET
- *Control your blood sugar* to help stave off mood swings. Eat breakfast within a half hour of waking up. Eat a *hard chew* fruit or vegetable snack (carrots, broccoli, apple) every two hours. Eat lunch by 1:00, which should always be a protein and veggies. Eat *hard chew* or *soft chew* snacks (orange, cantaloupe) every three hours in the afternoon. Dinner must include protein and veggies. It can also include a complex carbohydrate (a potato, rice, or couscous), if desired. Limit pasta to dinner every third night, if desired.

If you see △, please check Appendix C for further information.

VITAMINS, MINERALS, AND OTHER NUTRITIONAL SUPPLEMENTS
TAKE DAILY:
- *High-potency multivitamin and mineral supplement.*
- *B complex.* Critical in maintaining health of nervous system. Take 100 mg.
- *Pantothenic acid.* A B vitamin necessary to support the body when under great stress. Take 250–500 mg. Divide dose into several equal amounts.
- *Vitamin C.* Helps support adrenal glands, which produce antistress hormones. Take 1000 mg.
- *Calcium/magnesium.* Two nutrients depleted during stress; involved with

the muscles and the nervous system. Take 1000 mg calcium and 500 mg magnesium.

⚠ *Inositol.* Helps reduce stress due to calming properties. Take 300 mg.

• *Flaxseed oil.* Take 2 capsules.

HERBS

• *Valerian.* Soothes the nervous system. Take as a tincture, as directed on bottle, or as a tea, as directed on box.

• *Vervain.* Helps in reducing stress. Take as a tincture, as directed on bottle, or as a tea, as directed on box.

---

may create not only malnutrition or an upset stomach but also symptoms such as overwhelming fatigue, insomnia, and depression that can become *bankruptcy* conditions.

Here are some insights into those common psychological and stress-related *bankruptcies.*

ALCOHOLISM

JUST THE FACTS, PLEASE . . . THE MYSTERY EXPOSED.
When a bartender asks, "What's your poison?" she isn't kidding. Alcohol in any guise is a poison, pure and simple. Although one or two occasional glasses should not harm most people, a consistent dose to your system—a continuous withdrawal—and alcohol will eventually undermine your well-being. Because alcoholism creates metabolic havoc within every bodily function, your cells will not get the nutrients they need for a strong, healthy body.

Thanks to ethanol, an ingredient in alcohol that is toxic to your intestinal lining, many nutrients are malabsorped, including vitamin B_1 (thiamine) and folic acid, both important for proper metabolism, a strong immune system, and calm nerves.

Zinc, too, is lost in long-term alcohol abuse, owing to excessive fecal and urinary elimination. Some of the symptoms of zinc deficiency are impaired taste and smell, decreased appetite, stunted growth, infertility problems, poor wound healing, and a malfunctioning immune system.

Your withdrawals can occur throughout the gut, and the liver, the giant strainer for your body, will be so busy trying to cope with your alcohol consumption that it will be unavailable to perform its other jobs efficiently. In short, nutrients vital for a properly running Body Bank are simply eliminated, leaving your body as empty as the bottom of the glass.

THE EVIDENCE . . . EXHIBITS A TO Z.

There is no system, no organ, no part of the body that alcohol does not affect. And contrary to popular opinion, wine or beer is just as hard on you as the supposed "hard" liquors, vodka, gin, and whiskey.

GRADE-A DETECTIVE WORK.

I believe many alcoholics are hypoglycemic. They have low blood sugar, but whether they were born with hypoglycemia or developed low blood sugar from abusing their liver with the alcohol is not clear. The potential alcoholic can grow up craving the carbohydrates (starches, sweets, and alcohol) that low blood sugar calls for. (See Chapter 9 on gastrointestinal problems for more information on carbohydrate addiction.)

Now here's where the overweight eater and the alcoholic go their separate ways. Some hypoglycemics are seduced by the foods that provide the simple sugars, overeating and bingeing until it becomes impossible to lose weight. But others turn their cravings to alcohol. You might not think a drink is as much a potential carb-loader as candy, but it can be more lethal. Alcohol, too, is a simple carbohydrate and is rapidly converted into sugar by the body, creating an addictive high that is quickly followed by a low—unless another drink is poured.

This condition of low blood sugar from drinking alcohol creates the same roller-coaster ride, the same mood swings, as eating too much sugar to lose weight and gain energy. It's just a difference in personality. Perhaps your parents drank; perhaps drinking helps you forget your problems; perhaps it is socially acceptable among your peers; perhaps you simply like the smoky bar, B-movie romance aspect. Alcohol is a substance that can be escalated by the same chemical cravings as those that demand extensive sugar and simple carbohydrates. (One of my future goals is to work with support groups to explore these ideas.)

A BOUNCED CHECK:
CHRONIC INSOMNIA

There are many reasons for chronic insomnia, and most of them are not psychological. Yes, stress and tension play a role, but for most insomniacs, the inability to get a solid forty winks is due to:

- Low blood sugar
- Indigestion
- Too much caffeine
- Decongestants
- Antidepressants
- A sedentary lifestyle
- A lack of calcium and magnesium in the body

If these sound familiar, it's because they are. They are some of the same links found in a *leaky gut* and a *toxic liver*. Fix these two foundations with the Foundation Regimens and you just might find yourself getting a great night's sleep.

If your insomnia has reached crisis proportions, here are some regimens that may help you close your eyes and rest—at last!

- Reduce or eliminate caffeine, chocolate, and alcohol. They act as stimulants.
- Control your blood sugar. A blood-sugar crash can cause an abrupt awakening in the middle of the night.
- Take 600 mg of calcium and 300 mg of magnesium. Take them before bedtime to help you sleep. (See possible contraindications in Appendix C.)
- Inositol will help you relax. Take 300–600 mg before going to bed. (See possible contraindications in Appendix C.)
- Sip valerian tea. It will calm your nerves and help you rest.

Think about it. At support group meetings, tables are laden with sugary desserts and sweet juices. When alcoholics stop drinking, the carb craving doesn't go away. It is just substituted—from gin to gumdrops, from beer to bagels, from Chablis to cake.

Worse, keeping the blood sugar low contributes greatly to the jittery, nervous feelings the recovering alcoholic always has. The body continues to be malnourished—and more. A recovering alcoholic has little protection from stimuli in the outside world. The banished alcohol had served so many years as a buffer, muffling the external environment. It had served to deaden and block out the outside world.

If you are a recovering alcoholic, you have surrendered your

KEEPING YOUR CONDITION "BEHIND BARS"
RESCUE REGIMEN FOR ALCOHOLISM

Follow Preventive Regimen for stress for two weeks. Then add this Rescue Regimen.

If you see △, please check Appendix C for further information.

TIPS
- Do the Foundation Regimens for a *leaky gut* and a *toxic liver* for three weeks before beginning this regimen. Both need to be restored and supported.
- Follow the blood-sugar control diet in my Preventive Regimen (page 279). Controlling blood sugar is crucial to avoid cravings and confusing mood swings.

VITAMINS, MINERALS, AND OTHER NUTRITIONAL SUPPLEMENTS
TAKE DAILY:
- *Vitamin B₁* (thiamine). Deficient in alcoholics because ethanol, an ingredient in alcohol, is toxic to the intestinal lining and creates malabsorption. Take an additional 100 mg a day.
- *Vitamin B₃* (niacin). Helps restore nervous system and brain function. Take 100 mg.
- △ *Vitamin E.* Take 200–400 IU.
- △ *Inositol.* Add 300–600 mg. Split dose into several equal amounts.
- △ *GABA (gamma-aminobutyric acid).* An amino acid that helps decrease stress and provide feelings of calmness. Also helps promote proper brain function. Take 300–350 mg on an empty stomach. *Discontinue after 2 months.*
- △ *Zinc lozenge.* Enhances immune function. Often deficient in alcoholics. Take 25 mg.
- *Folic acid.* Take 400 mcg.

A JUMPING JACK . . . FLASH

You're exhausted. Your mind is frazzled. All you want to do is close your eyes and take a nap for a half hour. That's all. Just thirty minutes.

Don't touch that pillow! Studies have found that taking a short nap can actually make you more tired. It takes approximately half an hour to reach REM (rapid eye movement) sleep. This is the deep sleep in which you dream, the sleep that allows you to wake up refreshed and revitalized. But if you wake up before your REM, or interrupt it, you can become irritable, disoriented, and much more tired.

A better way to get the blood pumping and feel refreshed? Get up from your desk or your sofa and do ten jumping jacks. Walk around the block. Dance a few steps. That's it. You'll feel invigorated. Call it a fast healthy deposit!

---

buffer; you gave it up. You may feel battered by an influx of stimuli from the outside world. Every sight, sound, and smell comes flooding in. So you might end up eating more sugar in an unconscious attempt to control the alcohol cravings, substituting different carbohydrates. Instead of reducing anxiety and pain, the reverse happens: the sugar creates even *more* jitters. The mood swings continue. The noise of the world batters the brain, making it difficult to say no on a daily basis.

ATTENTION DEFICIT HYPERACTIVITY DISORDER (ADHD)

JUST THE FACTS, PLEASE . . . THE MYSTERY EXPOSED.

This condition comes in all guises. A child can have ADHD and be running around the room, hyperactive and uncontrollable. On the other hand, a child can be perfectly still in class; he or she just doesn't hear a word the teacher says. Adults can also suffer from ADHD. In fact, one study found that 20 percent of compulsive gamblers have ADHD.

WITH ADELE'S COMPLEMENTS!

A twelve-step program might say, "One day at a time," but for additional freedom from alcoholism, I say, "One bite at a time." Eating the right foods can help stop the cravings for alcohol. It can control the blood sugar and reduce some of the jittery, anxious feelings, truly helping the recovering alcoholic stay away from the bar.

KEEPING YOUR CONDITION "BEHIND BARS"
RESCUE REGIMEN FOR
ATTENTION DEFICIT HYPERACTIVITY DISORDER

Follow Preventive Regimen for stress for two weeks. Then add this Rescue Regimen.

If you see △, please check Appendix C for further information.

ON AN ONGOING BASIS:

DIET
- Do an *elimination diet* to determine if a food allergy is possibly causing the ADHD symptoms. (See Chapter 11.)
- *Avoid sugar.* It can exacerbate symptoms.

VITAMINS, MINERALS, AND OTHER NUTRITIONAL SUPPLEMENTS
TAKE DAILY:
△ *Inositol.* A vitamin-like substance that has a calming affect. Add 300 mg.
△ *GABA (gamma-aminobutyric acid).* An amino acid that helps keep the brain from being overwhelmed by stressful signals and messages. Take as directed on an empty stomach. *Discontinue after 2 months.*
- *L-Taurine.* An amino acid that is beneficial in dealing with hyperactivity and anxiety. Take as directed on an empty stomach. *Discontinue after 2 months.*

THE EVIDENCE . . . EXHIBITS A TO Z.
ADHD is a complicated problem; some of it is already in place in the genes or created by chemical alterations. For example, mothers who smoke show a higher risk of having children with ADHD.

Preservatives in food, especially salicylates (which are also naturally found in foods such as apricots, berries, tomatoes, cucumbers, oranges, plums, almonds, and peaches) and BHT, a preservative used in frozen, processed foods, may help cause ADHD. The same holds true for a diet too rich in simple carbohydrates.

GRADE-A DETECTIVE WORK.
I had experience with ADHD in my own family and in my practice; I knew it wasn't just the sugar in the cookies children loved, but also the additives, that caused the problem. Copper or lead toxicity may also create ADHD symptoms. A hair analysis can determine if there is any metal poisoning in your body.

CHRONIC FATIGUE SYNDROME (CFS)

JUST THE FACTS, PLEASE . . . THE MYSTERY EXPOSED.
More and more physicians are recognizing the validity of CFS. In fact, researchers have found a real connection between CFS and the Epstein-Barr virus (a mononucleosis-like condition that weakens the immune system). But CFS goes further than a viral infection. Recent studies have found that excess yeast can contribute to the symptoms of CFS. In fact, one study found a high occurrence of candidiasis (yeast infection) in people with chronic fatigue syndrome.

THE EVIDENCE . . . EXHIBITS A TO Z.
Other withdrawals that can create CFS *bankruptcy* include a recently re-peated antibiotic regime, a poor diet laden with simple carbohydrates (cookies, candies, white bread), and stress. (If you think this sounds like a *leaky gut* connection, you've been doing your Health Detective home-work.) A study done of Dade County, Florida, survivors of Hurricane

Andrew found that CFS patients were at greater risk for more severe symptoms, and there were relapses in those people who once had had CFS.

There are also reports that, if extensive fillings have been done, the mercury in a person's dental work can create toxicity, a withdrawal that can lead to CFS. Many dentists are no longer using amalgam with mercury. Ask your dentist for a different type of filling.

Studies have also found CFS in people who may have unresolved emotional conflicts, as well as in people who are pushing themselves too hard physically. This is the body's message to please slow down and reevaluate your life.

On a more happy note, a study of CFS patients found that their symptoms went away with good life events. Don't wait for that wonderful event to enter your life. Make it happen yourself by adjusting your lifestyle, by choosing health!

GRADE-A DETECTIVE WORK.

Chronic fatigue syndrome might not be all in your head, but it might be in your mouth. Researchers have been able to find two red markers at the back of the mouths of CFS sufferers. These small, crescent-shaped lesions are redder when symptoms are strong and more pink when symptoms have quieted down. The chief of the Infectious Disease Division of Winthrop University Hospital in Mineola, New York, found these markers in 80 percent of his CFS patients.

News flash: A link has been made between chronic fatigue syndrome and salt deficiency. Table salt should still be *verboten*, especially if you are suffering from high blood pressure, but eliminating all the salt from your diet may promote symptoms of dizziness, light-headedness, overwhelming fatigue, and faintness—all symptoms of CFS.

BANK S-TELLARS

Happiness depends upon ourselves. —Aristotle

KEEPING YOUR CONDITION "BEHIND BARS"
RESCUE REGIMEN FOR
CHRONIC FATIGUE SYNDROME

Follow Preventive Regimen for stress for two weeks. Then add this Rescue Regimen.

If you see △, please check Appendix C for further information.

VITAMINS, MINERALS, AND OTHER NUTRITIONAL SUPPLEMENTS
TAKE DAILY:

- *Pantothenic acid.* Add 250–500 mg. Divide dose into several equal amounts.
- *Coenzyme Q10.* Aids energy and the immune system. Take 100 mg.
- △ *Zinc lozenge.* Helps strengthen immune system. Take 25 mg.
- △ *L-Tyrosine.* An amino acid that helps elevate mood and reduce stress. Take 500 mg on an empty stomach. *Discontinue after 2 months.*
- *Dimethylglycine (DMG).* An amino acid that helps restore energy and revitalize brain function. Take sublingual form as directed. *Discontinue after 2 months.*
- *Echinacea.* An herb that supports the immune system. Take as directed.

DEPRESSION

JUST THE FACTS, PLEASE . . . THE MYSTERY EXPOSED.
To paraphrase Tolstoy, each depressed person suffers in his or her own way. Depression takes many forms, and sometimes it is disguised as a different symptom. An underactive thyroid gland, for example, can have the symptoms of clinical depression, but the treatment is different.

THE EVIDENCE . . . EXHIBITS A TO Z.
There are various types of depression—and guises. Doris suffered from clinical depression, triggered by unvoiced anger and enhanced

by a poor diet and a calcium and magnesium deficiency, which also exacerbated her insomnia.

Bipolar illness (or manic-depression) is exactly what it sounds like: a depressive state always followed by a mania in an ongoing cycle. When you are in a manic state, the sky's the limit; people have been known to drop their whole life's savings at a roulette wheel or on an all-day shopping spree. But the depression swiftly follows, like a deadweight, often bringing suicidal thoughts to mind.

Dysthymia is forever—or at least long term. It's a mild, ongoing depression like a continuous low-grade fever, whereby you don't feel great but you're able to work and even laugh—on occasion. Sometimes people suffering from dysthymia have full-blown attacks of depression that eventually recede.

Then there's anxiety and panic attacks. They can be symptoms of depression or a *bankruptcy* all by themselves. A panic attack can feel like a heart attack; you feel completely out of control. Stress-reducing therapies and a diet that controls blood sugar are health deposits for anxiety and panic.

Seasonal affective disorder (SAD) is a type of depression triggered by the lack of sunlight in the winter months. Sunlight helps regulate melatonin, a hormone released in the brain that helps keep depression at bay. Magically, SAD disappears with the last snow and the first crocus. Light therapy (literally sitting in front of a special high-intensity light for half an hour a day) can help chase the blues away. (A trip to the sunny Bahamas in January doesn't hurt, either!)

These are some of the more common psychological and stress-related *bankruptcies*. As you can see, they are physically linked to the body. Stress, diet, lifestyle, nutritional malabsorption, allergies—all play a role in the emotions. And emotions play a physical role, creating aches and pains, fatigue, and rashes in a vicious game between mind and body in which no one wins.

But your emotions don't have to control you. You can link your mind and body in a positive, exhilarating whole that is truly greater than the sum of its parts. Start now to make some very real changes in your body with the foods you eat and the supplements you take. You might be amazed at how your mood, your whole outlook on life, changes as well. A strong body *plus* a strong mind—now, I call that empowerment.

It's time to leave the deep recesses of the mind with its emotions and memory and go to the "sticks and bones" that enable us to jump, to dance, to run: the muscles, bones, and joints of our body.

GRADE-A DETECTIVE WORK.

Foods high in complex carbohydrates, such as potatoes, whole-grain breads, legumes, apples, and squash, all increase tryptophan, an amino acid that raises serotonin production (one of the neurotransmitters responsible for mood enhancement). Turkey contains tryptophan, which is one of the reasons everyone feels sleepy and cozy after a big Thanksgiving Day meal.

Beans, fish, chicken, and other high-protein foods help increase the levels of dopamine and norepinephrine, two neurotransmitters responsible for keeping your brain active and your mind alert. Nibble some chicken if you find yourself "drifting off" in a meeting or at a boring social gathering.

KEEPING YOUR CONDITION "BEHIND BARS"
RESCUE REGIMEN FOR DEPRESSION

Follow Preventive Regimen for stress for two weeks. Then add this Rescue Regimen.

If you see △, please check Appendix C for further information.

VITAMINS, MINERALS, AND OTHER NUTRITIONAL SUPPLEMENTS
TAKE DAILY:

- △ *L-Tyrosine.* An amino acid that affects mood owing to its influence on the neurotransmitter dopamine and the adrenal glands. Take 500 mg once a day on an empty stomach. *Discontinue after 2 months.*
- *Pantothenic acid.* A B vitamin that helps support the adrenal glands in stressful or anxiety-provoking circumstances. Add 250–500 mg. Divide dose into several equal amounts.
- *B complex.* Provides additional folic acid to help prevent depressive disorder. Take an additional 100 mg.

- *B_{12} sublingual.* To prevent homocysteine buildup. Take 500 mcg.
- ⚠ *GABA (gamma-aminobutyric acid).* An amino acid with a calming effect similar to some prescription tranquilizers. Take 750 mg once a day on an empty stomach. *Discontinue after 2 months.*

HERBS

⚠ *Saint-John's-wort.* Helps alleviate symptoms of depression naturally. Studies have found it may work as well as certain prescription antidepressants. Take as directed.

13

Muscular, Joint, and Skeletal Bankruptcies

I was too young to have such aches and pains. My back hurt. My shoulder. My knees. And I'd tried everything—pills, surgery, heat, cold, you name it. Who knew that all it took was some changes in the foods I ate? Some vitamin supplements. And patience. Now, for the first time in my life I wake up in the morning and stretch! —A 24-year-old graphic designer who had begun my Rescue Regimens only three months before

If Nancy had been famous, she'd have been a poster model for the American Dairy Council. She adored milk. She loved the creamy texture, the ice-cold satisfaction. When she was a young girl, her mother never had to tell her to finish her glass. In college, when everyone else was drinking diet sodas, she remained faithful.

But her healthy diet didn't stop with milk. Thanks to her mother, a nurse who was ever diligent that her children eat properly, Nancy had also learned to love broccoli, steamed or mixed in her salad. She learned to love fish and yogurt. She'd actually choose a carrot after school instead of a cupcake.

Nancy didn't try to pass along advice or proselytize. She didn't tell her friends and colleagues to stop eating their too-rich, high-fat food. She didn't lecture her students that candy would hurt their teeth.

In her late twenties, she married a man she met at a singles' dance. George was a thoughtful guy, a hardworking accountant. They moved to the suburbs, to a small house on a tree-lined street.

BANK S-TELLARS

*You are growing when you get to the point where you can do your best,
seen or unseen.*   —Booker T. Washington

When George was made a partner in his firm, Nancy was able to quit teaching. She was thrilled; she wanted to start a family. A year later she gave birth to their first child, a beautiful little boy. Their daughter followed two years later.

Suddenly, Nancy was a housewife, busy changing diapers, taking care of toddlers, running from one to the other, feeding, burping, comforting, and playing. She didn't have much time for herself anymore. She used to love to try new recipes. Now she was lucky if she even opened a can. The garden she'd once filled with vegetables and flowers was full of weeds. Nothing seemed the same; Nancy didn't feel she could do anything right.

Nancy loved her children, she loved her husband, but she needed some peace and quiet. She needed some stress release. She found it, as so many of us do, in food. In the creamy, rich texture of ice cream. In the soft mounds of mashed potatoes. In puddings, cream pies, and custard.

In less than a year, the young mother had gained twenty-five pounds. Nothing fit; she couldn't stand to look in the mirror. But more than hating her weight, Nancy was beginning to be concerned about her health. She didn't like the fact that she couldn't catch her breath when she walked up the stairs or that her blood pressure was creeping up to higher levels. She didn't have to add 2 and 2 to realize she was headed for disaster.

With fresh resolve, Nancy started the newest diet at the time, an extremely low-fat diet aimed at cardiovascular health. She was so determined to lose weight that she compulsively followed the program to the letter, measuring her food and refusing all salad dressings and even stir-fried or lightly sautéed foods.

Nancy became what I call "fat phobic," a person who believes that all fat is bad and that any amount of fat is poison. She avoided fat like the plague, exhaustively checking labels when she went to the super-

market, purchasing only nonfat products and eating steamed vegetables, whole grains, fruit, and her nonfat milk products. While her
family continued to use salad dressings, oils, and a pat of butter, she
ate her food dry.

The vigilance began paying off. Within three months she had lost
eighteen pounds and should have been ecstatic, but it was right about
then when the symptoms began.

Aches in her joints. Pains in her legs and her arms. An overwhelming feeling of fatigue. Nancy was miserable and had little patience for
her children. She barely spoke to her husband when he came home
from work, preferring to stay in bed, feeling as if she were going to die.

Finally, George demanded that she see the doctor, who gave her a
battery of tests and blood work. Nothing showed up. Finding no evidence of any disorder, Nancy's physician diagnosed her with fibromyalgia, an arthritis-like condition that does not have a clear medical
cause. The doctor could only give her ibuprofen for her pain and send
her on her way. He suggested she seek counseling.

Nancy's symptoms grew worse. The only thing that kept her going
was her diet. She became even more fanatical. As her life was falling apart
around her, her diet remained, steadfast and pure. A solid friend. But
the pains increased. Nancy had to do something. She decided to come
see me.

THE MYSTERY OF THE
KITCHEN CUPBOARD: SOLVED

I have worked with many clients who suffered from fibromyalgia. It's a
very real *bankruptcy*. Sufferers can't sleep; their immune systems are
suppressed; they have no energy; their pain is almost continuous. I
have also observed that, among my clients, more women than men
seemed to suffer from the condition (unless it is true that more
women seek help for their problems).

But on that first visit to my office, the Health Detective in me wasn't
yet ready to label Nancy's condition as fibromyalgia, or to even say she
already had a *bankruptcy*. Certainly she was *running in the red*, but disease? I wasn't sure.

As far as I was concerned, the intelligent, forty-something woman sitting in front of me had aches and pains in her muscles and joints. Period. There were many possibilities that needed to be explored. Did Nancy have low blood sugar, owing to a diet too high in sugar and simple starches? Had she been out in the grass lately, contracting Lyme disease, which would cause many of the same symptoms? Did Nancy drink enough water? Insufficient amounts of water may trigger arthritic-like aches. And what about a *leaky gut* and a *toxic liver*? Were they involved in Nancy's condition?

Clearly, there was much Health Detective work we had to do together. There were deposits Nancy could make to stop her spiral down into *bankruptcy*, but we had to determine which would have the most impact and why.

When it comes to aches and pains, I automatically think of bones. And bones make me think of calcium. So my first thought was that perhaps Nancy was not getting enough calcium in her diet.

Wrong. She told me she consumed lots of calcium every day, in nonfat milk, calcium-fortified cottage cheese, nonfat yogurt, vegetables, and supplements. Although it would seem she was getting enough calcium, we had to probe deeper.

I wasn't convinced. Was there a chance that she was not absorbing that calcium? She certainly seemed to be getting enough of her daily requirements, but something was amiss. We continued talking about Nancy's life, her habits, her routines, her diet; we needed to try to find the withdrawals behind her *running in the red* symptoms and the links that would make sense of it all.

She didn't drink a lot of water, which could cause dehydration, but I still could not accept this as the sole cause of such severe discomfort.

And then I had the most important clue yet. Nancy suddenly burst out, "I recently lost twenty-five pounds!" She went on to mention how successful her diet was and that her cholesterol levels and her blood pressure had also improved.

The diet Nancy used to lose weight was a very restrictive one that allowed only the tiniest amount of fat—and she had followed it to the letter. She refused to eat fat in any form, no animal protein except the nonfat milk products, and not even the "good oils" touched her lips. She had thrown out the bottles and containers of olive oil, canola oil, peanut butter, and more that she had in her kitchen cupboard. If she was going to go on a diet to improve her health, she would follow it *perfectly*.

WITH ADELE'S COMPLEMENTS!

People are just waking up to the fact that they, themselves, can affect their quality of life in ways they never realized.

Women are beginning to take to competitive sports, such as crew and running, in their fifties. Eighty-year-olds are graduating from colleges and universities. People in their forties are going back to medical school. Families are reveling in the beauty of nature. Some people are changing their jobs, opting for a less stressful lifestyle. They want to make a difference in their lives, in their children's lives, and in the lives of future generations. You have only to look at the memoirs stacked on the bookstore shelves. People are suddenly unafraid to say "Look at me, here is who I am." We have become survivors. Healers. Believers.

Maybe you didn't realize how far-reaching the benefits of a lifestyle choice or the food you eat could be. Maybe you didn't know how you were able to actually *prevent* illness.

Now that you know some of the wonderful things you can do, some of the health deposits you can make, you can never go back to your old ways with quite the same mind-set. You cannot ignore the benefits of health.

Enjoy! Celebrate your life! Don't wait. Embrace what you are and what you can be.

CHOOSE HEALTH!

And that's where the culprit lay, the clue that solved Nancy's mystery, the item that led, like a smoking gun, to withdrawal after withdrawal.

Vitamin D, which is essential for calcium absorption, is a fat-soluble vitamin, which means that it will not be absorbed by the body *without any fat in the diet*. Nancy ate absolutely *no* fat. Even with all the calcium-rich foods and supplements she took every day, there was no chance she was getting the calcium she needed. Without fat, her body could not absorb it. Like ships passing in the night, Nancy's Body Bank account and her healthy deposits of calcium were so close, but yet impossibly far apart.

Nancy needed a preventive program to get her body back on the healthy track. She didn't have fibromyalgia. She didn't have osteoporosis (although she could wind up with that *bankruptcy* if she continued her unwittingly destructive "no-fat" withdrawals). She didn't have any other full-blown condition—yet. Now was the time for her to take control of her life. Now was the time to restore and maintain a healthy Body Bank—a proactive stance instead of reactive behavior later.

The first recommendation I made was to immediately begin to add some oil or take essential fatty acid supplements so that her calcium would be absorbed by her body. I also suggested she drink lots and lots of water to ensure that dehydration wasn't the cause of her back pain. I added my own Rescue Regimens for reducing stress, strengthening the immune system, and supporting the muscles and bones.

A few weeks later, Nancy's aches and pains began to decrease. She could walk, jog, even dance. Her depression had lifted. She was getting back the energy she thought she'd lost for good. She had learned the secret of healing from the inside out.

DO YOU HAVE *RUNNING IN THE RED* MUSCLE, JOINT, AND SKELETAL SYMPTOMS?

Symptoms are not necessarily signs of a complete and total *bankruptcy*. As we have seen in the other chapters, symptoms can be merely a yellow caution, a reminder to do something *now* to prevent a condition from taking root. Symptoms on the outside alert us to the healing needed on the inside.

Look over these brief statements and see if any of them sound familiar. If so, you could very well develop muscular, joint, or bone pain that could turn into an actual condition if you don't start making some health deposits in your Body Bank. Like Nancy, you can gain control over your body. You can experience the joy and strength of taking charge of *your* health.

- Even a simple paper cut takes forever to stop bleeding.
- Milk is only to add color to my coffee, but I get enough calcium from the cheese I eat a couple of times a week. Right?
- When I was a child, I seemed to be allergic to everything: dairy products, wheat, dust, even eggs. But I grew out of it.
- Lately, I've been too busy to go to the gym to burn off steam. I

BANK S-TELLARS
Don't ask the doctor, ask the patient. —An old Yiddish proverb

---

stopped listening to my relaxation tapes. I started biting my nails again. Sure, I have stress in my life. But I can cope . . . I think.

- I'm around fifty and I'm just waiting for those first "flushing" signs of menopause.
- I spend every summer in the country. When it's really hot, I put on shorts and a T-shirt and take my dogs for long walks in the woods.
- I'd give anything for a decent night's sleep. I'm always tossing and turning. My body never seems able to rest.
- Someone once said I'm like a coiled spring, ready to pop. My legs shake all the time. I'm always tapping my fingers like a drum on my desk.
- I dread my period. A few days before, I start getting such bad cramps that I stay home from work. I go through an entire box of super protection with one cycle!
- I think I'm lactose intolerant. I get nauseous every time I drink or eat a milk product.

You don't have to resign yourself to a life of aches and pains. Nancy didn't and neither do you. And as in Nancy's case, the reasons behind your cramps, your stabbing pain, or your stiffness might be subtle—or they can be as obvious as the onset of menopause (which decreases not only estrogen levels but also absorption of calcium) or past pregnancy (which used your calcium to create a tiny little body, bones and all).

Once you have done your Health Detective work, you can prevent your pain from getting worse. Even better, you may be able to get rid of it—for good!

But you have to know what to look for and why. (See Melissa's story in Chapter 16 for more on muscle and joint pain that could have been seriously misdiagnosed without extensive Health Detective work.)

Here are some major links to muscular, joint, and skeletal symptoms—all of which can be broken with the right health deposits.

STRUCTURAL DAMAGE 1: "I CAN'T TAKE IT ANYMORE!"

One of the most stress-vulnerable nutrients is calcium. When you're working on overload, the immune system sends out corticosteroids (such as those "fight-or-flight" hormones released by the adrenal glands) and catecholamines (substances that affect the flow of the "mood chemicals" in the brain, such as norepinephrine). They are calcium leachers, sent out by stress to deplete your stores of magnesium in the muscles and reduce calcium storage.

How do you know if you have a calcium deficiency? It's not always easy. You have to change the way you think. Thanks to the parathyroid gland, whose main job is to maintain calcium balance in the blood, your blood work readings will most likely appear normal even if your bones are weakening. But within the realm of *Healing from the Inside,* it's not enough for your blood tests to come back negative. It's not enough for your heart to sound good through a stethoscope. It's all of you, your entire body, that needs to be in sync. Balance must exist in every system of your body for the energy and vitality you seek. So, in true Health Detective fashion, you must delve deeper than the surface facts. You must expose any possible links that are creating an imbalance and make the right healthy deposits to correct the situation.

Like Nancy's, your calcium deficiency might have been created by a self-imposed, rigid, no-fat diet. Other clues a good Health Detective looks for include sleeplessness, heavy menstrual cramping, finger tapping, throbbing headaches, dizziness, and stress.

STRUCTURAL DAMAGE 2: THE DRINK OF THE GODS

People assume that it's their age, or it was that one sneeze while they were brushing their teeth or stretching to reach the book on the top shelf that caused the paralyzing pain in their back or shoulder or neck. *Wrong.* They are vulnerable, true, but it is also possible that they are not drinking enough water. Add the diuretic effect of the coffee, tea, or soda they've been drinking, and dehydration becomes a fast-accumulating withdrawal.

How is dehydration linked to back pain? Drs. Nancy Brand and Sally Brooke-Smith find in their chiropractic office that when dehydration fatigues the muscles, people are more at risk for injury. And if a person is very dehydrated, it can contribute to back pain.

WITH ADELE'S COMPLEMENTS!

I know a vibrant, strong, seventy-five-year-old woman named Lillian who takes a brisk walk every morning. When our schedules permit it, we have heated debates over lunch about the political climate, the latest movies and books, the newest supplements to come out. A learned health educator, she still travels to give lectures to large, interested audiences.

This woman, more than anyone else I know, personifies what I have always believed: *aging should not be synonymous with disease*. If you take care of yourself now, putting healthy deposits in your Body Bank, your quality of life need not change in the future.

Unfortunately, not everyone is aware of this fact. When people accept the discomforts of aging as natural or normal, they do not seek any answers, and those aches and pains become a self-fulfilling prophecy. By now, it might sound like an Adele mantra, but I can't stress it enough: the food you eat can make all the difference in the world. You have to choose health!

Another major connection involves transportation. Fluids are vital vessels in the body, carrying nutrients throughout the body. If you're not drinking enough (or drinking too much caffeine), your juices may not be flowing properly and there's a problem with delivery. When that's combined with a nutrient deficiency owing to stress, your joints are not going to be well nourished. There may not be enough fluid to pass through the kidneys, setting the stage for development of kidney stones. All the more reason to drink lots of water; it helps flush waste from the kidneys.

This situation is easy to remedy. Simply drink lots of water—between eight and twelve glasses a day—and reduce your consumption of caffeinated beverages. You'll reduce your risk of muscle and joint pain!

If you're not accustomed to drinking water, you'll find it easier to chug down an eight-ounce glass of room-temperature water. Most people who don't like to drink water mistakenly add ice, which means they can only slowly sip—never downing the amounts of water they need.

STRUCTURAL DAMAGE 3: RASH ACTION

I remember a client who came to see me with a variety of seemingly unrelated symptoms. She had joint pain and headaches; she couldn't sleep at night; she was irritable during the day; and she had bouts of anxiety. Her primary care physician wanted her to see a mental health practitioner, but a friend had recommended that she try a nutritional approach first.

I would never rule out a mental health exam, but after careful questioning, I wasn't so sure her symptoms were a result of an inability to cope with life's ups and downs. In fact, everything I saw pointed to an allergy.

Yes, an allergy. As we have seen in Chapter 11, allergies can be more encompassing than seemingly possible. They also build up over time, with no apparent symptoms at first, until a threshold is reached, and boom!

Dr. Marshall Mandell, one of the first experts to study the far-reaching aspects of allergies, had patients who almost immediately experienced arthritic pain when they were given wheat. His work has linked allergies to muscular weakness and pain, joint swelling, stiffness, arthritis, backaches, and limping, among other symptoms. These reactions can usually be seen in people who are sensitive to the nightshade family of plants, including tomatoes, potatoes, peppers, and eggplant.

If you learn which foods cause an allergic reaction, you can stop eating them for now while you repair that *leaky gut*—repairs that could help prevent the aches and pains that mimic osteoarthritis, fibromyalgia, and more. (See Chapter 11 for details on identifying food allergies and clearing them up.)

STRUCTURAL DAMAGE 4: AMINO ACID TANGO

When you eat protein, it's not the protein as a whole that's crucial; it's the amino acids that are vital for life. When dietary proteins are broken down in a healthy Body Bank, the subsequent amino acids are then "stacked like blocks," refurbished and packaged into the body's own brand of protein. Depending on how the amino acids line up, the protein may create bone density. Or it might make muscles strong. Leucine helps give your muscles the energy they need to walk, to stretch, to dance. Lysine helps bones grow strong and healthy. Taurine helps your entire body utilize calcium.

PREVENTIVE REGIMEN
TO KEEP MUSCLES TONED, JOINTS FLEXIBLE, AND BONES STRONG

This Preventive Regimen is designed to combat flare-ups in muscles, joints, and bones—while keeping your body flexible, strong, and toned.

Be sure to start slowly, introducing supplements gradually, to help prevent any possible reactions. Do the Foundation Regimens for a *leaky gut* and/or a *toxic liver* for three weeks, if applicable, then add this Preventive Regimen.

TIP

- *Practice stress reduction.* This type of pain is associated with anxiety, stress, and depression. Try yoga classes, massage, meditation, deep breathing, or simply some quiet time off by yourself.

ON AN ONGOING BASIS:

DIET

- *Do an elimination diet to pinpoint any food allergies.* The most common allergens for flare-ups in muscles, joints, and bones are gluten-containing foods (wheat, oats, barley, rye), citrus fruits, milk and dairy products, beef, eggs, and the nightshade vegetables (eggplant, tomatoes, potatoes, and peppers). Remove all suspected foods from your diet for two weeks, gradually introducing one potential allergen at a time. If there is no reaction within another two weeks to wheat, for example, add another suspect. Keep going until you've "separated the wheat from the chaff" and can identify your allergy foods. Avoid these as much as possible.
- *Drink 8 to 12 glasses of filtered or bottled water daily.* Important for many bodily functions.

If you see △, please check Appendix C for further information.

VITAMINS, MINERALS, AND OTHER NUTRITIONAL SUPPLEMENTS

TAKE DAILY:

- *High-potency multivitamin-mineral supplement.*
- *B complex.* Helps relieve swelling and inflammation. Add 100 mg.
- *Pantothenic acid.* Helps strengthen adrenal glands and reduce stress and fatigue. Take 250 mg.

- *Vitamin C.* An antioxidant that decreases inflammation. Take 1000–2000 mg.
- ⚠ *Vitamin E.* An antioxidant with properties that decrease damage on the joints. Add 200 IU.
- *Calcium/magnesium.* Calcium is a major component of bone. Magnesium is required to utilize calcium properly. Both help to maintain proper nerves and muscles. Take 1000 mg calcium and 500 mg magnesium.
- *Fish oil capsules.* This essential fatty acid, rich in Omega-3, helps provide the fat needed for proper calcium absorption. Take 2 capsules.
- *Coenzyme Q10.* A powerful antioxidant that helps support immune function. Take 60 mg.
- *Quercetin.* A bioflavonoid that helps ease aches and pains in the legs and back. Take 500 mg.
- *Grape seed extract.* Protects muscles from damage and helps strengthen the immune system. Take 50 mg.

But what if the proper amino acids aren't available because you aren't eating enough protein? What if there is an imbalance in your system, interfering with digestion or the particular system's chemical processes? If the amino acids are not available, you may wind up with a loss of muscle tone, brittle bones, aches and pains, or a lack of energy.

Like a plant that's underwatered and kept out of the sun, your body won't function well without the right food, the right ingredients, or the right chemical messages. Nurture your structure by taking care of yourself, making healthy deposits into your Body Bank. Don't be an untended plant. Face the sun and raise your arms. Stretch your legs. Run. Jump. You just might—with my Preventive Regimens for healthy muscles, joints, and bones.

But even if you have been making so many withdrawals that your symptoms have turned into a full-fledged *bankruptcy* condition, there's no reason to despair. Let's go over a few common muscular, joint, and skeletal conditions, do a little Health Detective work on each, and see what we can come up with.

CHRONIC PAIN, BACK PAIN, AND FIBROMYALGIA

JUST THE FACTS, PLEASE . . . THE MYSTERY EXPOSED.
Albert Schweitzer wrote that "pain is a worse master even than death."
If you are one of the 40 million people who suffer from chronic pain,
you understand this sentiment completely. Although pain is subjec-
tive, unique to your tolerance, your feelings, your descriptions, there
are some basic truths behind the words "my aching back" or "my
stiff neck."

THE EVIDENCE . . . EXHIBITS A TO Z.
When pain begins, a neurological system is activated that travels from
your nerve endings to your brain; this passage of the pain sensation involves complex biochemical processes. If the electrochemical signals

---

A DEPOSIT SLIP:
TAKING CARE OF LYME DISEASE

Sometimes your symptoms have nothing to do with poor lifestyle
choices or nutrient deficiencies. Sometimes your symptoms are "out of
your control." Lyme disease, for example, looks very much like fibromyalgia on the surface. You're tired. You're sore. Your muscles always ache
in the same spot. But here, your symptoms occurred because of a
hungry tick while you were out strolling on a bright summer day.

If you're not sure if you've been making withdrawals or merely suffering a casualty of fate, get a Lyme test done. Go to a specialist. Lyme disease is tricky and has a propensity to hide. The evidence is not always
present in the bloodstream, ready to be counted. Finding an expert is
worth your peace of mind.

If you discover that you do have Lyme disease, you will most likely
have to take a regimen of antibiotics to rid your body of the organism.
If so, be sure to do the full Foundation Regimen for a *leaky gut* and a
toxic liver for the entire time listed. It is imperative to restore your good
bacteria that the antibiotics may have destroyed.

In addition, do the Preventive Regimen for this chapter.

And take echinacea, an herb that enhances immunity, as directed.

that travel to the brain happen to damage cells along the way, or if they cannot do their job, the pain you feel can persist long after you've fallen, pulled a muscle, or burned your hand. In fact, pain can exist without any outward cause and the reasons for it may not show up on X rays.

Your chronic pain might also be accompanied by other symptoms, including depression, insomnia, dizzy spells, ringing in your ears, or gastrointestinal distress.

GRADE-A DETECTIVE WORK.

We've already seen the connection that allergies, stress, dehydration, and nutrient deficiency have with chronic pain. But did you know that studies show a link between lower back pain and premature menopause? Or that women who suffer from fibromyalgia have their most intense pain before their periods? The immune system is weakest in women at ovulation, when their bodies prepare to allow a sperm, a "foreigner," to enter to fertilize an egg. (This is also one of the reasons why women get yeast infection outbreaks right before menstruation.)

A *running in the red leaky gut* and *toxic liver* may also help allow an onslaught of invaders to seep into your bloodstream. Toxins can ultimately cause inflammation and aches in your joints and muscles, causing pain.

KEEPING YOUR CONDITION "BEHIND BARS"
RESCUE REGIMEN FOR CHRONIC PAIN, BACK PAIN, AND FIBROMYALGIA

Follow Preventive Regimen for bones and muscles for two weeks. Then add this Rescue Regimen.

If you see △, please check Appendix C for further information.

TIPS
- It is possible that your pain may be a sign of Lyme disease. Have an examination by a Lyme specialist.
- This condition may be present owing to parasites. See a parasitologist to determine if you have parasites lurking in your gastrointestinal tract.

VITAMINS, MINERALS, AND OTHER NUTRITIONAL SUPPLEMENTS
TAKE DAILY:
- *Vitamin C.* Take an additional 1000 mg daily.
- *Malic acid with magnesium.* Helps keep muscles energized. Take as directed.
- *Proteolytic enzymes.* Helps reduce inflammation. Take as directed between meals.
- Foundation programs for the *leaky gut* and *toxic liver* are generally indicated (refer to Chapters 6 and 7).

If you suffer from fibromyalgia, chronic pain, or back pain, it would be useful to do my Foundation Regimens for a *leaky gut* and *toxic liver*. It's very possible that once these conditions are strengthened, your symptoms will ease.

OSTEOPOROSIS

JUST THE FACTS, PLEASE . . . THE MYSTERY EXPOSED.
The name might be from Latin, but translated, it is "brittle bones." And that's exactly what this condition is: a decrease in bone mass that leaves your skeletal infrastructure fragile and brittle. You might have what is called "dowager's hump," a bent-over posture resulting from tiny fractures in your spinal cord. Or perhaps you fall easily, breaking bones. Your clothes seem to be getting longer. Your shoulders stoop. It might be painful to take even one step.

THE EVIDENCE . . . EXHIBITS A TO Z.
What makes osteoporosis so insidious is the fact that after age thirty, your body slows down the process of making bone mass. You can help protect yourself from this condition by taking more calcium supplements with magnesium and vitamin D. In fact, if you begin to take calcium as an adolescent, it provides a "backbone" for the skeletal system, a "retirement fund" for your Body Bank's skeleton. By getting the nutrients early, especially calcium, in the proper amounts and with the

proper absorption, you can help keep yourself from losing what it took your growing years to accumulate.

Because women have less bone mass than men to begin with, they are more prone to this condition. But men beware! A study of over 100 men at the Indiana University School of Medicine found that osteoporosis was prevalent in men who smoked and drank. In fact, these lifestyle withdrawals were more potent than heredity in causing the condition.

GRADE-A DETECTIVE WORK.

We're so used to thinking "estrogen and menopause" when it comes to osteoporosis. In reality, the clues were in place years before. Think about progesterone, too. This hormone is vital not only for stimulating ovulation but also for helping the mineralization process of bone production. In other words, throughout your life, it is also progesterone that keeps bone mass at optimum levels, not just estrogen. Even more important, during perimenopause, progesterone output begins to slide, so that your bones begin to lose their mass even before menopause. Add the drop in estrogen at menopause, and boom! Rapid depletion that you might have been blissfully unaware of as you went about your day.

Then there's the all-important calcium issue. We've already discussed the link between calcium and bones, as well as the other vitamins and minerals needed for calcium to be properly absorbed by those hungry bones. But a good Health Detective knows that calcium deficiency is caused by more than a low-calcium diet. It's more than not drinking your milk.

A BOUNCED CHECK:
OSTEOPOROSIS

Many people think that the fracture they get when they fall, or the sprain, the tear, or broken bone, was the cause of their problem. When they are treated for their broken bones and joints, they might find that, as an added minus, they have osteoporosis.

In actuality, the osteoporosis may have come first. It's the brittle bones that caused the break. The fall was due to osteoporosis and a cracked bone *already in place*. Not the other way around.

Take care of yourself now, before the broken bones. Your body will thank you for years to come.

Salt, too, may deplete your body of calcium. One study found that women who consistently ate a high-salt diet (over 3,900 milligrams a day) lost 30 percent more calcium than those eating a low-salt regimen (1,600 milligrams a day).

Other materials "steal" calcium away from the bones. These include caffeine, alcohol, and the phosphorus found in sodas.

Another possible culprit? Hyperthyroidism. Although this is an endocrine *bankruptcy* (see Chapter 15), the results, as with all conditions, are far-reaching and connected to every system in the body. In hyperthyroidism, too much thyroxin, a hormone, is secreted. What does this mean in everyday terms? Thyroxin stimulates the bones to release minerals. Too much, and too many minerals are taken away. Bone mass can be depleted.

KEEPING YOUR CONDITION "BEHIND BARS"
RESCUE REGIMEN FOR OSTEOPOROSIS

Follow Preventive Regimen for bones and muscles for two weeks. Then add this Rescue Regimen.

If you see △, please check Appendix C for further information.

TIP
- *Weight-bearing exercise* will help build bones, regardless of calcium loss. Walk with hand weights. Lift weights. Wear weights in the water. Studies have found that women increased their spinal bone mass with vigorous exercise—about an hour four times a week.

ON AN ONGOING BASIS:
DIET
- *Limit carbonated drinks and caffeine.* Both contribute to potent calcium deficiency.
- *Avoid excessive protein intake.* It may hinder calcium absorption.

VITAMINS, MINERALS, AND OTHER NUTRITIONAL SUPPLEMENTS
TAKE DAILY:
- *Boron.* Enhances absorption of calcium. Add 1–2 mg.

- *Calcium/magnesium.* Take an additional 500 mg each.
- *Multienzyme with HCl.* Aids calcium absorption. Take as directed with meals.

OSTEOARTHRITIS AND
RHEUMATOID ARTHRITIS

JUST THE FACTS, PLEASE . . . THE MYSTERY EXPOSED.

When we think of arthritis, it's usually in general terms—cramping, painful walking, aching joints, swelling, especially before rain. Osteoarthritis usually occurs in people over forty; it affects specific joints in the body and may be a result of a lifetime of withdrawals, such as calcium deficiency and a *leaky gut.* Rheumatoid arthritis, on the other hand, can be found in young children; it is an autoimmune condition. It usually affects all the joints of the body.

THE EVIDENCE . . . EXHIBITS A TO Z.

I have found two varied profiles of arthritis in my practice, and each has its own personality. The "Type O oven cooker" is osteoarthritis, officially a condition found primarily in the elder population. Basically, it's a wearing away of the cushiony cartilage at the joints, usually at the hips or knees. There's a profile of a Type O and I've found it to be incredibly accurate. This arthritic has a history of eating lots of protein and lots of processed foods (which always leads the Health Detective in me to the possibility that there is a lack of nutrients to nourish the body or provide the proper materials it needs for its varied functions). A Type O almost always cooks an entire meal; eating just fresh salads or vegetables is considered unusual.

The "Type R pressure cooker" is rheumatoid arthritis, officially a condition that affects all the joints in the body, not just specific tender spots. It, too, eats away at the cartilage and tissues surrounding the joints, but sometimes also the bones themselves. I find that Type R people tend to be quieter; they drink very little water, if any, and will most likely be dehydrated. They do not eat enough protein, instead of too much (which always leads the Health Detective in me to consider the possibility of an amino acid deficiency). They may be tense, hyperactive, nervous. Rheumatoid arthritis can be crippling, causing fever, fatigue, even anemia and weight loss.

Different personalities, different symptoms, different roots, but still pain that, unfortunately, just doesn't seem to go away.

GRADE-A DETECTIVE WORK.
Allergies, as we have seen, can affect every system in the body. (See Chapter 11.) Allergic reactions can be particularly insidious when the symptoms don't include your typical sneezing, coughing, or nest of hives, but rather excruciating pain in the joints of your knees, your elbows, your hips. Toxins that escape from the *leaky gut* can often cause arthritis-like symptoms.

Imagine dancing under a starlit moon. Swimming brisk laps in the pool. Hiking through a sun-filtered woods. Pain free. Vital. Strong. This doesn't have to be just a dream. It can be reality. Your reality—if you make the appropriate healthy deposits in your Body Bank now.

There is always hope. Combined with knowledge, you too can have healthy muscles, joints, and bones. It's in your control. You can do it. You can change things—right now. To help your motivation stay strong, read on. There's more information to come, more preventive measures to glean, more empowerment awaiting . . . in the next chapter.

RESCUE REGIMEN FOR
OSTEOARTHRITIS AND RHEUMATOID ARTHRITIS

Follow Preventive Regimen for bones and muscles for two weeks. Then add this Rescue Regimen.

If you see △, please check Appendix C for further information.

OSTEOARTHRITIS

TIP

- The *elimination diet* in the Preventive Regimen is important to remove allergic foods and clear up toxicity that may be causing your arthritis (see page 208).

VITAMINS, MINERALS, AND OTHER NUTRITIONAL SUPPLEMENTS
TAKE DAILY:

- *Vitamin C.* Acts as an antiinflammatory. Take an additional dose of 1000 mg daily.
- *Glucosamine sulfate.* A substance necessary for proper bone and cartilage formation. Take 1500 mg. Divide dose into several equal amounts.
- *Sea cucumber.* Helps lubricate the joints. Take 1500 mg.
- △ *Green drinks, containing alfalfa.* Alfalfa provides minerals necessary for bone composition. May help provide relief from pain. Take as directed.

RHEUMATOID ARTHRITIS

ON AN ONGOING BASIS:

DIET

- Drink plenty of *water.*
- Eat a diet rich in *high-quality protein foods,* like lean chicken or fish.

VITAMINS, MINERALS, AND OTHER NUTRITIONAL SUPPLEMENTS
TAKE DAILY:

- *Vitamin C.* Take an additional 1000 mg daily.
- *Quercetin.* Take an additional dose of 1000 mg daily.
- *Bromelain.* An enzyme that helps the body digest. Take 3 times a day before meals.
- *Multi–amino acid complex.* Provides raw materials necessary for formation of bones. Take as directed on an empty stomach. *Discontinue use after 2 months.*
- *Feverfew.* Acts as an antiinflammatory. Take as directed.

14

SKIN AND HAIR BANKRUPTCIES

When I started to lose my hair, I tried all these expensive remedies. Nothing.
Figured it was heredity, like my dad. Now I've shared what I learned with <u>him</u>.
I might not be able to wear a ponytail, but the loss has greatly diminished. It's
a great feeling! —A 35-year-old artist who came to see
me about his premature baldness

When Roger entered a schoolroom at the beginning of a new year, his first thought wasn't what his new students would be like. He wasn't planning his syllabus or wondering if these kids would be ready to read some Melville. No. Although an excellent, devoted high school English teacher, Roger would have to confess that it wasn't scholarly pursuits on his mind. It was his dandruff.

Within minutes of writing his name on the blackboard, he knew he would feel an annoying itchiness on his scalp. He'd start to scratch and the flakes would start to fall.

Roger wouldn't be surprised if the kids in school called him "Mr. Shoulders" behind his back. He felt very self-conscious, which only increased with his belief that his condition put off some of the other teachers as well. He saw the quick glances of disgust they'd try to hide.

To add to his misery, Roger was ill a great deal with minor infections, something that had been with him since childhood. He was always catching a cold or developing a sore throat.

His diet had never been good. It started with high-fat, carbohydrate-laden dinners his mother painstakingly made each night, and it became even more unhealthy as he grew up. Starting his morning with sugary cereal and milk, Roger would eat his feelings as he went through his day. It was amazing that he was thin, considering the high-fat foods he ate. Although loaded with calories, these foods did not total more than he burned each day. Nor did Roger especially love what he ate. He always complained that he had "no taste buds," that he couldn't tell the difference between a jelly and a cream donut by taste. Neither did the foods help his moods; he became quite irritable and cranky as the day worn on.

No, Roger was not happy. He might have had an unsightly exterior, but inside he was a kind man, an excellent teacher who really seemed to care. He believed all his problems stemmed from his dandruff, and he'd try anything, from dermatologists to expensive specialty shampoos. Because he hadn't a clue that his healing could only occur from within, the solution was short-lived. His dandruff would always return.

Roger and I would have continued on separate paths, except for the two new symptoms he developed: pain upon urination and swollen glands. His doctor diagnosed him with an enlarged prostate and prescribed antibiotics.

He was tired of all this, of one thing after another. He had to do something else. He was sick of his whole life and he needed a new answer. He came to see me at a fellow teacher's suggestion.

We began our Health Detective work to try to figure out the connections between Roger's ailments and the underlying conditions that might be causing his symptoms. Even more important, we had to discover if Roger could regain both his physical and emotional health.

THE MYSTERIOUS CRIME OF
MR. SHOULDERS: SOLVED

We started with the obvious: Roger's dandruff. As always, a symptom so pronounced, so dramatic, signaled some kind of imbalance in the body. Dandruff may be a signal of excessive stress, a suppressed immune system, a lack of nutrients coming in, or an inability of the body to absorb them. The biggest links between Roger's symptoms and the possibilities that caused them were the nutritional deficiencies—in particular, selenium, zinc, and essential fatty acids.

The stress was easy to determine. Roger was miserable; he had been angry and resentful a long time, keeping the physical stress mechanisms overworked in his body. His adrenal glands were in high drive; his entire body was overtaxed.

Even if Roger was getting enough vitamins and minerals, this stress could deplete his nutrient reserves and increase his requirements, which could in turn alter the proper nutrient absorption of what little he was getting. This stress could also be linked to an alteration in digestive flow that would interfere with absorption. Further, thanks to his recent regimen of antibiotics and his high-sugar diet—both high-level withdrawals—his digestive system was "primed and ready" to become a *leaky gut*. This, in turn, would challenge his liver, which, once overwhelmed, would be unable to carry out its filtering and transporting jobs.

Then there was the clue of Roger's enlarged prostate, which has been linked to an infectious bacterium. If he'd had a proper reserve of zinc, his immune system, which guards against invasion, might have had the energy it needed to fend off attack. The same lack of protection might be leaving the door wide open to constant colds; a starving immune system is too weak to fight. An additional clue to this apparent zinc deficiency link was Roger's decreased sense of taste and smell.

We were getting closer. Here were links leading to other links. But we had to know more facts before a solution could be found. I asked Roger more about his eating habits and his daily routine.

The answers became clearer as Roger discussed his diet. He ate very few salads, very few fresh fruits and vegetables. His daily dose of donuts, starchy foods, and cola all contributed to an excessive amount of carbohydrates in his diet, which could certainly lead to a lack of some nutrients (and, ultimately, that *leaky gut*). He was getting fat, but not the right kind. An overabundance of saturated fats left no room for the "good oils." This poor diet could also lead to a whole host of other vitamin and mineral deficiencies, including a lack of the B vitamins, which could contribute to an enlarged prostate, a suppressed immune system, and dandruff.

These links kept coming back to Roger's withdrawals and their results: nutrient deficiency and unrelenting stress. His *running in the red* symptoms signaled a need to start his deposits on the ground floor, starting with my *leaky gut* and *toxic liver* regimens. We worked to "relieve" his liver by limiting some of his direct assaults, reducing fats in

---

WITH ADELE'S COMPLEMENTS!

We give disease names to our *bankruptcies* instead of nourishing them with health deposits. Look at your *running in the red* warning signals. Why are they there? What are some of the healthy deposits you can make to balance your account? Remember, prevention is key. Do something before a *bankruptcy* takes hold.

Make a deposit right now. It's as easy as opening your refrigerator and grabbing an apple. Or taking a brisk walk. Exploring the shelves of your local health food store. Taking some deep cleansing breaths. Calling a loving friend.

---

his diet, decreasing and eventually eliminating his caffeine while increasing his intake of water. Roger began my Foundation Regimens with flaxseed oil capsules (an Omega-3 essential fatty acid), digestive enzymes, and some probiotics.

Over the next few weeks, we added more to Roger's new regimens. He started taking other nutritional supplements. We slowly added more of my Foundation Regimens until he was on the full program and doing well. His diet became more and more of a health deposit, a support for his now-healthy life.

Within a few months, for the first time in his life, Roger's dandruff subsided. His skin looked better; he smiled more often. His prostatitis was under control and—as Roger learned—so could be his destiny. He could choose health.

DO YOU HAVE *RUNNING IN THE RED* SKIN AND HAIR SYMPTOMS?

Remember, a symptom is not a *bankruptcy*. A *running in the red* account can be saved. "No" and "never" are not in my vocabulary. I continue to observe that if you start making health deposits today, you can help your Body Bank in immeasurable ways.

Start now, with these quick, brief statements that, even if they sound unconnected, can signal symptoms of a skin or hair *running in the red* account. If any of them ring true, don't despair. Help is only a page away, in my Rescue Regimens. Try my remedies for a month or so. See if you, like Roger, begin to feel better. See if you too can rejoice in the feeling of empowerment that taking control of your body gives you!

- My hair is prematurely gray.
- It seems as if I'm always angry or anxious about something. Nothing ever goes the way I want it to!
- When I think greens, I think of that little piece of wilted lettuce that comes with my burger.
- I drink a lot of diet sodas. In fact, I must have at least two cans in the afternoon at work.
- Even though I buff and polish, I continue to get small white dots on my nails.
- I end up going to the periodontist almost as much as the regular dentist; my gums are in the worst shape, even though I floss.
- I know I can't wear black.
- I can eat anything. In fact, unless food is extremely spicy, all of it tastes and smells the same to me.
- If I get even the slightest cut from a piece of paper, it hurts horribly and takes forever to heal.

When someone says you have tough skin, it isn't just a figure of speech. Your skin is the primary barrier between you and the world; it *has* to be tough to ward off infection, toxins, and other foreign substances that could interfere with the proper working of your Body Bank.

But skin doesn't do just that. It's also a window on the rest of your body. A rash, acne, dry scalp—these can be the first hints that something, somewhere inside, past your surface, past your epithelial layers, is out of balance. Disrupted. *Running in the red.* Understanding and taking care of these outer symptoms can help you prevent a full-fledged *bankruptcy* from erupting.

Psoriasis, dandruff, and bruises that don't heal may be symptoms of a nutrient deficiency. They may also signal a *leaky gut* or a *toxic liver*. When toxins and other substances seep into the bloodstream where they don't belong, they can create havoc, putting your entire body out of balance, including your skin. Before you know it, your face takes on a sallow cast. Perhaps your wounds don't heal fast enough. Your hair begins to fall out.

Other symptoms, seemingly unconnected, may begin to flourish: constant infections, overwhelming fatigue, an uncomfortable feeling in your gut. One following another—all linked. All affected by withdrawals. In addition to a possible underlying *leaky gut* and *toxic liver*, there are a few surface issues that may specifically cause skin and hair symptoms, all of which can be stopped if you learn, if you understand, if you choose health.

SURFACE ISSUE 1: SELENIUM—THE "SALT" OF THE EARTH

It might sound like the name of a planet in a sci-fi thriller, but selenium is actually very much a part of earth. In fact, it is one of the most important nutrients *in* earth—literally. Selenium is found in soil, the same soil in which food is grown. Unfortunately, as you have seen in Section I, earth's selenium may be sorely depleted or compromised and, therefore, the fruits, vegetables, and grains grown in the soil may not have this mineral to absorb. The result? Selenium deficiency—and possible dandruff.

The dry scalp that causes itchy, white flakes has been linked to lack of selenium, among other nutritional deficiencies. What else in your body might be affected when you lack selenium? As people who are rushing to health food stores to stock up know, it is a powerful antioxidant that, when ingested and absorbed, has potential antiaging properties. When combined with vitamin E, another powerful antioxidant, selenium also helps to decrease the risk of certain cancers, maintain a strong heart and a well-functioning liver, and support prostate function. Last but not least, selenium aids in keeping the skin elastic and smooth, keeping dandruff at bay.

SURFACE ISSUE 2: ZINC—THE NEW NUTRITION BUZZWORD

Like oat bran in the 1980s, zinc has become the new miracle nutrient for immunity, anti-aging, and most popular of all, relief from the common cold. According to news reports, pharmacies and health food stores can't keep enough zinc lozenges on the shelves. There's no denying the fact that zinc can be a mighty healthy deposit!

The first and easiest place for a Health Detective to find clues of a zinc deficiency are your skin, your nails, and your hair. Finding and

---

A BOUNCED CHECK

Your nails can often save you hours of detective work:
- Brittle nails might signal an iron deficiency.
- Flat nails may mean a circulation problem.
- Square, wide nails might be a sign of hormonal problems.
- Nails that chip and crack easily may signal digestive problems—that *leaky gut*!
- A nail fungus usually means to stop using the nail polish you've been wearing. It may also signal a food allergy or a yeast invasion.
- White spots on your nails may be a sign of zinc deficiency.

---

acting on any *running in the red* symptoms here may prevent a full-fledged, serious *bankruptcy*.

You'll find the "zinc conspiracy" in:

- *White spots on your nails.* Zinc is an active ingredient in over 2,000 enzymes that assist metabolic functions throughout the body. A lack of zinc can inhibit growth; nails grow slower and nutrients aren't absorbed as efficiently. Zinc is stored in the nails (as well as the hair, skin, and bones). If you don't have enough in your system, those telltale spots can appear.

- *Wounds that don't heal.* Having too little zinc affects your immune system, preventing it from performing normal wound healing. Zinc not only stands alone as a powerful antioxidant but is also necessary for the creation of yet *another* antioxidant, an enzyme called superoxide dismutase (SOD). Add its help in forming collagen, and you have a "superhero" that goes after germs fast and heals up wounds with a single blast.

- *Drinking too much milk.* Despite what the ads proclaim, you *can* overindulge in calcium. Although zinc is absorbed in the small intestine during the digestive process, calcium intake can hinder that absorption. If you love your milk, make sure you increase your zinc every day. Other zinc depleters are excessive amounts of grains (thanks to the phytic acid they contain) and other foods high in fiber (which grab hold of the zinc and eliminate some of it before it can be absorbed).

- *A lack of taste and smell.* If you can't smell your grandmother's apple pie in the oven or taste the garlic in her tomato sauce, don't blame your nose, your taste buds, or your family. Zinc is needed for the taste buds to work properly. A lack of zinc and a bud simply won't "bloom." And since zinc is necessary to keep the liver from chemical harm, too little zinc may mean a *toxic liver.*
- *Broken-out skin.* Acne can be more than a sign of eating too much shrimp (iodine can make skin break out in food-sensitive people). Zinc is also a great regulator for the skin's oil glands. Not enough zinc and oil may erupt.
- *Drinking tap water.* We already know about the parasites that lurk in tap water (see Section I), but did you ever take copper into account? Even trace amounts of copper can contaminate water. Copper pipes that lead to your sinks and your shower, traces found in pipes and chemicals of your swimming pool—these can cause too much copper to be absorbed by your system. And, unfortunately, copper vies for the same absorption sites in the small intestines as zinc does. Too much copper and it simply pushes the zinc away. The zinc isn't absorbed and a withdrawal begins. . . .
- *Prematurely graying hair.* It can be your genes, but premature gray hair, especially when combined with the other signs I've described here, can be caused by a zinc deficiency. Some zinc is stored in the hair follicles. If the body needs more than it's getting, it will go to any storeroom it can find, and that includes your hair. The result? Loss of color in your locks.

SURFACE ISSUE 3: FROM C TO SHINING C—
THE LINK BETWEEN VITAMIN C AND YOUR SKIN

Some things are so much a given, they tend to be taken for granted. Vitamin C is one of them. As a child, you learned how important vitamin C was in history class, when you heard about sailors who didn't get scurvy because of the citrus fruit they ate aboard ship. You heard the reports about vitamin C preventing the common cold. Although the evidence is still out on the "C cold cure," vitamin C *is* a powerful antioxidant, a cancer-fighter par excellence. It is also a strong immune system builder, especially in combination with bioflavonoids. In short, you know how potent a healthy deposit of vitamin C can be—even many of the most conservative experts have accepted its value.

But now take a look as a Health Detective at this miracle vitamin, and you may begin to see the subtle signs of a *running in the red* account that needs to be examined, to help prevent more serious symptoms and a possible Body Bank *bankruptcy*. There are links between a vitamin C deficiency and split ends, brittle nails, sore gums and gingivitis, bruises that remain black and blue for weeks, and aches and pains in the joints (which need "vitamin C–dependent" connective tissue as a "cushion"), as well as more serious conditions in the future.

How does a vitamin C withdrawal occur, despite your loading up on fresh fruits and vegetables? In a word, stress. Whether emotional or physical, ongoing, unrelenting stress depletes your body of almost every nutrient, affecting your hormonal balance and your immunity. It also affects the absorption of vitamin C.

Sulfa drugs, taken for urinary tract infections, also deplete the body's vitamin C stores; they can cause excess excretion of too much of the vitamin.

SURFACE ISSUE 4: THE ESSENTIAL FATTY ACID TEST

Fat has become such a bad word in today's world that it's difficult to believe there are some fats that are actually good for you—essential, as a matter of "fat." These essential fatty acids (EFA) cannot be manufactured in the body; they must be ingested. Omega-3 and Omega-6 essential oils help maintain a strong heart and a healthy immune system. Omega-3 oils may also be potent antiinflammatories, helping ease the aches and pains of osteoarthritis and irritated skin. Deficiencies of EFAs have been found in people who suffer from psoriasis. (See Sections I and II for more on essential fatty acids and how they affect the body.)

These are only some of the "surface issues" that reflect on the skin, that open a window onto a Body Bank that could very well be *running in the red*. Treat your skin and hair to some of my Preventive and Rescue Regimens and you may begin to see the signs of healthy, glowing skin and shiny, thicker hair within weeks.

But perhaps your symptoms are more severe than others. Perhaps your dandruff or your acne has grown into a full-blown *bankruptcy*. Don't despair. Read the following *bankruptcy* descriptions and see if any of my accompanying Rescue Regimens can be of some help.

PREVENTIVE REGIMEN
FOR KEEPING SKIN AND HAIR HEALTHY

Here are the deposits to help your body create glowing skin and healthy hair.

Do the Foundation Regimens for a *leaky gut* and/or a *toxic liver* for three weeks, if applicable, then add this Preventive Regimen. Be sure to start slowly, introducing supplements gradually, to help prevent any possible reactions.

If you see △, please check Appendix C for further information.

VITAMINS, MINERALS, AND OTHER NUTRITIONAL SUPPLEMENTS
TAKE DAILY:

- *High-potency multivitamin and mineral supplement.*
- *Vitamin B complex.* Helps to maintain healthy skin and hair. Take 100 mg.
- *Vitamin C.* An antioxidant that enhances immune function. Take 1000 mg.
- *Biotin.* A B vitamin that helps maintain hair and skin health. Take 400 mcg.
- *Pantothenic acid.* Helps promote proper skin and hair health. Also supports body under stress. Take 250 mg.
- △ *Zinc.* Helps to promote wound and tissue healing. Take gluconate lozenge. Take 25–50 mg.
- *Flaxseed oil.* Helps promote hair and skin health. Take 2 additional capsules daily.
- △ *Multienzyme with HCl.* Helps ensure proper digestion. Take with warm water with meals as directed.
- *Calcium.* Necessary for basic health. Take 800 mg–1000 mg.
- *Magnesium.* To support calcium balance. Take 400 mg–500 mg.

HERBS
- *Dandelion root tea.* Helps cleanse the liver. Take 1 or 2 cups.

ACNE

JUST THE FACTS, PLEASE . . . THE MYSTERY EXPOSED.
Who hasn't been a teenager spending hours in front of a mirror trying, against all odds, to hide that blemish before a big date? Nine times
out of ten, it only got worse the more cover-up or hot compresses you
used. Unfortunately, pimples are almost synonymous with the teenage
years. Hormones are flowing; glands, along with emotions, body hair,
and growth, are highly dramatic, acting out in all sorts of ways. These
overactive glands include the sebaceous glands, which are situated
at the base of each hair follicle. When they are working right, these
glands lubricate the skin and keep skin soft. But if oil gets trapped in

A BOUNCED CHECK PAIR:
ECZEMA AND DERMATITIS

Many people think these two conditions are the same. But in reality,
eczema is a type of dermatitis. The grand dame of irritating skin conditions, dermatitis is recognized by flaking, itchy, scaling, and thickening
skin, and with red lesions. It may be caused by contact with allergic
substances, such as perfume, latex, cosmetics, metals, and poison ivy.
It can also be triggered internally, by food allergies, such as to the
gluten found in wheat, barley, oats, and rye, and dairy products.

Eczema goes one step further: the surface of the skin blisters; pus-
filled boils may appear that ooze and spread.

Help your dermatitis and eczema with:

- Vitamin B_6, which helps maintain healthy skin. Take 100 mg daily.
- Niacin, another B vitamin, which also helps maintain healthy skin.
  Take 100 mg daily.

Help reduce the appearance of boils by increasing your intake of vitamin C, which acts as an antiinflammatory—up to 3000 mg daily. Split
the dosage and use the buffered type; it is easier on your stomach.
(See Appendix C for further information.)

Tea tree oil, an antibacterial substance, may help soothe irritated,
inflamed skin. Studies have found that 5 percent tea tree oil applied
topically worked as effectively in reducing acne as 5 percent benzoyl
peroxide (the traditional medical prescriptive), with fewer side effects.

these glands, bacteria gather, plugging up your pores and causing the inflammation you know as a pimple.

Other problems you may still dread: a blackhead is the result of this oil-bacteria mixture being exposed to skin pigmentation. A whitehead is the accumulation of inflamed oil and bacteria under the surface of the skin. A boil is an inflamed infection, filled with pus.

THE EVIDENCE . . . EXHIBITS A TO Z.

Sebaceous gland activity is not just a teenage phenomenon. Premenstrual hormonal activity, stress, contraceptives, food allergies—all these can cause red, inflamed eruptions. Men are also more prone to acne

KEEPING YOUR CONDITION "BEHIND BARS"
RESCUE REGIMEN FOR ACNE

Follow Preventive Regimen for skin and hair for two weeks. Then add this Rescue Regimen.

If you see △, please check Appendix C for further information.

ON AN ONGOING BASIS:
DIET
- *Avoid milk products, saturated oils, fatty foods, sugars, and preservatives.* These foods can contribute to acne flare-ups.

VITAMINS, MINERALS, AND OTHER NUTRITIONAL SUPPLEMENTS
TAKE DAILY:
- △ *L-Cysteine.* An amino acid that contains sulfur, an important substance for healthy skin. Take 500 mg on an empty stomach. *Discontinue use after 2 months.*
- △ *Vitamin A.* Helps promote healthy skin. Take 20,000 IU. *Discontinue after 2 months.*

HERBS
- *Dandelion tea.* One or two cups daily.
- *Tea tree oil.* Has antibacterial and antifungal properties. Apply topically as directed.

than women because the male sex hormones, called androgens, are most responsible for producing sebum and keratin, the two key culprits in clogged pores.

Although acne is considered a dirty word, the reality is that too much washing can irritate the skin. People with blemishes or boils are usually very clean, scrubbing their faces many times a day, which ironically stimulates the production of more oil and androgens.

GRADE-A DETECTIVE WORK.
Broken-out skin is a nuisance all by itself, but it may also signal an underlying condition: a *toxic liver* and/or a *leaky gut.* Many toxins are expelled through the skin when you sweat. If your body is overburdened by toxins, the kidneys and the liver can't filter them all out; it becomes an impossible job. If you have regular bouts of acne or red, inflamed skin or boils, it's possible that your Body Bank could be calling for healthy deposits for your *toxic liver* and *leaky gut* now! (See Chapters 6 and 7.)

DANDRUFF

JUST THE FACTS, PLEASE . . . THE MYSTERY EXPOSED.
Those embarrassing white flakes on your shoulders are actually first cousins to acne. Dandruff may be the result of overactive or underactive sebaceous glands on your scalp.

THE EVIDENCE . . . EXHIBITS A TO Z.
Dandruff has been linked to various vitamin and mineral deficiencies, especially the B vitamins, which help maintain proper metabolic function, and zinc and selenium. This deficiency may be the result of a high-carbohydrate diet and/or a *leaky gut,* which may prevent the complete breakdown of foods.

GRADE-A DETECTIVE WORK.
Take a look at a bottle of dandruff shampoo. One of its first ingredients is selenium. No surprise here. A real clue to selenium deficiency is dandruff.

A BEAUTY BONUS

When my clients have been on my regimens for several months, they come into my office with special delight. Not only are they beginning to feel better but they cannot believe how beautiful and strong their nails are. Why? Because they are eating right and taking care of themselves. It's a wonderful side effect!

If you are having problems with your nails, make them stronger with:

- My Foundation Regimen for a *leaky gut*. It is very possible that your gut is the culprit behind your nail problems.
- *Silica.* A mineral that helps make your nails strong. Take as directed.
- *Multi–amino acid complex.* Provides the building blocks for healthy nails. Take as directed.

Stress, both emotional and physical, as well as an overtaxed body, may also trigger a bout of dandruff. All your functions are on "quick time," creating hormonal imbalances, inefficient digestion, and malabsorption of vitamins and minerals.

KEEPING YOUR CONDITION "BEHIND BARS"
RESCUE REGIMEN FOR DANDRUFF

Follow Preventive Regimen for skin and hair for two weeks. Then add this Rescue Regimen.

If you see △, please check Appendix C for further information.

VITAMINS, MINERALS, AND OTHER NUTRITIONAL SUPPLEMENTS
TAKE DAILY:

- *Vitamin E.* Take 400 IU.
- *Kelp.* Rich in minerals and important for a healthy scalp. Take 1000 mg.

HAIR LOSS

JUST THE FACTS, PLEASE . . . THE MYSTERY EXPOSED.
Androgenetic alopecia (AGA) is known by its more familiar term, male pattern baldness, much to many a gentleman's—and gentlewoman's—chagrin. It is a slow hair loss, owing to heredity and the male sex hormones, that orders hair to literally stop growing. Alopecia can also be triggered by your genes (yes, sometimes it is your grandfather)!

THE EVIDENCE . . . EXHIBITS A TO Z.
Even if it runs in the family, severe hair loss does not necessarily have to figure in your life if you diminish your other withdrawals or other contributing factors. These factors include:

- *The downside of the stress curve.* Years ago, when I was a consultant to a hair clinic, I learned that the trichologists expected that they would see exacerbated hair loss six weeks to three months *after* the stressful situation had disappeared. Remember that the "aftershocks" of stress can occur long after the event that triggered it, so keep up your stress-reducing regimens.

- *Vitamin and mineral deficiences.* If your scalp is not getting the nutrients it needs, the result can be hair loss.

- *Poor circulation.* If your heart is not pumping as effectively as it should or if arteries are clogged with plaque, your circulatory system may not be up to par. It's hard enough getting to all your limbs and organs, let alone your scalp! Without enough blood at the scalp, hair roots, like plants, cannot survive. They can fall out.

- *Topical abuse.* Hot blow-dryers, hot curlers, hair dye, and gels, sprays, and mousses—all of these and more in excess can make your hair brittle, damaged, and at risk to fall out.

- *A toxic liver.* If your liver is overburdened and overwhelmed, it cannot perform its detoxification task properly, nor can it help aid digestion in the gut. The resulting malabsorption and toxicity can interfere with bodily processes, including hair growth.

- *An underactive thyroid.* Hair loss can be a sign of a malfunction of this gland.

GRADE-A DETECTIVE WORK.
While nutritional supplements can support, inappropriate use can cause problems. Too much vitamin A can cause hair loss, taken either

KEEPING YOUR CONDITION "BEHIND BARS"
RESCUE REGIMEN FOR HAIR LOSS

Follow Preventive Regimen for skin and hair problems for two weeks. Then add this Rescue Regimen.

If you see △, please check Appendix C for further information.

TIP
- Do the Foundation Regimen for a *toxic liver* for three weeks before beginning both the Preventive Regimen and, two weeks later, this Rescue Regimen.

VITAMINS, MINERALS, AND OTHER NUTRITIONAL SUPPLEMENTS
TAKE DAILY:
- *Pantothenic acid.* A B vitamin that helps support the body during stress. Add 250 mg.
- *Coenzyme Q10.* Helps to enhance circulation. Take 50 mg.

as a supplement or as a topical cream (such as the popular Retin-A). The good news is that as soon as you stop taking the excess vitamin, hair growth goes back to normal.

PSORIASIS

JUST THE FACTS, PLEASE . . . THE MYSTERY EXPOSED.
This skin condition makes its appearance as silvery scales on the limbs, scalp, back, and behind the ears. A normal skin cell begins life deep within the bottommost layer of skin. This skin cell rises to the surface and matures within twenty-eight days. As it reaches the top layer of skin, the epidermis, it dies and eventually flakes off. In psoriasis, a skin cell begins life nearer the surface and reaches the top layer within eight days. The result is an "immature" patch of inflamed silver that can cause discomfort.

BANK S-TELLARS

To wish to be well is part of becoming well. —Seneca

THE EVIDENCE . . . EXHIBITS A TO Z.

It usually comes down to "you are what you eat." And a condition such as psoriasis is no exception. A diet poor in oily fish, such as sardines,

---

KEEPING YOUR CONDITION "BEHIND BARS"

RESCUE REGIMEN FOR PSORIASIS

Follow Preventive Regimen for skin and hair problems for two weeks. Then add this Rescue Regimen.

If you see △, please check Appendix C for further information.

TIP

- Do both the Foundation Regimens for a *leaky gut* and a *toxic liver* for three weeks before starting the Preventive Regimen and, two weeks later, this Rescue Regimen. It is possible that they are the underlying conditions for your psoriasis.

ON AN ONGOING BASIS:
DIET

- *Avoid caffeine, alcohol, and acetaminophen.* These all tax the liver.

VITAMINS, MINERALS, AND OTHER NUTRITIONAL SUPPLEMENTS
TAKE DAILY:

- *Shark cartilage.* May help to prevent outbreaks. Take as directed.
- △ *Carotenoid complex.* Helps promote healthy tissue. Take as directed.

HERBS

- *Silymarin, or milk thistle.* Helps to support liver detoxification. Take 70 mg twice daily.

salmon, herring, and mackerel, may bring on an attack. One of the culprits behind this skin condition is a deficiency of essential fatty acids.

Stress can also trigger an attack if you are already predisposed to psoriasis.

GRADE-A DETECTIVE WORK.
Perhaps you are eating fish five times a week. You even take an essential fatty acid supplement. But psoriasis still makes an unwelcome appearance. The reason might not be that you aren't getting enough EFAs, but that they aren't being utilized properly. This can be a result of a *leaky gut* and a *toxic liver* that, overwhelmed, vulnerable, and sluggish, cannot do the proper job of digesting, metabolizing, and eliminating.

Arachidonic acid (AA), a substance that contributes to the redness, inflammation, and number of lesions in psoriasis, may also be "outsmarted" by the EFAs. Supplementing your diet with more EFAs may prevent the effect of these AAs, which are found in milk products.

Other culprits "beyond the surface"? Nonsteroid antiinflammatory medication such as ibuprofen, a severe sunburn, beta-blockers prescribed for high blood pressure, and alcohol abuse.

It's time now to go below the skin, to the hormones that can create so much havoc not only on the surface but also within every system of the body. It's time to see if you have any symptoms of endocrine *bankruptcies* and, even better, find out how you can prevent hormonal problems now and in the future.

15

ENDOCRINE BANKRUPTCIES

*If someone told me that some supplements, some changes in my routine,
could make all the difference between being miserable and living a full life, I'd
never believe it. But I've been able to cut my insulin in half for the first time in
years!*   —A 70-year-old retired businessman
who'd had diabetes for twenty years

Bonnee could tell without looking at her watch: it was 3:00 in the afternoon. She had begun what she came to call "the ritual." First came the
sleepiness, the constant yawning, the feeling faint. Fifteen minutes
later came the walk down the hall to her marketing assistant, who kept
a jar of chocolate candies at her desk. She'd grab a handful of chocolates, unwrapping one as she walked back to her office. Bonnee
needed her sugar fix now. She had a meeting at 3:30 and she needed
to be alert.

If she weren't so busy, Bonnee would be worried about this ritual.
It happened every day of the workweek, at approximately the same
time. She dreaded afternoon meetings, because she knew she'd be too
tired to think clearly. She didn't even make plans for after work; she
needed to go home, eat something fast and convenient, or even skip
dinner altogether; she needed to go to sleep.

Unfortunately, this ritual had been with Bonnee a long time. Even
in the days when she was an assistant herself, she'd take the elevator
down to the newsstand in the lobby at 3:00 for chocolate. Since it was
second nature, she never thought of her afternoon slumps as living a
life that was only half satisfying, half fulfilling. She never realized that

271

her lack of energy stopped her from trying out new things, to accomplish goals she'd not thought possible.

Lately the ritual had taken on a new urgency, one that began to alarm her. She could no longer wait until the afternoon. Bonnee was worried at how out of control she felt when she needed this fix and there were no chocolates left in the jar. She began to grow tired right after lunch, so tired that she could barely keep her head up. To compensate, she drank another two cups of coffee in the afternoon, which like the chocolate provided only a "quick fix." Within an hour, she was just as exhausted as she'd been before. Ironically, Bonnee had insomnia and, despite her overwhelming fatigue, couldn't sleep at night.

Bonnee went to see her physician, who suggested doing a fasting glucose test. Her sugar levels recorded in the normal range. He told her to learn to relax, to try to eat better and get out more often.

Bonnee felt even worse than she had before. She had no idea what was wrong with her; she wondered if she was losing her mind. She became extremely irritable, nervous. She couldn't stop eating. She was hungry all the time. She did join a gym, but she was too tired to go after work, and because she didn't sleep at night, she couldn't face the gym in the morning. Her workload was too heavy; it became an overwhelming task to get through the papers on her desk.

Bonnee had heard me speak and was intrigued enough by what I had to say about blood-sugar control to make an appointment. She wondered if she was one of those people who have hypoglycemia even though the tests show nothing.

THE CASE OF THE
IRRITABLE ACCOUNT EXECUTIVE: SOLVED

As we began our Health Detective work and I asked Bonnee about her eating habits, her family, and her moods, all the symptoms pointed to hypoglycemia. But nothing had shown on her fasting glucose test. Why? We needed to know what was causing her to *run in the red*.

The clinical aspect of the fasting glucose test doesn't always show hypoglycemia; it doesn't show the impact foods have on blood-sugar levels, nor the role the adrenal glands may play in hypoglycemic-like behavior. Are you, like Bonnee, adding more and more sweets to your diet, putting more stress on your body, further overwhelming your adrenal function? The result is excess insulin production, which leads to low blood-sugar levels—levels that are usually not picked up in the fasting glucose test, even though you exhibit hypoglycemic-like symptoms. But if you support your adrenal glands with healthy deposits, such as eating right and changing the way you react to stress, these symptoms may disappear.

In short, stress can contribute to a low blood-sugar state. The ongoing stress that Bonnee and others like her experience keeps adrenal gland activity constantly poised in a "fight-or-flight" formation. Eventually, the adrenal glands grow weary and less adrenaline is pumped into the bloodstream. This hormonal imbalance could set the stage for hypoglycemic reactions. The more stress you experience, the more your blood sugar is affected. It might not be the sweets you eat, but the stress, that "does the dip."

Although Bonnee's stress was a major factor in her hypoglycemic-like symptoms, her sugar-rich, high-fat diet did not help. You needn't be diagnosed as hypoglycemic to have low blood sugar if your diet is poor. If you are tired in the late afternoon, if you are listless, irritable, and crave sugar and carbohydrates, you are probably experiencing the swings of low blood sugar caused by the foods you eat. The sugar in the foods you eat is absorbed too quickly; blood glucose first rises, then crashes down, causing you to crave more starches or sweets to bring you back up. And the roller-coaster ride goes on.

The low blood sugar that creates this craving becomes your ventriloquist, a voice that speaks to you and tells you what to eat, pulling your strings without your even realizing it.

Because Bonnee's hypoglycemic behavior might have been triggered by stress, I suggested some relaxation exercises. We also worked together to reorganize the way she worked to reduce her feelings of being overwhelmed. Knowing that her healing would begin from within, I also paid special attention to her diet, which would help strengthen her adrenal glands and her immune system, as well as reduce the highs and lows of a blood-sugar imbalance. Over the ensuing months we added various supplements to her regimen; she had also begun to exercise, simply walking thirty minutes during her lunch break three times a week. Slowly, Bonnee made progress. She began to feel better and more in control of her behavior. She knew that she could decide the course her body took. She was the one who could decide "to chocolate or not to chocolate." Her lethargy and irritability gave way to energy and a sense of well-being she'd never before experienced. She realized that she could find the solution to her problem within herself; she could find control within herself. You can, too.

DO YOU HAVE *RUNNING IN THE RED* ENDOCRINE SYMPTOMS?

Take a few moments to look through these brief statements. See if any of them sound familiar to you. Be honest with yourself. As with Bonnee, they could be vital clues in your Health Detective work.

- My friends call me a worrywart. I'm always anxious about something. I can never relax.
- I could eat anytime, anywhere, anything. I'm always hungry.
- I must be getting old; I can nod off in the middle of a conversation.
- I feel light-headed when I stand up too quickly. It doesn't feel right. I wonder if my blood pressure is okay.
- One problem I *don't* have is water. I drink quarts of it every day—but I'm still thirsty.
- I've recently gained about ten pounds, even though I didn't think I was eating more than usual.
- My skin is so dry; I'm always using a heavy-duty moisturizer.
- I must be losing my hair. I find strands floating in my sink.
- I always take a sweater with me wherever I go. I'm always freezing. My heating bills are costing me a small fortune!
- I get terrible, sharp, shooting pain in my back that radiates to my pelvis.

What do sensitivity to cold, numb lips, and constant hunger have in common? Plenty—and it's called glands. The endocrine system is a vast umbrella. It's responsible for the glands that secrete the hormones that keep us going, from our sexual drive to our metabolism, from our ability to act to the way we feel. The endocrine system requires a delicate balance of chemicals, enzymatic action, and nutrients to perform its functions.

There are several reasons why the glands get sidetracked, and symptoms may not only seem totally unrelated but caused by a completely different *running in the red* account. The good news is that once you've discovered the links between your hormones and your symptoms, you can begin to establish stability once again. You can start to have a body and mind that's strong in spirit, energy, and vibrancy.

And those links—even for burgeoning Health Detectives—are not impossible to find. Here are four "secretion secrets" that may reveal hormonal imbalance.

SECRETION SECRET 1:
THE ADRENAL GLAND CALL TO ARMS—STRESS
The boss calls you into her office. Your teenager slams the bedroom door. A million and one things to do—in an hour. You pay the bills when there's not enough in your account. You walk to the lectern for your first presentation. We all know the signs of stress and how stress can build. We've all felt that surge of energy as we walk down the corridor, walk out on the stage, or get ready for a confrontation.

It's the adrenal glands at work, secreting adrenaline to give us the extra zip we need to make it through a stressful situation. In primitive times, this situation was necessary every time a woolly mammoth lumbered out of the forest; the adrenal glands calmed down once the prehistoric creature went on to greener pastures.

Today, however, the stress seems endless; the adrenal glands keep pumping adrenaline, with no outlet. Production is stretched to the limit, causing an imbalance. Adrenal insufficiencies result that may contribute to such *bankruptcy* conditions as food allergies, a suppressed immune system, arthritis, and blood-sugar highs and lows (because, as you have seen in Bonnee's story, one of the adrenal glands' jobs is to monitor insulin production to help maintain optimal blood-sugar levels).

The small adrenal glands, one on each side of the kidneys, secrete two different hormones. The center of each, the medulla, spurts out its adrenaline, but the outer area, the cortex, is responsible for producing cortisone and the sex hormones and for regulating metabolism.

Vitamin C supports the adrenal glands, helping to regulate adrenaline production and strengthen the adrenal glands in times of stress. If you don't have enough vitamin C to support them, symptoms of adrenal gland malfunction—such as fatigue, dizziness, memory lapses, and sugar cravings—may occur. What's the fastest way to deplete the amount of vitamin C in your body? Ironically, the answer is stress. And the vices we often turn to in stressful times? Alcohol, caffeine, and tobacco, which are toxic to the body and the adrenal glands.

Depression is another factor. A study at the Medical College of Pennsylvania actually found that the adrenal glands were larger in people who were depressed. After treatment, the glands went back down to normal size.

The cortisone-producing arena of your adrenal glands can be disrupted by the use of cortisone medication. If you are taking any type of cortisone drug for arthritis, osteoporosis, or skin irritations, it can seriously impact your adrenal hormone production. Even polycystic ovary syndrome has been linked to a malfunctioning adrenal gland—too much production of the sexual hormones secreted by the cortex. (Women taking infertility drugs should be particularly wary of this link.)

But the adrenal glands rarely work alone. Like hunters in many primitive tribes, they work in teams.

SECRETION SECRET 2: THE H-TEAM—HYPOTHYROID, HYPOGLYCEMIA, AND HYPOADRENAL ENDOCRINE DISORDERS

Call them the terrible triad, the troubling trio, the telltale troubadours. Whatever you call them, you should be aware that if you have one, you could have another. Here's what happens:

Hypothyroidism can result in *hypoglycemia*, creating major imbalances in the body. When the hormones are out of whack, many of your body's systems try to compensate. The adrenal glands soon become worn down with these unrelenting messages from the body, and with the constant pressure of stress, a sluggish metabolism, and the quick blood-sugar "hits" and "drops." This situation adds the third member of the "condition club," *hypoadrenal disorder.*

You are left with a hormonal whirlwind from three powerful glands that signals more than a craving for sugars and simple carbohydrates. You feel exhausted, unable to focus. You are depressed, moody, forgetful. In short, you have all the symptoms of *hypothyroidism, hypoglycemia,* and *hypoadrenal disorder*—the insidious H-team.

A BOUNCED CHECK: ADRENAL GLAND ALERT

Adrenal gland malfunction can be a double whammy: not only do you suffer the symptoms of stress but you can also get high blood pressure. A hormone secreted by the pituitary gland (ACTH, or adrenocorticotropic hormone) when you are experiencing heavy stress leads to a biochemical transaction that can cause salt retention—and potassium elimination. A potential result over a long period of time? Hypertension.

To help combat the effects of stress on a battered adrenal gland, try my Preventive Regimen for keeping a healthy hormonal balance.

SECRETION SECRET 3: TO B OR NOT TO B—
A NECESSARY VITAMIN COMPLEX FOR THE ENDOCRINE SYSTEM

The entire vitamin B complex is vital for enzymatic function in our bodies. These vitamins help break down fats, carbohydrates, and proteins. They also help regulate body fluids. In short, the question might be, "What don't the B vitamins do?"

Deficiencies in vitamin B_6 (pyridoxine) in particular are linked to hypoglycemia and, possibly, diabetes and kidney stones. Symptoms are similar to other endocrine conditions: fatigue, dizziness, aches and pains in the muscles, excessive urination, and in the case of kidney stones, painful elimination.

In fact, many people in later life who develop carpal tunnel syndrome might not have a neurological or arthritic disorder; they might, in actuality, have a vitamin B_6 deficiency and diabetes.

To ensure that this doesn't become your problem, increase your intake of the vitamin B_6–rich foods, such as chicken, carrots, beans, brown rice, broccoli, cabbage, corn, and cantaloupe.

The B vitamin pantothenic acid, in particular, provides support for the adrenal glands. If you are under stress, you may want to also take a pantothenic acid supplement. (See my Crisis Regimens later in this chapter.)

Hormonal balance may become reality with a bit of sleuthing and action, using my Rescue Regimens.

SECRETION SECRET 4: WATER RETENTION—
EVEN WHEN THE SALTSHAKER IS NOWHERE IN SIGHT

When you are under stress and you're not eating, you might be surprised that the scale doesn't show a weight loss. For this link, look once more at your adrenal glands. They help regulate the sodium:potassium ratio in your body. When the stress in your life is unrelenting and the adrenal glands are working overtime, sodium levels increase while potassium is excreted and you retain fluid. The result may be water weight gain.

The endocrine system is mysterious, both complex and orderly at the same time. Hormonal balance is one of perfect precision, coenzymes and nutrients working in perfect tandem. Because the endocrine system is all-encompassing, involving all bodily functions, it is easy to point to a hormonal problem first. (How many people do you know who blame their excess weight on their slow thyroid—as they're gobbling up a burger?)

That's why it's important to look beyond the obvious, to go below the surface and understand the links between symptoms and causes. Eventually, your role as Health Detective will become second nature. As you become more aware of your body—the way it works, the habits you do on a daily, weekly, and monthly basis—you'll start to identify what healthy deposits you need to make to nourish your Body Bank account, to keep it strong and stable.

I'll be there as a guide and helper. And it is possible that your *running in the red* endocrine symptoms have become *bankruptcy* conditions. No need to panic. Look over the common *bankruptcies* that follow. Add some of the healthy deposits I describe in my specific Rescue Regimens. By taking these important steps, you'll be halfway home on the road to a healthy Body Bank.

PREVENTIVE REGIMEN
FOR KEEPING HEALTHY HORMONAL BALANCE

Create hormonal harmony by developing body balance.

Do the Foundation Regimens for a *leaky gut* and/or a *toxic liver* for three weeks, if applicable, then add this Preventive Regimen. Be sure to start slowly, introducing supplements gradually, to help prevent any possible reactions.

If you see ⚠, please check Appendix C for further information.

VITAMINS, MINERALS, AND OTHER NUTRITIONAL SUPPLEMENTS:
TAKE DAILY:

- *High-potency multivitamin and mineral supplement.*
- *Vitamin B complex.* Necessary for proper carbohydrate metabolism, thyroid function, and fluid balance. Add 50–150 mgs. Divide dose into several equal amounts.
- *Pantothenic acid.* A B vitamin that helps support the adrenal glands during stress. Take 250 mg.
- ⚠ *Vitamin E.* Helps support immune system and has powerful antioxidant properties. Take 400 IU.
- *Calcium.* Important for pH and mineral balance. Take 1000 mg split doses.
- *Magnesium.* Supports enzyme system while protecting against coronary artery spasms. Take 500 mg.

DIABETES

JUST THE FACTS, PLEASE . . . THE MYSTERY EXPOSED.
We all know about diabetes, the disease where you can't eat a lot of sugar, where rich desserts are a no-no, and pastas can make you sick. But it doesn't have to be a state of deprivation. It can be controlled.

No one yet knows what you can do to prevent Type I diabetes, which usually occurs in childhood. But adult-onset diabetes, Type II, is a different story. This usually occurs in people forty and older, and although your genes do play a role, it can usually be avoided by changing poor eating habits and a sedentary lifestyle.

THE EVIDENCE . . . EXHIBITS A TO Z.

Diabetes is, literally, the inability of your body to break down carbohydrates properly. There isn't enough insulin produced to convert glucose into energy to be used by the cells or the cells are resistant to taking it in. Consequently, glucose stays in the bloodstream, unabsorbed, creating blood-sugar levels that are much too high. Some symptoms of diabetes include muscle cramps, infection, impaired eyesight, extreme thirst, and extreme fatigue. It can ultimately lead to such *bankruptcies* as kidney failure, blindness, and even death, if not properly treated.

GRADE-A DETECTIVE WORK.

Stress and obesity are two main lifestyle culprits. There are some hidden agendas at work in diabetes, too. It's not just the sugar that creates diabetes; it's the animal fat and the simple carbohydrates.

Although it might sound contradictory, hypoglycemia, or low blood sugar, can be a *health-link* to this condition. It may precede diabetes as a warning sign for the late-onset type. It is not the opposite of diabetes; both are carbohydrate metabolic disorders affecting the levels of glucose in your bloodstream.

People with diabetes are also more at risk of having too much LDL, or "bad" cholesterol. Arteries get clogged faster, and therefore they are more susceptible to cardiovascular disease. What are your best healthy deposits for reducing this diabetes-induced LDL? Load up on antioxidant supplements: vitamin C, vitamin E, and beta-carotene. Increase your exercise and the amount of water you drink. Limit your dietary fat intake.

KEEPING YOUR CONDITION "BEHIND BARS"
RESCUE REGIMEN FOR DIABETES

Follow Preventive Rescue Regimen for endocrine system for two weeks. Then add this Rescue Regimen.

If you see △, please check Appendix C for further information.

TIPS
- *Insulin requirements* will lessen dramatically and should be monitored closely.
- *Try to lose weight.* Since obesity is a *health-link* to Type II diabetes, losing weight may halt the condition or reduce its severity.
- *Exercise* helps enhance insulin's effectiveness. Try to walk thirty to sixty minutes, four days a week.

ON AN ONGOING BASIS:
DIET
- *Eat a low-fat, high-quality protein diet,* with nonstarchy vegetables, some grains, and an occasional fruit to decrease the risk of heart disease and other diabetes-related conditions.

VITAMINS, MINERALS, AND OTHER NUTRITIONAL SUPPLEMENTS
TAKE DAILY:
- △ *Vitamin E.* Take 400 IU.
- △ *Chromium picolinate.* Enhances insulin's action to help lower blood-sugar levels for those diabetics who are chromium deficient. Take 200–600 mcg. Divide dose into several equal amounts.
- △ *L-Glutamine.* An amino acid that helps reduce sugar cravings. Take as directed on an empty stomach. *Discontinue use after 1 month.*
- *Pycnogenol.* An antioxidant that can help decrease the risk of diabetes-related diseases. Take 100 mg.
- *Magnesium.* Protects against retinal artery spasms. Take additional 300 mg.

HERBS
- △ *Gymnema sylvestre.* An Indian herb that may help increase production of insulin. Take as directed.
- • *Bilberry.* Helps control insulin levels. Use capsules. Take as directed.

HYPOGLYCEMIA AND LOW BLOOD SUGAR

JUST THE FACTS, PLEASE . . . THE MYSTERY EXPOSED.
When glucose, the food that feeds every part of your body, from the heart to the brain to the muscles, is too low in the bloodstream, the result is called hypoglycemia.

THE EVIDENCE . . . EXHIBITS A TO Z.
When glucose levels are stable, all is well. The proper amounts of insulin and glucagon—two hormones that regulate blood-sugar levels—are produced properly and cells receive the right amount of sugar. But if there is too little glucose in your bloodstream, you have low blood sugar. Your body responds with a craving. It longs for food rich in glucose, which usually makes you think of alcohol, fruit, starches, and sugar. Symptoms of hypoglycemia include overwhelming fatigue, confusion, a lack of energy, insomnia, irritability, mood swings, heart palpitations, dizziness, and depression.

GRADE-A DETECTIVE WORK.
With low blood sugar, you have little control over the physiological mechanisms of a craving. Your body, in a chemical state of deprivation, wants to eat—immediately. It demands the most glycemic—or quickest, easiest to convert to sugar—foods for fast gratification. You comply with a sugar "hit" of this glycemic food, by eating chocolate, candy, ice cream, cake, cookies, alcohol, even pasta, bagels, and bananas. When broken down in the liver, these foods are quickly converted into the

glucose the body craves. Unfortunately, they are rapidly "eaten" by the cells and it isn't long before your body responds with a drop in blood sugar. You need another hit. And the cycle continues.

KEEPING YOUR CONDITION "BEHIND BARS"
RESCUE REGIMEN FOR HYPOGLYCEMIA

Follow Preventive Regimen for endocrine system problems for two weeks. Then add this Rescue Regimen.

If you see △, please check Appendix C for further information.

ON AN ONGOING BASIS:
DIET
- *Control your blood sugar* with the 5-Day Miracle Diet. Eat breakfast within a half hour of waking up. Eat a *hard chew* fruit or vegetable snack (carrots, broccoli, apple) every two hours. Eat lunch by 1:00, which should always be a protein and veggies. Eat *hard chew* or *soft chew* snack (orange, cantaloupe) every three hours in the afternoon. Dinner must include protein and veggies. It can also include a complex carbohydrate (a potato, rice, or couscous), if desired. Limit pasta to dinner every third night, if desired. Vegetarian meals may include beans, lentils, soy cheese, tofu, or soymilk as protein.

VITAMINS, MINERALS, AND OTHER NUTRITIONAL SUPPLEMENTS
TAKE DAILY:
- *Pantothenic acid.* Helps maintain proper adrenal function. Take 250 mg twice daily.
- △ *L-Glutamine.* An amino acid that helps reduce sugar cravings to maintain stabilized blood sugar levels. Take as directed on an empty stomach. *Discontinue after 2 months.*

HYPOTHYROIDISM

JUST THE FACTS, PLEASE . . . THE MYSTERY EXPOSED.

You're overweight. Perhaps you're tired, irritable. You have constipation and seem to be allergic to everything. You have headaches and bad PMS, and are even experiencing hair loss. Help! You could very well have undiagnosed hypothyroidism.

THE EVIDENCE . . . EXHIBITS A TO Z.

The thyroid secretes a hormone that helps regulate your metabolism. It determines how fast your calories are burned and used as energy. When too little thyroid hormone is produced, you experience symptoms that mimic everything from depression to hypoglycemia, irritable bowel syndrome to chronic fatigue, compulsive overeating to circulatory problems.

Although over 5 million people suffer from hypothyroidism, many more people only think they have hypothyroidism. More times than not, there are other conditions at work causing your symptoms.

Unfortunately, laboratory tests don't often pick up hypothyroidism. To determine if you have this *bankruptcy*, try taking your temperature under your arm with a basal thermometer first thing in the morning. Keep it on your night table so you won't move before taking your temperature and disrupt the results. Leave it under your arm for fifteen minutes. If you show a reading below 97.5, you could have hypothyroidism.

GRADE-A DETECTIVE WORK.

Studies have found vitamin B_{12} deficiency in people with hypothyroidism. If you do not eat any animal products, or have gastrointestinal problems or a full-fledged *leaky gut*, it is possible that this nutrient is not being properly absorbed by the body.

Be careful if you are taking levothyroxine, a common thyroid medication. A study done at the University of Massachusetts found that it can decrease bone mass by 13 percent.

An offshoot of hypothyroidism, Wilson's disease throws the thyroid offbalance. It occurs when the thyroid hormone thyroxine is not able to efficiently convert into another hormone, triiodothyronine. It is usually triggered by unrelenting emotional or physical stress. Symptoms are very similar to those of its "parent," hypothyroidism. They include overwhelming fatigue, anxiety, insomnia, dry skin, and depression.

A BOUNCED CHECK: HYPERTHYROIDISM

This *bankruptcy* is the flip side of hypothyroidism. Instead of sluggishness, weight gain, fatigue, and an inability to handle cold, people who have hyperthyroidism are nervous and irritable. They usually lose weight and have a hard time tolerating heat. Another sign of hyperthyroidism are eyes that protrude.

If you think you might have hyperthyroidism, it would be wise to see your doctor.

Here are some healthy deposits I recommend to my clients who suffer from hyperthyroidism:

- *Eat veggies from the cruciferous family.* These include cabbage, Brussels sprouts, cauliflower, broccoli, and kale. They may suppress excess thyroid function. (For this reason, I recommend minimizing these foods if you have hypothyroidism.)
- *Vitamin B₂ (riboflavin)* helps maintain proper function of all glands and organs. Take 50 mg in addition to the B complex vitamin on my Basic Health and Preventive Rescue Regimens.

KEEPING YOUR CONDITION "BEHIND BARS"
RESCUE REGIMEN FOR HYPOTHYROIDISM

Follow Preventive Regimen for endocrine system problems for two weeks. Then add this Rescue Regimen.

If you see △, please check Appendix C for further information.

ON AN ONGOING BASIS:
DIET
- *Avoid cabbage* and other veggies in the cruciferous family. These include Brussels sprouts, broccoli, and cauliflower. They contain goitrogens, antithyroid substances.

VITAMINS, MINERALS, AND OTHER NUTRITIONAL SUPPLEMENTS
TAKE DAILY:
- *Vitamin B₂.* Necessary for proper thyroid function. Take 50 mg.
- △ *L-Tyrosine.* An amino acid that has been found to be low in

people suffering from hypothyroidism. Take 500 mg on an empty stomach. *Discontinue use after 2 months.*
- *Kelp.* A good source of iodine, a main component of thyroid hormone. Take capsules. Take 1000–1500 mg.

KIDNEY STONES

JUST THE FACTS, PLEASE . . . THE MYSTERY EXPOSED.
You have excruciating pain whenever you try to go to the bathroom. Sometimes there's blood. You know the signs. You've been there before: kidney stones that must be passed.

Actually, kidney stones are not really "pebbles"; they can be as big as a sparrow's egg! They are formed of calcium phosphate (80 percent of all stones), uric acid, or cystine. Stones grow rapidly in urine that is not acidic.

THE EVIDENCE . . . EXHIBITS A TO Z.
Some scientists believe that kidney stones are formed when the parathyroid gland, a tiny gland in the neck adjacent to the thyroid, is overactive. The hormones it secretes keep too much calcium floating around in the bloodstream; it isn't properly absorbed and calcium-containing stones may form.

Other links? Dehydration, irritable bowel syndrome (remember the imbalances caused by a *leaky gut*?), and a diet that has too much protein and sugar—and not enough vitamin A–rich fruits and vegetables. The urine becomes more alkaline and the minerals, especially calcium, you ingest are left like sediment to settle in the kidneys.

GRADE-A DETECTIVE WORK.
Calcium malabsorption may be the major *health-link* between kidney stones and an endocrine *bankruptcy*—the same deficiency that can cause osteoporosis (see Chapter 13). This inability for calcium to be used by the body can be caused by a deficiency of vitamin B_6 and magnesium. These nutrients may help prevent kidney stones, while deficiencies of them may lead to many other ailments, including osteoporosis, carpal tunnel syndrome, and restless leg syndrome.

LIKE A KIDNEY STONE

The Southeast is called the "Stone Belt" because more people get kidney stones in that area of the country than anywhere else. Which region has the least amount? The Northwest. Although scientists don't know exactly why, they believe it has to do with the humidity, the hot climate, and dehydration.

KEEPING YOUR CONDITION "BEHIND BARS"

RESCUE REGIMEN FOR KIDNEY STONES

Follow Preventive Regimen for endocrine system problems for two weeks. Then add this Rescue Regimen.

If you see △, please check Appendix C for further information.

ON AN ONGOING BASIS:

DIET

- *Limit products with high vitamin D.* This includes some milk products and supplements. They enhance calcium absorption, which in turn may increase the heavy load of calcium your body already cannot handle.
- *Avoid excessive animal protein.* Meat may cause excess calcium excretion, resulting in calcium buildup in the kidneys.
- *Avoid spinach and rhubarb.* Both are high in oxalic acid, a substance found in people with kidney stones.
- *Increase your veggies.* They are also high in fiber and low in salt, both of which help reduce kidney stone formation.

VITAMINS, MINERALS, AND OTHER NUTRITIONAL SUPPLEMENTS

TAKE DAILY:

- *Magnesium.* Helps moderate low levels of substances that contribute to kidney stones. Take the citrate form. Take 500 mg.
- *Potassium.* Helps prevent stone crystallization. Take the citrate form. Take 99 mg.

HERBS
- *Corn silk tea.* Helps support proper kidney function. Take as directed.
- *Uva ursi.* Helps to relieve pain associated with kidney stones. Take as directed.
- *Dandelion root tea.* May enhance function of kidneys. Take 1 or 2 cups daily.

These are only a few of the common endocrine *bankruptcies* that may occur if you don't heed a symptom's call. But a healthy deposit made right now can begin working immediately. Think of what might be yours: fabulous energy, vitality, strength. It's all about prevention—*preventing* symptoms from getting worse, *preventing bankruptcies* from ruling your life, *preventing* hormonal problems from even beginning in the first place, *preventing* crime—the fifth section on how to heal from within.

Our journey is almost done. But there is still one more mystery the Health Detective must solve.

16

RESPIRATORY BANKRUPTCIES

My stuffed nose, my aches and pains, were part of me, something I lived with. And then things changed. I started making healthy deposits. I feel terrific. This is what it means to be in control of yourself. This is what it means to do good things for your body. Wow! Why did I wait so long?
— A 59-year-old magazine editor and grandmother

Looking back, I could see how easy it might have been to mistake Melissa's problem. It took all my skills as a Health Detective to determine the cause of her symptoms and for us, together, to stop a mode of treatment that might have had disastrous results.

Melissa's story began in the late fall, when the weather suddenly climbed from just above freezing to a hot, humid Indian summer. She had had asthma for many years and it grew worse in this heat. She always carried an inhaler or two in her pocketbook; she never knew when an attack would hit.

When the weather was particularly bad, Melissa didn't go out. She was lucky enough to work at home as a graphic designer; most of the time, she was able to communicate with her clients via computer. She kept an air filter going constantly and used the air conditioner in her apartment window whenever the temperature went over sixty-five degrees.

She was aware that she was living a life hampered by illness, but she didn't know what to do about it. Melissa was terrified of getting an attack on the street, in a conference room, or on a vacation.

During this warm fall, things went from bad to worse. Melissa's joints started to ache; she couldn't sit at her computer for more than fifteen minutes at a time before her fingers began to throb. The pain became almost unbearable. Her skin started to break out and it seemed as if she was tired from the moment she woke up.

The few times Melissa did go out—for dinner with friends, the occasional movie, a family visit—dwindled. She was in excruciating pain in many parts of her body. On top of that, there was the ever-looming possibility of an asthma attack. When she had to leave her apartment, Melissa would make sure she had several working inhalers in her pocketbook.

Melissa's fatigue and her deteriorating condition were starting to affect her work. She began to go to specialist after specialist. No one could find anything wrong, except her asthma. She was given prescriptions for antihistamines and steroids, which she kept tucked in her pocketbook alongside her inhalers.

Finally, an endocrinologist told her he thought she had lupus.

The news startled her. She was glad to finally put a name to her problems, but lupus was so exotic, so frightening. The endocrinologist explained that there was no cure, but they could try to keep it in check with a long-term regimen of antidepressants, aspirin, and even more powerful steroids. She would have to learn to live not only with the condition but with the side effects brought on by these medications.

The thought of lupus alarmed Melissa so much that when she heard how I had helped a friend with her migraine headaches, she decided to make an appointment. It was time to try a natural approach for healing her *bankruptcy* conditions.

THE CASE OF THE POCKETBOOK
AND THE INHALER: SOLVED

I wanted us to begin our Health Detective work immediately. Lupus is a serious diagnosis, a chronic, potentially life-threatening inflammation of the connective tissues surrounding the joints, muscles, skin, even the lungs and heart. It causes symptoms very similar to the terrible aches and pains Melissa was experiencing.

But when I saw Melissa opening her pocketbook and clutching her inhaler just in case she had an asthma attack, I realized that we had to talk about her, and me, for a bit. Melissa needed to have her hope restored. Some health practitioners seem to become uninterested or frustrated when a client doesn't get better right away. Unconsciously, they may give up instead of redoubling their efforts. That attitude is, in turn, picked up by the client.

Melissa was becoming one of these people, a woman who was so scared of getting sick that she scarcely left the house. And now her fear had a name, a frightening name: lupus. She didn't know where to turn or what to do. Hope was not in her vocabulary.

I wanted to help change all that. The first healthy deposit I wanted to help Melissa make came before our Health Detective work could begin. It was something we needed to share. It was the nurturing, compassionate, and understanding presence that a good health practitioner must have for his or her clients. Like the placebo effect of many medications, in which a sugar pill helps as much as the real stuff, the support this atmosphere instills is an extremely valuable healthy deposit. It provided motivation, resolve, and hope.

We talked about Melissa's life, her goals, her dreams, and her work; she needed to know that she could talk and be heard. We discussed Melissa's feelings about her illness and how I believed that, together, we could uncover how to improve her health.

As Melissa grew more animated and more comfortable, we were able to begin our Health Detective work in earnest. I discovered that she was under a great deal of stress about her work. Her days and nights were the same; when she had a deadline, she'd stay up all night and sleep all day; she had no regular routine. And lately, the freelance jobs had dried up and she didn't even have the energy to try to hustle up more work. Money was a constant strain. Melissa coped with her stress by eating foods that, unfortunately, didn't support her well.

The stress, the lack of nutrients, the irregularity of her hours—all these were hefty withdrawals from Melissa's Body Bank. But they still didn't explain the lupus link. We had to delve deeper.

I thought about Melissa's pocketbook, how often she'd open and close the clasp to take out her inhaler, terrified she was going to have an asthma attack. Asthma, aches and pains, broken-out skin, fatigue. I had to ask: "Melissa, how many times a day do you think you use your inhaler?"

She told me that she didn't count the times; she used it at least once every hour.

This was an important clue. I asked Melissa if she experienced any symptoms after she used the inhaler, or if it only provided relief. She had to think for a moment; she said that it had become less and less effective, which was why she was using it so much. And although the terrible wheezing stopped, the aches and pains briefly intensified. She usually got a headache.

I believed that Melissa's *running in the red* complaints could have been something other than lupus. Her symptoms could have been caused by a toxic reaction, initiated by the constant use of her inhaler and the steroids and antibiotics she was taking. These withdrawals could create an altered digestive system that was also *running in the red.* This *leaky gut,* in turn, could set the scene for those terrible aches and pains, which were the body's reaction to the toxins allowed into the bloodstream by the weakened gut wall. It was a snowball effect, one assault building on another.

Melissa's symptoms might have mimicked lupus, but her aches and pains had a different source. Melissa's bad diet and her poor habits helped to create the perfect atmosphere for a *leaky gut.* Her "fast food" eating style contributed to this condition. And even when some nutrients did make it down her gut, there was a problem with absorption, thanks to the excessive amount of medications and antibiotics that destroyed her good flora.

I told Melissa that we were going to work on her body as a whole. We were going to start her healing from the inside out, helping her to gain control over herself. We were going to turn years of withdrawals into deposits and create a healthy Body Bank account.

We began that hot, humid fall day with my Foundation Regimens for a *leaky gut* and a *toxic liver.* I suggested she try to use her inhaler only when absolutely necessary instead of from anxiety. Over the next few weeks, we added more supplements and stress-reducing exercises, and worked on creating a more balanced diet and routine.

Thanks to the inhalers, Melissa appeared to have lupus and had almost undergone an intensive, lifelong medical regimen that would only have made her symptoms worse. And, in a bitter irony, inhalers have been shown to decrease bone density over time, which meant that, instead of lupus, Melissa could have been at risk for osteoporosis.

Today, no one would ever imagine that Melissa had been diagnosed with lupus. The inflammatory reactions in her joints and muscles have receded. And she has more energy than she has ever had in her life. The best news? After so many healthy deposits, her asthma has been under better control and she carries only one inhaler in her pocketbook, barely using it at all.

DO YOU HAVE *RUNNING IN THE RED* RESPIRATORY SYMPTOMS?

I admit that Melissa's story is more complicated than most. But over time you too can uncover what is ailing you. As you do your Health Detective work, you will learn how to listen to your body, to heed its signals that something is wrong in order to know which healthy deposits to make. You will begin to understand that *health-links* are not always obvious, that you must look back, searching for connections between seemingly unrelated events and symptoms.

You will begin to take back your health by asking yourself questions: "What am I feeling? Where does it hurt? When did it start to hurt? Was it after I ate a certain food? What else happened at the time? Am I under a great deal of stress?" and more.

You can be a first-rate Health Detective. See for yourself with the following quiz. Determine whether any of the statements pertain to you and your respiratory symptoms. I hope you won't find these situations so unrelated anymore and that the links are becoming easier to see. Perhaps you are beginning to understand how important making healthy deposits to your Body Bank account is, and you'll even begin to know some of the ones to make for the most return.

- If someone near me is wearing perfume, my throat gets hoarse. I start to cough.
- There's nothing much going on in my life right now, just the usual stress: too much work, not enough play. It's not very dramatic, but it is relentless.
- I never suffered from allergies, never. Then suddenly, just like that, my eyes started to water when I munched on a strawberry or ate an egg.
- I've taken so many antibiotics for my bronchitis that I can't even remember all the times. Worse, the bronchitis keeps coming back!
- I get really bad headaches in the middle of the afternoon. It hurts the most around my eyes. The first thing I do? Take acetaminophen.

BANK S-TELLARS

In the Orient people believed that the basis of all disease was unhappiness. Thus to make a patient happy again was to restore him to health.
—Donald Law

- Milk products are a large part of my diet.
- I blow my nose so much that I literally have chapped skin around my nostrils. Sometimes I think I keep the tissue companies in business.
- I often get constipated, just like the rest of my family. I remember waiting in line to get into the bathroom. Each one of us would be in there for ages!

If these statements sound familiar to you, it's very possible that your respiratory symptoms have less to do with "catching a cold germ" and more to do with congestion caused by a poor diet, allergic reactions, an antibiotic regimen, excessive yeast, an overwhelmed *leaky gut*, or a *toxic liver.*

I know. It's difficult to believe that every time you blow your nose, it may be because you're not properly absorbing some vitamins or minerals. It's hard to imagine that the very antibiotics you've been taking to stop your sore throat may be making it worse. It's strange to think that your sinuses, way up in your head, may be connected to a *toxic liver.* You might not even drink!

The fact is that all these situations can be linked to—and indeed may be responsible for—respiratory ailments. They are all part of the ongoing withdrawals you've been making all your life. But you have the power to reverse them by starting to make healthy deposits. It is possible for you, yourself, to turn a *bankruptcy* condition around and create a healthy, wealthy, and wise Body Bank account. Let's go over some of the "breathing lessons" to give you a better understanding of these respiratory links.

BREATHING LESSON 1: PASS THE TISSUES, PLEASE
True, infection can cause respiratory symptoms, especially if your immune system doesn't happen to have a "match" for the bug in the anti-

body department. You can catch a cold from that nearby stranger on the bus, the one sniffling and sneezing and touching the same handlebar as you.

But respiratory symptoms can also be caused by congestion, pure and simple. In fact, this congestion provides a rich, fertile soil for infections to grow. If you just get rid of the bug, it will simply grow back.

Instead, you have to look at mucus-making foods, a withdrawal that can cause congestion in the lungs. But what exactly are these mucus-producing items? It sounds unpleasant at worst, interesting at best. These can be foods you eat all the time: milk products, tofu, yogurt, wheat, barley, oatmeal, rye bread, refined sugar, and potatoes, among others.

BREATHING LESSON 2: FORGET THE BUNSEN BURNER

You don't have to "scratch" the surface to know that if you have an allergy, there's a good possibility you also have a *leaky gut*. (See Chapter 11 on allergies.) When toxins, partially digested food, and excess yeast seep into the bloodstream through the intestinal walls, the body may react with a sore throat, watery eyes, headache, aches and pains, or other signs of an allergy.

In addition to a *leaky gut*, an allergic response involves the immune system. Specifically, the antigens in the immune system are unable to recognize a specific food, which becomes an allergen. The antigens start battling seemingly innocuous items like bread or eggs.

But just as you had learned in English class, there is an exception to every rule, including allergies. Sometimes what appears to be an allergic response is, in fact, something different that will require a different healthy deposit. An experienced Health Detective will suspect that the answers lie in the particular items a person is seemingly allergic to. Chemical hypersensitivity is one of these situations. Here, it's not the actual eggs or the wheat, but the *chemicals* in the food that cause palpitations or headache. The immune system is not the problem. Instead, substances called histamines are released by the cells, causing those who are sensitive to itch or feel dry in their throat, whenever they drink coffee, alcohol, or soft drinks, or whenever they breathe in dust mites or chemical pollutants. (The over-the-counter medications—antihistamines—are purposely formulated to go after these chemicals. But a better route is to get rid of the offending food chemicals themselves and to fix the underlying situation.)

AND IT TASTES GOOD, TOO!

Chicken soup is good for the soul . . . and your respiratory tract. Not only is chicken soup warm and soothing, but studies have shown that it is better at breaking up mucus than plain hot water. Like all animal proteins, it contains the amino acid cysteine, which eases congestion.

BREATHING LESSON 3: STOP THE WORLD!

The *New York Times* recently published the results of some studies done at Carnegie-Mellon University that dealt with stress and colds. The conclusion? Stress can actually double the risk of a person coming down with a stuffed nose, a sore throat, and bouts of sneezing.

As you have seen in Chapter 12, the stress you experience literally lowers your resistance to illness; it weakens your immune system. Your adrenal glands go into overdrive, taxing your hormonal production; the liver becomes overwhelmed in its detoxifying tasks; and your frontline battalion, the antibodies, lose their "drive"; they slow down, allowing germs to enter cells. It's as if your castle walls began to erode.

The Carnegie-Mellon study found a direct relationship between stress and the incidence of developing a cold with the antibody immunoglobulin-A. The less A, the more colds. There are other criteria: the stress has to be around for at least a month and it has to be difficult for you to handle. A bad boss, an eroding relationship, a sick relative—these all keep anxiety levels high, especially if you don't make appropriate relaxation deposits, such as scheduled massages, exercise, or a warm bath.

BREATHING LESSON 4: THE ULTIMATE CONNECTION

The upper respiratory arena has a direct connection to the liver. When you develop sinusitis or bronchitis, you should be learning to suspect that another part of your body may be causing the problem. If the liver is congested, it isn't properly detoxifying the substances that enter your body. The result could be allergies, a nonstop runny nose, a hoarse throat, and other respiratory *bankruptcies*.

I have found that my clients who suffered from recurring sinusitis improved dramatically when they used my Foundation Regimens for a *toxic liver* and a *leaky gut*. I have noticed that the more toxic their liver seemed to be, the more congested were their sinuses. I have also observed that clients who did not go through the Foundation Regimens rarely achieved the same satisfactory results, regardless of the healthy deposits they made.

It might be a new idea for you that respiratory health can be so linked to a *leaky gut* and a *toxic liver.* Hard to connect, but connected they are! You tend to think of your respiratory system as part of your upper body, your head and your chest. You think of your liver and your gastrointestinal tract as "below the waist." You don't usually think of them as related entities, as vital parts of a complete whole. But as you know from reading *Healing from the Inside*, every part of the body is very much related, including the respiratory system and the liver and gut. Yes, you can get germs and infections from other people, but only if the withdrawals—stress, a poor diet, and chemical toxins—are already in place and have created a *running in the red* Body Bank for a long time.

By trying my Preventive Regimen for strong, healthy breathing, you may be able to protect your respiratory tract from infection and congestion. You can breathe deeply, smelling the spring rain, the simmering soup, the ocean's waves. I call it making simple, healthy deposits to your Body Bank account. Like Melissa, you might call it freedom.

But what if a respiratory *bankruptcy* has taken hold of your account? What if you've "bounced" one too many "checks"? Do not despair. It is never too late to make healthy deposits. Begin some of my specific Rescue Regimens for common ailments that follow and you should begin seeing an improvement soon!

HUGS ARE BETTER

A leading allergist, Dr. Marshall Mandell, once observed a group of severely asthmatic children in a hospital. Conventional wisdom at the time was that they didn't receive "mother love." They needed nurturing. How did the nurses help with the hugs? By offering cold milk, cookies, and bread—three "biggies" in the allergy department. Instead of getting better, these kids suffered even more from asthma!

PREVENTIVE REGIMEN
FOR HEALTHY BREATHING

Ease chronic breathing problems by revitalizing your respiratory system.

Do the Foundation Regimens for a *leaky gut* and/or a *toxic liver* for three weeks, if applicable, then add this Preventive Regimen. Be sure to start slowly, introducing supplements gradually, to help prevent any possible reactions.

If you see ⚠, *please check Appendix C for further information.*

VITAMINS, MINERALS, AND OTHER NUTRITIONAL SUPPLEMENTS

TAKE DAILY:

- *High-potency vitamin and mineral supplement.*
- *Vitamin C.* Helps enhance immune function. Take 1000 mg twice daily.
- ⚠ *Pantothenic acid.* A B vitamin that helps support adrenal function during stress. Take 250 mg.
- *B complex.* Helps support immune function. Take 100 mg twice daily.
- ⚠ *Vitamin E.* Helps adrenal hormones and oxygenate tissues. Take 400–600 IU.
- *Coenzyme Q10.* Helps enhance immune function and may improve breathing. Take 60 mg.
- *NAC.* An antioxidant that helps to replenish glutathione. Take 500 mg for two months and discontinue.
- *Calcium/magnesium.* Increases vital capacity of lungs. Take 1000 mg calcium and 500 mg magnesium.
- *Proteolytic digestive enzymes.* Helps to reduce inflammation. Take as directed between meals.
- *Quercetin with bromelain.* Helps to reduce inflammation. Take 1000 mg divided into several equal amounts.
- *Flaxseed oil.* Take 2 capsules daily.

ASTHMA

JUST THE FACTS, PLEASE . . . THE MYSTERY EXPOSED.
Your breathing isn't silent. It's more like a wheeze, a whistle. You have
difficulty catching your breath when you walk just a few blocks. You're
restless; you can't sleep. You carry your inhaler, just in case. You never
know when your chest will start to tighten. When you will start to
cough out of control. When you won't breathe. When the next attack
will come.

THE EVIDENCE . . . EXHIBITS A TO Z.
If you have asthma, you're in good company. More than 15 million
Americans suffer from the condition, many of them children. It is a
condition that affects the act of breathing out, not in, and it occurs in
sporadic episodes. When you have an attack, the tiny bronchiole tubes
in the lungs swell, narrowing the passageways that allow air to pass
through the lungs. These passages become clogged with mucus and
you are forced to gasp for air.

Bronchiole tubes do not swell and constrict air on their own. Nor .
does the mucus covering their walls automatically get released. Something has to trigger this chemical reaction. For approximately 90 percent
of people, that trigger is an allergy or a hypersensitivity.

GRADE-A DETECTIVE WORK.
Although allergy is a common trigger, it is more prevalent in children than in adults. And different foods and materials evoke hypersensitivity, depending on where you live and your surroundings. In
Spain, for example, asthma sufferers were found among those who ate
tropical fruits or shellfish, and who came into contact with latex and
pollen.

More Health Detective data: Asians are less likely to develop
asthma than westerners, even if they both grow up in the same area.
Presumably, the diet Americans eat is more conducive to asthma than
the low-fat, high-fiber and fish meals of typical Asians.

Deficiencies in certain vitamins and minerals might be linked with
asthma. One study of 2,633 random adults found low magnesium levels in those suffering from asthma.

Simply breathing in the proper fashion can be powerful. "Breathing exercises have helped almost every asthmatic I treat," says Dr. Richard Firshein, the author of *Reversing Asthma.* "Breathing exercises teach patients how to breathe correctly with their diaphragm and strengthens the muscles used during respiration. It also gives asthmatics the confidence to get through emergencies. Based on ancient yoga techniques, they form an essential part of the treatment of asthma, which includes diet, exercise, environmental controls, and nutritional support."

KEEPING YOUR CONDITION "BEHIND BARS"
RESCUE REGIMEN FOR ASTHMA

Follow Preventive Regimen for respiratory bankruptcies for two weeks. Then add this Rescue Regimen.

If you see △, please check Appendix C for further information.

TIP
- Do the Foundation Regimens for both a *toxic liver* and a *leaky gut* for three weeks before starting both the Preventive Regimen and this Rescue Regimen. Both a *toxic liver* and a *leaky gut* may be strongly linked to asthmatic symptoms.

DIET
- Check for possible food allergies.
- Reduce meat, egg, and dairy fats.
- Increase vegetarian diet.

VITAMINS, MINERALS, AND OTHER NUTRITIONAL SUPPLEMENTS
TAKE DAILY:
- *Magnesium.* Increases vital capacity of lungs. Take citrate form. Take additional 250 mg.
- *Calcium.* Also supports lung function. Take additional 500 mg.
- *Pantothenic acid.* Add 750 mg. Divide dose into several equal amounts.
- *Vitamin B6.* May help to lessen severity of asthmatic symptoms. Take 100 mg.

- *Vitamin C.* Take an additional 1000–2000 mg.
- *Flaxseed oil.* Provides antiinflammatory action.
- *Adrenal gland concentrate.* Helps support adrenal glands during stress. Take as directed.
- *Dimethylglycine (DMG).* Helps increase oxygen supply in lungs. Take as directed.

CHRONIC BRONCHITIS AND SORE THROATS

JUST THE FACTS, PLEASE . . . THE MYSTERY EXPOSED.
Perhaps you're coughing and you can't seem to stop. Maybe your throat is burning up and your chest hurts with every breath you take. You don't have asthma—yet. But you definitely have something besides phlegm, mucus, and congestion that won't go away. It feels like the flu, complete with aches and pains, chills, and fatigue. Help!

THE EVIDENCE . . . EXHIBITS A TO Z.
Chronic bronchitis is an almost constant irritation to your lungs. Oxygen and carbon dioxide "fight for space," and if you don't make a healthy deposit soon, this tug-of-war can lead to asthma, pulmonary hypertension, or heart problems. Some of the withdrawals for this condition include:

WITH ADELE'S COMPLEMENTS!

Remember me and the lemon? It works not only for a mucus-filled throat but also for other respiratory symptoms. It can be a major liver-cleansing tool. However, it's important to start small and slowly increase the amount of lemon juice you use. If you go too fast, you might find your sinuses draining so much that you'll go through box after box of tissues. Think of half a lemon, two times a day, as your ultimate goal. (See Section IV for all the "juice" on the lemon squeeze and the liver.)

- Cigarette smoking (for all the obvious reasons!)
- Cold weather (because there's a greater risk that a cold caught in winter can lead to bronchitis)
- Hazardous workplaces, such as coal mines, chemical plants, and office buildings with improper ventilation (which can all irritate the lungs)

GRADE-A DETECTIVE WORK.
Although vitamin A supplementation has been found to quiet flulike symptoms of the upper respiratory tract, be careful not to overdose— vitamin A may create other problems. One study found that children with respiratory infections, such as bronchitis, suffered from diarrhea after two weeks on megadoses of vitamin A.

And just in case you were looking for a new reason *not* to go on a diet, a study at the University of Medicine and Dentistry of New Jersey found that a low-calorie diet too restrictive in protein may cause damage to the lungs.

KEEPING YOUR CONDITION "BEHIND BARS"
RESCUE REGIMEN FOR CHRONIC BRONCHITIS AND SORE THROATS

Follow Preventive Regimen for respiratory problems for two weeks. Then add this Rescue Regimen.

If you see △, please check Appendix C for further information.

VITAMINS, MINERALS, AND OTHER NUTRITIONAL SUPPLEMENTS
TAKE DAILY:
- *Vitamin C.* Take an additional 1000–2000 mg.

- *Carotenoid complex.* Helps protect and maintain healthy lung tissue. Take as directed.
- *Coenzyme Q10.* Add 60 mg.
- ⚠ *Zinc.* Supports immune function and necessary for tissue repair. Use gluconate lozenge. Take 25 mg.
- *Calcium/magnesium.* Aids.

HERBS
- *Slippery elm.* Helps soothe inflamed mucous membranes. Use lozenge. Take as directed.

SLEEP APNEA

No one likes to sleep next to someone who is snoring. But this is more than just noise. In sleep apnea, the throat closes and the individual actually stops breathing for up to three minutes! The gargling sound you hear isn't snoring; it's the gasping of air and the restoration of regular breathing.

Although we're not sure of the exact cause of sleep apnea, we do know that losing weight will help. So will a good, brisk walk several times a week.

Other healthy deposits are:
- *Avoid alcohol.* It causes the throat to relax even more, bringing on more severe cases of sleep apnea.
- *Try vervain*, a flower remedy, to help calm you. Follow the directions on the bottle.
- *Do relaxation exercises.* Sleep apnea can be caused by emotional upsets and an inability to cope well with stress.

Purchase small bandages at your pharmacy that are especially designed to fit over the bridge of your nose. Wear them while you sleep to stop the "snores." They really work!

SINUSITIS

JUST THE FACTS, PLEASE . . . THE MYSTERY EXPOSED.

From burning, itchy, irritated eyes to a postnasal drip that just won't stop; from a thick, mucusy sniffle to a cough that just won't quit, this *bankruptcy* can be a misery for those who have it. The sinuses are the bony, air-filled compartments that surround the nasal passages, stimulating mucus secretion to protect the passages from toxins. The sinus cavities are all in your head, literally. They lead up from your nose, travel behind the eyes, encircle the cheekbones, and move into your forehead.

The sinuses have very tiny openings that close at the first sign of an irritating withdrawal, be it cigarette smoke, dust and air pollen, or infection. They swell and prevent these irritations from entering the nasal passages. As a further bastion against invasion, mucus is secreted into the compartments to "drown" the irritating substances and flush them out through the nose.

THE EVIDENCE . . . EXHIBITS A TO Z.

Combating potentially dangerous withdrawals takes work. In the nasal passageways, it is the nutrients—the healthy deposits of such items as good food and supplements—that nurture these mucus membranes and "bathe" the sinuses with a gentle but strong battalion.

Unfortunately, withdrawal after withdrawal of substances that are toxic to the system, such as caffeine, food preservatives, and medications, may deplete these nutrients and undermine the functioning of the body, including the mucous membranes; they can't do their job effectively. Further, the sinus passages can't differentiate from true irritation (secondhand smoke) and more eccentric, individualized varieties (the sensitivity people have to dust or flower pollen).

The result may be sinusitis, with symptoms very much like hay fever or a heavy cold at the onset: fatigue, thick mucous discharge from the nose, headache, a raspy voice, coughing (from the excess mucus leaking into the throat, which is so attractively called a postnasal drip), sneezing, and sniffling.

GRADE-A DETECTIVE WORK.

Sinusitis can become chronic if it is not treated properly. The clogged nasal passages degenerate the mucous membrane tissue and the mucus no longer functions properly. In addition to the drip, the cough, and the sniffle, chronic sinusitis may also cause a continuous dull pain in the affected sinus cavity, persistent nasal congestion, continual post-nasal drip, and a diminished sense of smell—all of them *running in the red* notices of a respiratory account that needs some healthy deposits fast. And with your very first healthy deposit, the congested liver may begin to drain and the inflammation in the sinuses begin to ease.

KEEPING YOUR CONDITION "BEHIND BARS"
RESCUE REGIMEN FOR SINUSITIS

Follow Preventive Regimen for respiratory problems for two weeks. Then add this Rescue Regimen.

If you see △, please check Appendix C for further information.

TIP
- Do the Foundation Regimens for a *toxic liver* and a *leaky gut* for three weeks before starting both the Preventive Regimen and, two weeks later, this Rescue Regimen. They can be strongly indicated in sinusitis.

ON AN ONGOING BASIS:
DIET
- *Check if food allergies* are contributing to your condition. Do an elimination diet (see page 208).

VITAMINS, MINERALS, AND OTHER NUTRITIONAL SUPPLEMENTS
TAKE DAILY:
- *Vitamin C.* Add 1000 mg–2000 mg.
- *Thymus tissue.* Helps support immune function and promote health of mucous membranes. Take 500 mg twice a day.

HERBS
- *Echinacea.* Enhances immune system. Take as directed.

Take a long, deep breath. This brings us to the end of the respiratory bankruptcies chapter and the completion of my Rescue Regimens to help ease symptoms and conditions. We've also completed the journey through various other "branches" of the Body Bank account.

You should now have a sound idea of your body: how to listen to its language, how to explore its signs, and how to be a Health Detective in discovering its secrets and links.

It's time now to look forward—to *your* healthy future, one where you have control over your body, where you can choose health with a destiny filled with celebration, where you can master healing from the inside out.

Epilogue: Your Healthy Future with *Healing from the Inside*

"At least you've got your health."

It's a saying that's been around for decades. Whenever something traumatic occurs, something terrible, something shattering, you can hold your head up high and murmur, "At least I've got my health."

But why is it *least*?

And why do you think of health only when everything else has fallen by the wayside?

Good health is not a *least*. It's a wonderful celebration of life. It's a miracle—with a difference. It's a miracle that you, yourself, can make happen. That you, yourself, can control. That you, yourself, can help sustain.

CHOOSE HEALTH!

In the pages of this book I have tried to help you see how to choose health. I hope I have also given you the spark to *want* to make that choice—for your mind, your body, and your soul.

When I look back over the years, I remember what made me want to become a nutritionist in the first place. Helping my clients resolve their health problems has always given me great personal satisfaction. One of the most compelling reasons I chose to work in this field was the great potential to help others—to make a lasting difference in their lives and to help them make positive changes for themselves.

THE SECRETS' MESSAGE

Between the lines of the Rescue Regimens, my basic good health
tenets, the Health Detective work, and the Body Bank concept, I've
tried to impart a message, loud and clear: a vision of empowerment, of
taking charge of your health, of determining what's wrong and fixing
it. And preventing it from getting worse.

Simple.

Powerful.

A message that can have far-reaching benefits for your long life.

AGING DOESN'T HAVE TO BE OLD

No, we cannot predict the future. We cannot look into a crystal ball
and see exactly what will be. I don't think I'd even want to attempt it!

After all, if you change the way you feel, if you have an attitude of confidence and vitality, you can look forward to that unknown as an exciting
adventure. You can stay youthful, your curiosity strong as long as you live.

Perhaps your image of an aging person is the woman down the
block who is so crippled by osteoporosis that she stoops over her cane,
barely walking. Or it might be the man who trembles, who cannot hear
or see too well.

But these are only clichés. They are your fears talking, not your
soul. You can actually feel and behave twenty years younger than your
birth certificate says.

Want proof? Think about the eighty-four-year-old woman who ran
a marathon—and who had taken up jogging when she turned eighty!
Or the man who invented Scrabble—after he was well past seventy. Or
the eighty-four-year-old who just got her bachelor's degree from Harvard. Vital minds, vital bodies.

Study those senior citizens whom you admire, who seem to have
more energy than you could ever have. They have instinctively learned
how to make healthy deposits to their Body Bank. They exercise. They
eat a bounty of healthful foods. They take vitamins and they know how
to relax with, perhaps, a bath or a good mystery.

But there's something else. Hear it? Laughter. The ability to laugh,
to cope with life's ups and downs.

And they are laughing all the way to the healthy Body Bank.

5 HEALING GIFTS
YOU CAN GIVE YOURSELF RIGHT NOW

To help you on the road to a youthful future, here are five simple gifts that you can give yourself right now with very little effort. Besides a good laugh:

1. Begin taking a good multivitamin and mineral tablet every day. Make sure it doesn't contain any artificial colorings, preservatives, sugar, or starch.
2. Start shopping in the organic area of your supermarket's produce department. Try buying a new, different fruit or vegetable each week. And if you don't know how to slice it, cook it, or eat it, ask!
3. Buy a pair of good walking shoes and begin to walk a half hour three times a week. Take a friend, take your dog, take a Walkman—whatever. Don't think. Just put on your shoes and go! And if walking isn't your thing, buy a bathing suit and swim. Or put on some music and dance around the house.
4. Set your alarm for five minutes earlier than you normally get up. Lie in bed. Breathe deeply. Pause. Stretch your legs and your arms. Yawn. You'll start your day much more relaxed.
5. Locate your nearest health food store and visit it. Look at the items on the shelves. Read the labels on the bottles of herbs. Sample a natural body lotion or smell an essential oil. Taste a carrot juice drink. Look at the bulletin board and see if there's anything that interests you: a licensed massage therapist in your area, a personal trainer, a yoga class that's starting up.

5 PRINCIPLES TO HELP YOU
HEAL FROM THE INSIDE

I want to help you to think differently, to see your body in a whole new way—not just as a collection of parts and organs, not as a separate entity with a life of its own. I want you to be able to see yourself, mind and body, as one—to recognize that you, and only you, can change things for the better—and to rejoice in that knowledge. Use me. Use my sourcebook, my knowledge, my compassion. I want you to make *Healing from the Inside* yours:

- *Gain* the empowerment that comes from choosing health.
- *Learn* how to become your own Health Detective and read what your body is trying to tell you.
- *Know* the mastermind behind many of your ailments—the *leaky gut*—and how to repair and restore it to health.
- *Understand* the silent collaborator—the *toxic liver*—that works in tandem with the *leaky gut.* Together, these partners in crime make up your foundation. They can be as stable and as strong as you want them to be, with understanding, knowledge, and nourishment.
- Finally, I hope you have learned that by *preventing* "crime," in your body and your mind, you can stop the *running in the red* symptoms from becoming full-fledged *bankruptcies.*

Feel the flush of that first victory as you start to gain control of yourself, as you step out of your house for your first walk, as you expand your world of vegetables, as you have your first aromatherapeutic massage.

Feel the power.

Feel the vitality.

Feel the strength.

It's you. It's part of you. And it's always been there, waiting for you.

No, your good health is not *least*, not by a long shot. It's the best, the brightest, the most brilliant thing about you, because with good health, everything follows.

With good health, you can celebrate life.

Start now. With just one deposit. Just one.

One of my clients recently said, "Thank you, Adele, for giving me back my life."

My answer?

"Don't thank me. Thank *you. You.*"

To your good life.

Choose health!

Appendix A:
Finding a Health
Professional in Your Area

The following is a list of national organizations that can help guide you to the complementary medicine of your choice. These organizations can help you find a licensed health practitioner in your area.

Aromatherapy Organisations Council
3 Latymer Close
Braybrooke
Market Harborough
Leicestershire LE16 8LN
Tel: 01858 434242

Association of Reflexologists
27 Old Gloucester Street
London WC1N 3XX
Tel: 01273 479 020

British Acupuncture Council
Park House
206–208 Latimer Road
London W10 6RE

British Chiropractic Association
29 Whitley Street
Reading RG2 0EG
Tel: 01734 757 557

British College of Osteopathy and Naturopathy
6 Netherhall Gardens
London N3 5RR
Tel: 020 7435 6464

British Homeopathic Association
27a Devonshire Street
London W1N 1RJ
Tel: 020 7935 2163

British Massage Therapy Council
Greenbank House
65a Adelphi Street
Preston PR1 7BH
Tel: 01772 881 063

General Council and Register of Consultant Herbalists
18 Sussex Square
Brighton
East Sussex BN2 5AA
Tel: 01243 267 126

Integrated Medical Centre
43 New Cavendish Street
London W1M 7RG
Tel: 020 7224 5111
Fax: 020 7224 3114

Appendix B:
Finding the Right
Health Professional for You

You need more than a list of practitioners in your area. You need to know that you are in good, safe hands, that you have a rapport, that he or she is the best person to help you with your particular needs.

Remember that you are the important one in this equation. The health practitioner is only a vehicle to help you achieve optimal health. He or she should be there in every way possible for you: emotionally, spiritually, intellectually. Your good feelings about your health professional will be as instrumental in achieving well-being as they are in combating disease. If you are not happy with your current health practitioner, for whatever reason, move on to someone else. It is your life in the balance, and you should settle for nothing less to achieve your goals.

The best way to find the right health professional for you is to prepare a list of questions to ask *before* you make an appointment. Some questions to ask are:

- How long have you been certified and where did you receive your education?
- How many years have you been in practice?
- What therapies do you use? Do you recommend vitamin and mineral supplements?
- Do you specialize in any particular area?
- Are you affiliated with any medical professionals?
- Have you had experience working with my problem?
- Are you more inclined toward prevention than toward treatment of disease?

After your visit, determine if you felt that he or she was giving you enough time to explain your problem, if the individual sounded sympathetic. Make sure that the health professional answered your questions clearly and without any defensiveness.

APPENDIX C:
A BRIEF EXPLANATION OF
AND WARNINGS FOR
REMEDIES IN THIS BOOK

Here, in alphabetical order and divided by category, is a listing of some of the vitamins and minerals, nutritional supplements, herbs, and probiotics I suggest in this book. You'll find quick descriptions and contraindications. *It is especially important to check this appendix for further information if there is △, a warning icon, in front of a remedy.* In addition, be sure to consult with your health practitioner before using these remedies if you are being treated for any medical conditions, to avoid possible treatment interactions.

VITAMINS

Vitamin A. Necessary for normal growth and reproduction, healthy skin, the immune system, and night vision. *It is a fat-soluble vitamin and can be toxic in high doses. Do not take over 10,000 IU if you are pregnant, trying to conceive, or suffer from liver disease.* When you take beta-carotene, it is converted to vitamin A without ill effects.

Beta-carotene. A carotenoid, or substance that is converted to vitamin A in the liver. Taking beta-carotene, a precursor of vitamin A, is usually nontoxic. It is an important antioxidant, helping to combat damage from roaming free radicals. Beta-carotene can color your skin orange if taken in high dosages. *Do not take if you have hypothyroidism. Your body will not convert it.*

B Complex. Supplement containing all the B vitamins (see individual listings for function).

Vitamin B₁ (Thiamine). Necessary for normal nervous system function and metabolism of fat, carbohydrates, and protein.

Vitamin B₂ (Riboflavin). Necessary for metabolism of fat, carbohydrates, and protein. *Can color urine.*

Vitamin B₃ (Niacin). Crucial for fatty acid production and metabolic function. Aids oxygen transport in the blood. Helps to lower cholesterol. *Very high doses can cause liver damage.*

Vitamin B₆ (Pyridoxine). Crucial for the nervous system and the synthesis of DNA. Helps produce hydrochloric acid and metabolize fats and protein. Helps prevent water retention. *Can be toxic in very high doses, causing damage to the nervous system.*

Vitamin B₁₂ (Cobalamin). Necessary for RNA/DNA synthesis, maintenance of bone marrow, and folic acid production.

Biotin. A B vitamin necessary for healthy skin and hair and metabolism of carbohydrates.

Choline. Helps transmit electrochemical messages in the brain; promotes healthy liver function and fat and cholesterol metabolism. *Do not take if you have manic-depression.*

Inositol. Necessary for hair growth. It also helps maintain the circulatory system, reducing cholesterol levels and preventing hardening of the arteries. It aids the digestive process by helping metabolize fat and transport it from the liver. It can help calm you. *Do not take if you have manic-depression.*

Folic Acid. Necessary for normal growth and development, RNA/DNA synthesis, and prevention of birth defects. *Extremely high doses can hide a B₁₂ deficiency. Do not take high doses if you have a hormone disorder.*

Pantothenic Acid (Vitamin B₅). Helps fight the debilitating effects of stress by supporting adrenal gland function.

Vitamin C (Ascorbic acid). A powerful antioxidant that helps strengthen the immune system, aid in wound healing, promote adrenal gland function, and assist in collagen repair and formation. Enhances absorption of iron. Do not stop abruptly; it can create scurvy-like side effects such as bleeding gums, muscle weakness, and black and blue bruises.

Vitamin D. A fat-soluble vitamin that is crucial for healthy bones and teeth. Necessary for calcium absorption. Can be toxic in high dosages (over 1000 IU each day), causing an excess amount of calcium in the blood and affecting the liver and kidneys.

Vitamin E. A powerful antioxidant that may help improve heart health and circulation. Take your iron supplements at different times during the day than your vitamin E; iron as ferrous sulfate can destroy vitamin E. If you have high blood pressure, start slowly, with only 100 mg each day, gradually building to your necessary dosage.

Vitamin K. Necessary for normal blood clotting. *Synthetic vitamin K can be toxic in high doses. Do not take during the last month of pregnancy or if you are on blood-thinning medication.* Excess amounts can also cause flushing and sweating.

Vitamin P (Bioflavonoids). Helps decrease pain, enhance circulation, and increase bile production. *Quercetin* is a common bioflavonoid whose action is enhanced by *bromelain*, an enzyme found in pineapple.

MINERALS

Boron. Needed for strong bones and absorption of other minerals, including calcium and magnesium. Do not exceed 3 mg each day.

Calcium. Crucial for healthy bones, teeth, and gums, proper nervous system function, heartbeat, and blood clotting. *Do not take excessive amounts if you are prone to kidney stones.*

Chromium. Helps to maintain blood-sugar levels owing to its effect on insulin activity. The best form to take is chromium picolinate. Be careful to monitor glucose levels, as this nutrient can dramatically lower insulin requirements. Extremely effective for insulin-resistant diabetics. *Type I diabetics should take only under a health practitioner's care.*

Copper. Necessary for bone formation, hemoglobin, and red blood cell production.

Iodine. Necessary for normal thyroid function and proper physical and mental development. *Excess iodine can create an enlarged thyroid. It can also cause acne, diarrhea, vomiting, and a metallic taste in the mouth.*

Iron. Vital in the formation of hemoglobin in the blood and in muscles (where it's called myoglobin) that "feed" oxygen to the cells. Vitamin C can enhance its absorption. *Excess iron can be toxic by increasing free radical formation. Excesses can increase vitamin E needs and have been linked to cancer and heart attacks. May cause constipation.*

Magnesium. Necessary for proper bone formation, enzyme function, and normal function of heart, nerves, and muscles. Aids calcium utilization.

Manganese. Necessary for fat and protein breakdown, proper immune function, and healthy nerves.

Molybdenum. Necessary for proper cell function.

Phosphorus. Necessary for bone and teeth formation, heart muscle contractions, and the metabolism of fat, carbohydrates, and protein.

Potassium. Critical in maintaining fluid balance, which helps stabilize blood pressure. Promotes a healthy heart and nervous system. *Doses over 25,000 mg a day can cause kidney failure. High doses can also result in heart problems.*

Selenium. A powerful antioxidant that supports immune function and helps to maintain a healthy cardiovascular system. *An excess of selenium can be toxic to the liver and kidneys. Do not exceed 200 mcg.*

Zinc. Necessary for proper wound healing, immune function, taste and smell perception, prostate gland function, and liver detoxification. *Can suppress the immune system in doses higher than 100 mg a day.*

OTHER NUTRITIONAL SUPPLEMENTS

Borage Oil. Contains essential fatty acids that may help reduce inflammation and strengthen the heart and the immune system. *Do not take if you are pregnant.*

Bromelain. An enzyme that aids digestion.

Carotenoid Complex. A group of substances that possess antioxidant properties. *Do not take if you are diabetic.*

Chondroitin Sulfate. A component of cartilage that protects cartilage from destructive enzymes.

Coenzyme Q10. A powerful antioxidant that helps enhance the immune system, aids circulation, and has anti-aging properties.

Dimethylglycine (DMG). An amino acid that provides energy on a cellular level and increases oxygen in the lungs.

Evening Primrose Oil. Contains essential fatty acid that may reduce symptoms of menopause, inflammation, high blood pressure, and heart disease. *It can soften stools and, because it triggers estrogen production, should be avoided by women at risk for breast disease.*

Flaxseed Oil or Seeds. Contains essential fatty acids that may help lower cholesterol levels and relieve arthritic pain.

Fish Oil. Contains essential fatty acids that may reduce risk of heart disease and other conditions. *Do not take if you are taking blood thinner medication.*

Gamma-Aminobutyric Acid (GABA). An amino acid that is necessary for proper brain function. Supplements can relax you, but *an excess can make you more anxious. It can also create shortness of breath and numbness in the mouth and fingers.*

Gamma-Oryzonal. An amino acid that helps reduce flushing associated with a congested liver or menopause.

Glucosamine Sulfate. A critical ingredient in formation of collagen.

Green Drinks. These nutritional boosts are made from plants. They help cleanse the system and provide valuable minerals, enzymes, and nutrients to the body. They are sold as powders you mix with liquid.

Green Tea. Has antioxidant-like properties that may lower cholesterol. Alkalizes the stomach.

Kelp. Provides iodine, a necessary mineral for thyroid function.

L-Carnitine. An amino acid–like substance that aids in fat metabolism.

L-Cysteine. An amino acid that helps the liver detoxify toxins and may help treat arthritis. *Do not take if you have diabetes. It can interfere with insulin activity.*

L-Glutamine. An amino acid that enhances brain function, maintains a healthy digestive system, and reduces sugar cravings. *Do not take if you have Reye's syndrome, cirrhosis of the liver, or kidney problems.*

L-Lysine. An amino acid necessary for growth, formation of bones, and production of antibodies and tissue repair. Useful for herpes.

L-Methionine. An amino acid that helps break down fat, prevent heart disease, and aid the detoxification process. *Must be taken in conjunction with Vitamins B_6, B_{12}, and folic acid, as provided in Basic Health Regimen.*

L-Taurine. An amino acid that is a main component of bile. Necessary for proper use of many minerals and helps to control blood cholesterol levels.

L-Tyrosine. An amino acid that enhances mood and aids in adrenal, thyroid, and pituitary function. *Do not use if you are taking MAO inhibitors.*

Malic Acid. A naturally occurring acid found in fruit that helps provide muscles with energy.

Multi–Amino Acid Complex. Provides the building blocks for healthy skin, cells, tissues, and organs.

Multienzyme with HCl. Helps in the digestion and breakdown of foods. *Do not take if you have ulcers.*

N-Acety-cysteine (NAC). A form of the amino acid cysteine. *Do not take if diabetic.*

N-Acetyl-glucosamine (NAG). A form of amino acid that helps protect intestinal mucosa.

Pancreatin. An enzyme that aids digestion and may help with treating food allergies and autoimmune disorders.

Papaya Enzymes. Aid digestive process.

Proteolytic Enzymes. Aid in breakdown and digestion of food when taken with meals. Have antiinflammatory effect when taken between meals.

Psyllium Husk. Provides fiber to help regulate bowel function. *Always take with a lot of water.*

Pycnogenol. A bioflavonoid with antioxidant properties that can help decrease the risk of diabetes-related diseases. Has the same properties as grape seed oil.

Raw Adrenal Gland. Helps restore adrenal gland function.

Sea Cucumber. Marine animals used to help treat arthritis.

Shark Cartilage. A substance thought beneficial for psoriasis and rheumatoid arthritis. Also used to try to prevent growth of tumors. *Do not take if pregnant, undergoing surgery, or have heart problems.*

Silica. Provides the mineral silicone for gland and tissue health.

Thymus Tissue. May help enhance immune function.

HERBS

Alfalfa. Helps ease inflammation. *Do not take if you are on blood thinners. Contains vitamin K.*

Aloe Vera. When applied as an ointment, will relieve burns and heal cuts and scrapes. Can soothe stomach problems if taken as a capsule. Use the juicy inside of the leaves. *Allergic reactions have been noted.* Do a patch test first: put a dab behind your ear; if a rash appears, do not use.

Anise. Chewing the seeds can help digestion. It can also help clear sinus passages. May also help menopause discomfort.

Bilberry. Acts as a powerful antioxidant. Contains fatty acids and flavonoids. May help stabilize insulin levels, and reduce anxiety, hypoglycemia, and macular degeneration. Use the whole plant. *Can cause iron absorption problems.*

Burdock. Use the roots and the seeds to help strengthen the liver and gallbladder. *Can cause iron absorption problems.*

Cat's Claw. Can help cleanse the digestive tract. Also works as an antioxidant. Use the roots. *Do not take if pregnant.*

Cayenne. Aids digestion. Can help ward off respiratory ailments. Helps digestion and circulation. Use the berries. *Do not take if you have high blood pressure.*

Chamomile. Use the flowers, stems, or roots to reduce inflammation and aid digestion. May also relieve stress and anxiety. Do not take for long periods of time, because it can promote ragweed allergy. *Do not take at all if you are allergic to ragweed.*

Chaste Tree Berry. An herb that helps regulate pituitary gland function and, therefore, may help regulate menstrual cycle and menopausal changes.

Corn Silk. Helps support proper kidney function.

Dandelion Root. Helps cleanse the liver and make the production of bile more efficient. Use the leaves, roots, and flowers.

Echinacea. Use the leaves or the roots to help ward off colds, flus, and any other respiratory ailments. Will also strengthen the immune system. *Do not use if you are allergic to sunflowers.*

Fenugreek. Possesses laxative properties. Helps reduce inflammation and improve sinus problems.

Feverfew. Clears the lungs and bronchial tubes. May help arthritis, intestinal conditions, headaches, and muscle pain. Use the bark, leaves, or flowers, dried. *Do not use if you are pregnant.*

Garlic. A natural antioxidant. Protects and strengthens the immune system. Can lower blood pressure. An all-around excellent healer and health-enhancer. Use cloves or buy capsules.

Ginger. Enhances circulation, possesses antioxidant properties, and acts as a colon cleanser. *Can cause stomach distress if taken in excess.*

Ginkgo Biloba. A powerful antioxidant. Use the leaves for clearer thinking and a stronger circulatory system. May help depression, tinnitis, asthma, and eczema.

Goldenseal. Use the roots for a natural antibiotic that cleanses the body of toxins. Helps increase the efficiency of insulin. Promotes a healthy gastrointestinal tract. Helps ward off respiratory infections. *Do not use if you are pregnant or allergic to ragweed.*

Grape Seed Extract. A flavonoid with antioxidant properties.

Gymnema Sylvestre. Helps in the production of insulin. *Be careful to monitor glucose levels, as this nutrient can significantly lower insulin requirements.*

Hawthorn Berries. May help lower cholesterol and aid in heart health.

Licorice. Supports adrenal function. *Can elevate blood pressure.*

Passion Flower. The plant and the flowers may help you get to sleep. Acts as a natural sedative. *Do not use if pregnant.*

Peppermint. Aids digestive process by helping to create proper stomach acidity. *Can cause problems with iron absorption if taken in excess.*

Red Clover. Possesses antibiotic-like properties.

Saint-John's-Wort. Use the leaves and stems for a natural antidepressant. May also help ward off viral infections. *Do not sit in the sun if currently using. Can create deficiencies in iron and other minerals.*

Silymarin, or Milk Thistle. A potent liver strengthener. Also good for adrenal gland and kidney function. May help relieve psoriasis. Use the leaves, seeds, or fruits.

Slippery Elm. Helps ease diarrhea and the symptoms of respiratory infections. Reduces inflammation in the mucosal passages. Use the inner bark.

Tea Tree Oil. Has antibacterial and antifungal properties. Apply topically.

Uva Ursi. Helps to relieve pain associated with kidney stones.

Valerian. Enhances circulation and provides calming effect. *Do not take if currently using tranquilizers.*

PROBIOTICS

B. bifidum. Inhibits the overgrowth of "bad" bacteria and yeast in the *leaky gut. Start slowly. A too-rapid introduction can cause excessive gas activity.*

L. acidophilus. It is effective in restoring flora after a regime of antibiotics or a bout of stress. It can also be found in yogurt. *Start slowly. A too rapid introduction can cause excessive gas activity. Use only the dairy-free version if lactose intolerant.*

L. bulgaricus. Takes two weeks to travel down the gut and, during that time, it creates a climate that is inhospitable to harmful bacteria. It also helps reduce the symptoms of lactose intolerance allergies. Start slowly, with the smallest dose ($1/8$ of a teaspoon in $1/2$ cup water). *A too rapid introduction can cause excessive gas activity.*

Whey Protein. Enhances and stimulates the growth of "good bacteria" in the lower portion of the intestines. It provides a fertile ground for it to grow. *Start slowly. A too rapid introduction can cause excessive gas activity. Use a vegetable formulation if you are lactose intolerant.*

SOURCES

Adera, T., R.A. Deyo, and R.J. Donatelle, "Premature Menopause and Low Back Pain," *Annals of Epidemiology*, Vol. 4, No. 5, September 1994.

Alarcon-de-la-Lastra, A.C., M.J. Martin, V. Motilva, M. Jimenez, C. La-Casa, A. Lopez, "Gastroprotection Induced by Silymarin, the Hepatoprotective Principle of Silybum Marianum in Ischemia-Reperfusion Mucosal Injury: Role of Neutrophils," *Planta Medica*, Vol. 61, No. 2, April 1995.

Altman, D.R., and L.T. Chiaramonte, "Public Perception of Food Allergy," *Journal of Allergy and Clinical Immunology*, Vol. 97, No. 6, June 1996.

Altman, Lawrence K., "Illness Outbreak Puzzles Officials," *New York Times*, June 30, 1996.

Anderson, Richard, et al., "Beneficial Effect of Chromium for People with Type II Diabetes," *Diabetes*, Vol. 45, Supplement 2, 1996.

Andersson, S., and T. Lundeberg, "Acupuncture—From Empiricism to Science: Functional Background to Acupuncture Effects in Pain and Disease," *Medical Hypotheses*, Vol. 45, 1995.

Ashwell, M., "Obesity in Men and Women," *International Journal of Obesity-Related Metabolic Disorders*, Vol. 18, Supplement 1, June 1994.

Badiali, D., E. Corazziari, F.I. Habib, E. Tomei, G. Bausano, P. Magrini, F. Anzini, and A. Torsoli, "Effect of Wheat Bran in Treatment of Chronic Nonorganic Constipation," *Digestive Diseases and Sciences*, Vol. 40, No. 2, February 1995.

Balch, James F., and Phyllis A. Balch, *Prescription for Nutritional Healing: Second Edition*, Garden City Park, N.Y.: Avery Publishing Group, 1997.

Barnard, James R., et al., "Effects of Diet and Exercise on Qualitative and Quantitative Measures of LDL and Its Susceptibility to Oxidation," *Arteriosclerosis, Thrombosis, and Vascular Biology*, Vol. 16, No. 2, February 1996.

Baskaran, K., et al., "Antidiabetic of a Leaf Extract From Gymnema Sylvestre in Non-Insulin-Dependent Diabetes Mellitus Patients," *Ethnopharmacology*, Vol. 30, 1995.

Bassett, I.B., D.L. Pannowitz, and R.S. Barnetson, "A Comparative Study of Tea-Tree Oil Versus Benzoylperoxide in the Treatment of Acne," *Medical Journal of Australia,* Vol. 153, No. 8, October 1990.

Bellatoni, M.F., "Osteoporosis: Prevention and Treatment," *American Family Physician,* Vol. 54, No. 3, September 1, 1996.

Bendich, Adrianne, "Vitamins and Immunity," *American Institute of Nutrition,* Vol. 122, Supplement 3, March 1992.

Bergner, Paul, "Silybum Marianum and Liver Therapy," *Townsend Letter for Doctors,* August/September 1988.

Black, Kathryn, "The Miracle Cures," *Mirabella,* Vol. 7, No. 2, November/December 1996.

Blakeslee, Sandra, "Virus's Similarity to Body's Proteins May Explain Autoimmune Diseases," *New York Times,* December 31, 1996.

Bland, Jeffrey S., *Nutraerobics,* San Francisco: Harper & Row Publishers, 1983.

Bland, Jeffrey S., "Food and Nutrient Effects on Detoxification," *Townsend Letter for Doctors & Patients,* December 1995.

Bland, Jeffrey, with Sara Benum, *The 20-Day Rejuvenation Diet Program,* New Canaan, Ct.: Keats Publishing, Inc., 1997.

Bland, Jeffrey S., Eleanor Barrager, R. Graham Reedy, Kyle Bland, "A Medical Food-Supplemented Detoxification Program in the Management of Chronic Health Problems," *Alternative Therapies,* Vol. 1, No. 5, November 1995.

Boris, M., and F.S. Mandel, "Foods and Additives are Common Causes of the Attention Deficit Hyperactive Disorder in Children," *Annals of Allergy,* Vol. 72, No. 5, May 1994.

Braitstom, Lars, "Vitamins as Homocysteine-Lowering Agents: A Mini Review," Presented at The Experimental Biology, 1995 AIN Colloquium, Atlanta, Ga.

Britton, J., I. Pavord, K. Richards, A. Wisniewski, A. Knox, S. Lewis, A. Tattersfield, and S. Weiss, "Dietary Magnesium, Lung Function, Wheezing, and Airway Hyperreactivity in Random Adult Population Sample," *Lancet,* Vol. 344, No. 8919, August 6, 1994.

Brody, Jane, "Osteoporosis Can Threaten Men as Well as Women," *New York Times,* September 4, 1996.

Brody, Jane, "Research Hints Vitamin D and C May Slow Down Osteoarthritis," *New York Times,* September 4, 1996.

Budeiri, D.J., A. Li-Wan-Po, and J.C. Dornan, "Clinical Trials of Treatments of Premenstrual Syndrome: Entry Criteria and Scales for Measuring Treatment Outcomes," *British Journal of Obstetrics and Gynecology,* Vol. 101, No. 8, August 1994.

Burros, Marian, "A New Goal Beyond Organic: 'Clean Food,' " *New York Times*, February 7, 1996.

Burtis, W.J., L. Gay, K.L. Insogna, A. Ellison, and A.E. Broadus, "Dietary Hypercalciuria in Patients with Calcium Oxalate Kidney Stones," *American Journal of Clinical Nutrition*, Vol. 60, No. 3, September 1994.

Burton Goldberg Group, *Alternative Medicine: The Definitive Guide*, Fife, Washington: Future Medicine Publishing, Inc., 1994.

Camilleri, M., W.G. Thompson, J.W. Fleshman, J.H. Pemberton, "Clinical Management of Intractable Constipation," *Annals of International Medicine*, Vol. 121, No. 7, October 1, 1994.

Canty, D.J., and S.H. Zeisel, "Lecithin and Choline in Human Health and Disease," *Nutrition Review*, Vol. 52, No. 10, October 1994.

Carey, O.J., J.B. Cookson, J. Britton, and A.E. Tattersfield, "The Effect of Lifestyle on Wheeze, Atopy, and Bronchial Hyperreactivity in Asian and White Children," *American Journal of Respiratory Critical Care Medicine*, Vol. 154, No. 2, August 1996.

Carlin, Peter, "Treat the Body, Heal the Mind," *Health*, January/February 1997.

Carpentier, P., and P. Priollet, "Epidemiology of Chronic Venous Insufficiency," *Presse-Medicale*, Vol. 23, No. 5, February 10, 1994.

Carper, Jean, *Food—Your Miracle Medicine*, New York: HarperPerennial, 1994.

Carper, Jean, *Total Nutrition Guide*, New York: Bantam Books, 1987.

Castillo, R., J. Delgado, J. Quiralte, C. Blanco, and T. Carrillo, "Food Hypersensitivity Among Adult Patients: Epidemiological and Clinical Aspects," *Allergologia et Immunopathologia*, Vol. 24, No. 3, May–June 1996.

Cater, R.E., "Chronic Intestinal Candidiasis as a Possible Etiological Factor in the Chronic Fatigue Syndrome," *Medical Hypotheses*, Vol. 44, No. 6, June 1995.

Celiker, R., O. Basgoze, and M. Bayraktar, "Early Detection of Neurological Involvement in Diabetes Mellitus," *Electroencephalography and Clinical Neurophysiology*, Vol. 36, No. 1, January–February 1996.

Cheskin, L.J., N. Kamal, M.D. Crowell, M.M. Schuster, and W.E. Whitehead, "Mechanisms of Constipation in Older Persons and Effects of Fiber Compared with Placebo," *Journal of the American Geriatric Society*, Vol. 43, No. 6, June 1995.

Chilton, S.A., "Cognitive Behaviour Therapy for the Chronic Fatigue Syndrome: Evening Primrose Oil and Magnesium Have Been Shown to Be Effective," *British Medical Journal*, Vol. 312, April 27, 1996.

Cigolini, M., G. Targher, I.A. Bergamo-Andreis, M. Tonoli, F. Filippi, M. Muggeo, and G. DeSandre, "Moderate Alcohol Consumption and Its Relation to Visceral Fat and Plasma Androgens in Healthy Women," *International Journal of Obesity-Related Metabolic Disorders*, Vol. 20, No. 3, March 1996.

Colbin, Annemarie, *Food and Healing*, New York: Ballantine Books, 1986.

Collier, P.M, A. Ursaell, K. Zaremba, C.M. Payne, R.C. Staughton, and T. Sanders, "Effect of Regular Consumption of Oily Fish Compared with White Fish on Chronic Plaque Psoriasis," *European Journal of Clinical Nutrition*, Vol. 47, No. 4, April 1993.

Collinge, William, *The American Holistic Health Association Complete Guide to Alternative Medicine*, New York: Warner Books, 1996.

Colt, George Howe, "See Me, Feel Me, Touch Me, Heal Me," *Life*, September 1996.

Cornu, Thenard A., P. Boivin, J.M. Baud, I. DeVincenzi, and P.H. Carpentier, "Importance of the Familial Factor in Varicose Disease: Clinical Study of 134 Families," *Journal of Dermatologic Surgery and Oncology*, Vol. 20, No. 5, May 1994.

Crum, R.M., C. Muntaner, W.W. Eaton, and J.C. Anthony, "Occupational Stress and the Risk of Alcohol Abuse and Dependence," *Alcoholism: Clinical and Experimental Research*, Vol. 19, No. 3, June 1995.

Danby, F.W., W.S. Maddin, L.J. Margesson, and D. Rosenthal, "A Randomized, Double-Blind, Placebo-Controlled Trial of Ketoconazole 2% Shampoo Versus Selenium Sulfide 2.5% Shampoo in the Treatment of Moderate to Severe Dandruff," *Journal of the American Academy of Dermatology*, Vol. 29, No. 6, December 1993.

Denny, F.W., Jr. "The Clinical Impact of Human Respiratory Virus Infections," *American Journal of Respiratory Critical Care Medicine*, Vol. 152, No. 4, October 1995.

Derebery, M.J., "Otolaryngic Allergy," *Otolaryngologic Clinics of North America*, Vol. 26, No. 4, August 1993.

Despres, Jean-Pierre, et al., "Hyperinsulinemia as an Independent Risk Factor for Ischemic Heart Disease," *New England Journal of Medicine*, Vol. 33, April 11, 1996.

Dorant, E., P.A. Van Den Brandt, and R.A. Goldbohm, "Allium Vegetable Consumption, Garlic Supplement Intake, and Female Breast Carcinoma Incidence," *Breast Cancer Research and Treatment*, Vol. 33, No. 2, 1995.

Dunavskii, G.A., P.A. Karpenko, E.I. Denisiako, A.E. Tsimbal, and N.B. Iurkovskaia, "The Use of a Dried Protein Mixture in Treating Patients with Viral Hepatitis," *Vrachebnoe Delo* (Kiev), No. 7, July 1989.

Duplechain, G., and J.A. White, "Male Pattern Baldness," *Journal of Louisiana Medical Society*, Vol. 146, No. 1, January 1994.

Eaton, Charles B., et al., "Sedentary Life-Style and Risk of Coronary Heart Disease in Women," *Medicine and Science in Sports and Exercise*, Vol. 27, No. 11, 1995.

Editors of *Prevention* Magazine Health Books, *Symptoms: Their Causes & Cures,* Emmaus, Pa.: Rodale Press, 1994.

Editors of Time-Life Books, *The Medical Advisor: The Complete Guide to Alternative & Conventional Treatments,* Alexandria, Va.: Time-Life Books, Inc., 1996.

Eisinger, J., A. Planatamura, and T. Ayaou, "Glycolysis Abnormalities in Fibromyalgia," *Journal of the American College of Nutrition,* Vol. 13, No. 2, 1994.

Ellestad-Sayed, Judith J., Ralph A. Nelson, Martin A. Adson, W. Martyn Palmer, and Edward H. Soule, "Pantothenic Acid, Coenzyme A, and Human Chronic Ulcerative and Granulomatous Colitis," *American Journal of Clinical Nutrition,* No. 29, December 1976.

Elmer, G.W., C.M. Surawicz, and L.V. McFarland, "Biotherapeutic Agents: A Neglected Modality for the Treatment and Prevention of Selected Intestinal and Vaginal Infections," *Journal of the American Medical Association,* Vol. 275, No. 11, March 20, 1996.

Engel, Robert R., and Allan H. Smith, "Arsenic in Drinking Water and Mortality From Vascular Disease: An Ecological Analysis in 30 Counties in the United States," *Archives of Environmental Health,* Vol. 29, No. 5, September/October 1994.

Evans, R. III, "Environmental Control and Immunotherapy for Allergic Disease," *Journal of Allergy and Clinical Immunology,* Vol. 90, No. 3, September 1992.

Ferrell-Torry, A.T., and O.J. Glick, "The Use of Therapeutic Massage as a Nursing Intervention to Modify Anxiety and the Perception of Cancer Pain," *Cancer Nursing,* Vol. 16, No. 2, April 1993.

Feskens, Edith J.M., and Dan Kromhout, "Hyperinsulinemia, Risk Factors, and Coronary Heart Disease: The Zutphen Elderly Study," *Arteriosclerosis and Thrombosis,* Vol. 14, 1994.

Field, T., "Massage Therapy for Infants and Children," *Journal of Developmental Behavior in Pediatrics,* Vol. 16, No. 2, April 1995.

Finnegan, John, *The Facts About Fats: A Consumer's Guide to Good Oils,* Berkeley, Ca.: Celestial Arts, 1993.

Firshein, Richard, *Reversing Asthma: Reduce Your Medications with This Revolutionary New Program,* New York: Warner Books, 1996.

Florido-Lopez, J.F., P. Delgado-Gonzalez, B. Saenz de San Pedro, C. Perez-Miranda, J.M. Arias de Saavedra, and J.F. Marin Pozo, "Allergy to Natural Honeys and Chamomile Tea," *International Archives of Allergy and Immunology,* Vol. 108, No. 2, October 1995.

Fuller, R., "Probiotics in Human Medicine," *Gut,* Vol. 32, 1991.

Flynn, Margaret A. et al., "The Effect of Folate and Cobalamin on Osteoarthritic Hands," *Journal of the American College of Nutrition*, Vol. 13, No. 4, 1994.

Gasinska, T., M. Izbicka, and A. Kierat, "Association of Primary Autoimmune Hypothyroidism with Addison's Anemia," Endokrynologia Polska, Vol. 42, No. 3, 1991.

Gatto, Lissa M., et al., "Ascorbic Acid Induces a Favorable Lipoprotein Profile in Women," *Journal of the American College of Nutrition*, Vol. 15, No. 2, 1996.

Gertner, David, et al., "Irritable Bowel Syndrome and the Food Intolerance," *The Practitioner*, Vol. 238, July 1994.

Ghiz, L., and J.C. Chrisler, "Compulsive Eating, Obsessive Thoughts of Food, and Their Relation to Assertiveness and Depression in Women," *Journal of Clinical Psychology*, Vol. 51, No. 4, July 1995.

Gibson, G.R., and M.B. Roberfroid, "Dietary Modulation of the Human Colonic Microbiota: Introducing the Concept of Probiotics," *Journal of Nutrition*, Vol. 125, No. 6, June 1995.

Giller, Robert M., and Kathy Matthews, *Natural Prescriptions: Dr. Giller's Natural Treatments and Vitamin Therapies for More than 100 Common Ailments*, New York: Ballantine Books, 1994.

Gottesman, C., "Energy Balancing Through Touch for Health," *Journal of Holistic Nursing*, Vol. 10., No. 4, December 1992.

Gottlieb, Bill, ed., *New Choices in Natural Healing*, Emmaus, Pa.: Rodale Books, Inc., 1995.

Gray, D.S., "The Clinical Uses of Dietary Fiber," *American Family Physician*, Vol. 51, No. 2, February 1, 1995.

Hammes, W.P., and P.S. Tichaczek, "The Potential of Lactic Acid Bacteria for the Production of Safe and Wholesome Food," *Zeitschift fur Lebensmittel-Untersuchung und -Forschung*, Vol. 198, No. 3, March 1994.

Hanania, N.A., K.R. Chapman, W.C. Sturtridge, J.P. Szalai, S. Kesten, "Dose-Related Decrease in Bone Density Among Asthmatic Patients Treated with Inhaled Corticosteroids," *Journal of Allergy and Clinical Immunology*, Vol. 96, No. 5, November 1995.

Harris, Robert H., and Rolf Eliassen, "Industrial Waste Disposal," *Collier's Encyclopedia*, CD-ROM, February 28, 1996.

Hatch, G.E., "Asthma, Inhaled Oxidants, and Dietary Antioxidants," *American Journal of Clinical Nutrition*, Vol. 61, No. 3, March 1995.

Heller, Richard F., and Rachael F. Heller, *Healthy for Life: The Scientific Breakthrough Program for Looking, Feeling, and Staying Healthy Without Deprivation*, New York: Dutton, 1995.

Hermann, Mindy, "The Healing Power of Fruits and Vegetables," *McCall's*, December 1994.

Hertog, M., E. Feskens, P. Hollman, et al., "Dietary Antioxidant Flavonoids and Risk of Coronary Heart Disease: The Zutphen Elderly Study," *Lancet,* Vol. 342, 1993.

Hill, D.J., and C.S. Hosking, "The Cow Milk Allergy Complex: Overlapping Disease Profiles in Infancy," *European Journal of Clinical Nutrition,* Vol. 49, Supplement 1, September 1995.

Hodge, L., K.Y. Yan, and R.L. Loblay, "Assessment of Food Chemical Intolerance in Adult Asthmatic Subjects," *Thorax,* Vol. 51, No. 8, August 1996.

Hodge, L., C.M. Salome, J.K. Peat, M.M. Haby, W. Xuan, A.J. Woolcock, "Consumption of Oily Fish and Childhood Asthma Risk," *Medical Journal of Australia,* Vol. 164, No. 3, February 5, 1996.

Hoffman, David, *The Complete Illustrated Holistic Herbal: A Safe and Practical Guide to Making and Using Herbal Remedies,* New York: Barnes & Noble Books, 1996.

Horvilleur, Alain, *The Family Guide to Homeopathy,* Virginia: Health and Homeopathy Publishing, Inc., 1986.

Hotz, J., and K. Plein, "Effectiveness of Plantago Seed Husks in Comparison with Wheat Bran on Stool Frequency and Manifestations of Irritable Colon Syndrome with Constipation," *Medizinische Klinik,* Vol. 89, No. 12, December 15, 1994.

Hourihane, J.O., T.P. Dean, and J.O. Warner, "Peanut Allergy in Relation to Heredity, Maternal Diet, and Other Atopic Diseases: Results of a Questionnaire Survey, Skin Prick Testing, and Food Challenges," *British Medical Journal,* Vol. 313, No. 7056, August 31, 1996.

Hoy, M.K., S. Heshka, D.B. Allison, E. Grasset, R. Blank, M. Abiri, and S.B. Heymsfield, "Reduced Risk of Liver Function Test Abnormalities and New Gallstone Formation With Weight Loss on 3350-kJ (800-kcal) Formula Diets," *American Journal of Clinical Nutrition,* Vol. 60, No. 2, August 1994.

Husten, Larry, "A New Reason to B," *Harvard Health Letter,* Vol. 19, No. 7, May 1994.

Jacknow, D.S., J.M. Tschann, M.P. Link, and W.T. Boyce, "Hypnosis in the Prevention of Chemotherapy-Related Nausea and Vomiting in Children: A Prospective Study," *Journal of Developmental Behavior in Pediatrics,* Vol. 15, No. 4, August 1994.

Jacobs, J., L.M. Jimenez, S.S. Gloyd, et al., "Treatment of Acute Childhood Diarrhea With Homeopathic Medicine: A Randomized Clinical Trial in Nicaragua," *Pediatrics,* Vol. 93, 1994.

Jacobs, Jennifer, "Q: What's the Best Way to Cope With a Cold?" *Self,* April 1997.

Jain, S.K., R. McVie, J.J. Jaramillo, M. Palmer, T. Smith, Z.D. Meachum, and

R.L. Little, "The Effect of Modest Vitamin E Supplementation on Lipid Peroxidation Products and Other Cardiovascular Risk Factors in Diabetic Patients," *Lipids,* Vol. 31, Supplement S87-90, March 1996.

Jankowski, J.A., R.A. Goodlad, and N.A. Wright, "Maintenance of Normal Intestinal Mucosa: Function, Structure, and Adaptation," *Gut,* Supplement 1, 1994.

Janniger, C.K., and R.A. Schwartz, "Seborrheic Dermatitis," *American Family Physician,* Vol. 52, No. 1, July 1995.

Jarisch, R., and F. Wantke, "Wine and Headache," *International Archives of Allergy and Immunology,* Vol. 110, No. 1, May 1996.

Janssen, Matthijs, "Achlorhydria Does Not Protect Against Benign Upper Gastrointestinal Ulcers During NSAID Use," *Digestive Diseases and Sciences,* Vol. 39, No. 2, February 1994.

Jonnalagadda, S.S., E.A. Trautwein, and K.C. Hayes, "Dietary Fats Rich in Saturated Fatty Acids (12:0, 14:0, and 16:0) Enhance Gallstone Formation Relative to Monounsaturated Fat in Cholesterol-Fed Hamsters," *Lipids,* Vol. 30, No. 5, May 1995.

Kim, Young-in, "Can Fish Oil Maintain Crohn's Disease in Remission?" *Nutrition Review,* Vol. 54, No. 8, August 1996.

Kinnaird, S.W., N. McClure, and S. Wilham, "Latex Allergy: An Emerging Problem in Health Care," *Neonatal Network,* Vol. 14, No. 7, October 1995.

Kirschmann, Gayla J., and John D. Kirschmann, *Nutrition Almanac: Fourth Edition,* New York: McGraw-Hill, 1996.

Knoke, M., and H. Bernhardt, "Clinical Significance of Changes of Flora in the Upper Digestive Tract," *Infection,* Vol. 17, No. 4, July–August 1989.

Kuroki, F., M. Iida, M. Tominaga, T. Matsumoto, K. Hirakawa, S. Sugiyama, and M. Fujishima, "Multiple Vitamin Status in Crohn's Disease: Correlation with Disease Activity," *Digestive Diseases and Sciences,* Vol. 38, No. 9, September 1993.

Lam, R.W., R.P. Zis, A. Grewal, P.L. Delgado, D.S. Charney, and J.H. Krystal, "Effects of Rapid Tryptophan Depletion in Patients with Seasonal Affective Disorder in Remission After Light Therapy," *Archives of General Psychiatry,* Vol. 53, No. 1, January 1996.

Lane, Earl, "The Leftovers of the Nuclear Age," *Newsday,* August 3, 1997.

Lansdown, A.B.G., "Zinc in the Healing Wound," *The Lancet,* Vol. 347, March 16, 1996.

Larrey, D., "Liver Involvement in the Course of Phytotherapy," *Presse-Medicine,* Vol. 23, No. 15, April 1994.

Lederle, F.A., "Epidemiology of Constipation in Elderly Patients: Drug Utilization and Cost-Containment Strategies," *Drugs and Aging,* Vol. 6, No. 6, June 1995.

Leung, L.H., "Pantothenic Acid Deficiency as the Pathogenesis of Acne Vulgaris," *Medical Hypotheses,* Vol. 44, No. 6, June 1995.

Lieberman, Shari, and Nancy Bruning, *Design Your Own Vitamin and Mineral Program,* New York: Doubleday & Company, 1987.

Linde, Klaus, et al., "St. John's Wort for Depression—An Overview and Meta-Analysis of Randomized Clinical Trials," *British Medical Journal,* Vol. 313, 1996.

Linnoila, V.M., and M. Virkkunen, "Aggression, Suicidality, and Serotonin," *Journal of Clinical Psychiatry,* Vol. 53, Supplement, October 1992.

Loizeau, E., "Can Antibiotic-Associated Diarrhea Be Prevented?" *Annals of Gastroenterology and Hepatology, Paris,* Vol. 29, No. 1, January–February 1993.

Lutgendorf, S.K., M.H. Antoni, G. Ironson, M.A. Fletcher, F. Penedo, A. Baum, N. Schneiderman, and N. Klimas, "Physical Symptoms of Chronic Fatigue Syndrome Are Exacerbated by the Stress of Hurricane Andrew," *Psychosomatic Medicine,* Vol. 57, No. 4, July/August 1995.

Magni, G., M. Marchetti, C. Moreschi, H. Merskey, and S.R. Luchini, "Chronic Musculoskeletal Pain and Depressive Symptoms in the National Health and Nutrition Examination. I: Epidemiologic Follow-Up Study," *Pain,* Vol. 53, No. 2, May 1993.

Mandell, Marshall, and Lynne Waller Scanlon, *Dr. Mandell's 5-Day Allergy Relief System,* New York: PocketBooks, Inc., 1979.

Marable, Manning, "Our Neighborhoods Should Not Be Dumping Grounds," *The Weekly Journal,* January 12, 1995.

Margolin, Shoshana, "Emotional Detoxification," *Health Freedom News,* April/May 1996.

Marx, Louis, J., *Healing Dimensions of Herbal Medicine,* Ventura, Ca.: Neo-Paradigm Publishers, Inc.

Mengshoel, A.M., "Effect of Physical Exercise in Fibromyalgia," *Tidsskr kar den Enfermadades, del Aparato Digestiv,* Vol. 116, No. 6, February 28, 1996.

Meydani, Simin Nikbin, Michael Hayek, and Laura Coleman, "Influence of Vitamins E and B_6 on Immune Response," *Annals of the New York Academy of Sciences,* Vol. 669, September 1992.

Michaelsson, G., B. Gerden, M. Ottosson, A. Parra, O. Sjoberg, G. Hjelmquist, L. Loof, "Patients with Psoriasis Often Have Increased Serum Levels of IgA Antibodies to Gliadin," *British Journal of Dermatology,* Vol. 129, No. 6, December 1993.

Milberger, S., J. Biederman, S.V. Faraone, L. Chen, and J. Jones, "Is Maternal Smoking During Pregnancy a Risk Factor for Attention Deficit Hyperactivity Disorder in Children?" *American Journal of Psychiatry,* Vol. 153, No. 9, September 1996.

Miller, J.J., K. Fletcher, J. Kabat-Zinn, "Three-Year Follow-Up and Clinical Implications of a Mindfulness Meditation-Based Stress Reduction Intervention in the Treatment of Anxiety Disorders," *General Hospital Psychiatry,* Vol. 17, No. 3, May 1995.

Miskin, Seymour, "Inflammatory Bowel Disease, Dairy Products, Elimination Diet and Lactose Malabsorption," *American Journal of Clinical Nutrition,* Vol. 65, 1997.

Moore, Michael, "Q: What's the Best Way to Cope With a Cold?" *Self,* April 1997.

Moyer, Ellen, *Vitamins and Minerals: Questions You Have . . . Answers You Need,* New York: Wings Books, 1993.

Murphy, Kate, "Do Food Additives Subtract From Health?" *Business Week,* May 6, 1996.

Naldi, L., F. Parazzini, L. Peli, L. Chatenoud, and T. Cainelli, "Dietary Factors and the Risk of Psoriasis: Results of an Italian Case-Control Study," *British Journal of Dermatology,* Vol. 134, No. 1, January 1996.

Nguyen-HP, D.L. Le, Q.M. Tran, V.T. Nguyen, and N.O. Nguyen, "Chromassi: A Therapy Advice System Based on Chrono-Massage and Acupression Using the Method of ZiWuLiuZhu," *Medinformation,* Vol. 8, No. 2, 1995.

Nicoloff, George, and Thomas L. Schwenk, "Using Exercise to Ward Off Depression," *The Physician & SportsMedicine,* Vol. 23, No. 9, September 1995.

Nino, Murcia G., "Diagnosis and Treatment of Insomnia and Risks Associated with Lack of Treatment," *Journal of Clinical Psychiatry,* Vol. 53, Supplement, December 1992.

Novick, S.G., et al., "How Does Zinc Modify the Common Cold?" *Medical Hypothesis,* Vol. 46, 1996.

Nsouli, T.M., "Role of Food Allergy in Serious Otitis Media," *Annals of Allergy,* Vol. 73, September 1994.

Nygard, O., H. Refsum, P. Ueland, et al., "Coffee Consumption and Plasma Total Homocysteine: The Hordaland Homocysteine Study," *American Journal of Clinical Nutrition,* Vol. 65, No. 1, 1997.

Panjwani, U., H.L. Gupta, S.H. Singh, W. Selvamurthy, U.C. Raj, "Effect of Sahaja Yoga Practice on Stress Management in Patients of Epilepsy," *Indian Journal of Physiology and Pharmacology,* Vol. 39, No. 2, April 1995.

Panush, Richard S., "Food Induced ('Allergic') Arthritis: Clinical and Serologic Studies," *The Journal of Rheumatology,* Vol. 17, No. 3, 1990.

Percival, Mark, "Detoxification," *Nutritional Pearls,* January 1996.

Percival, Mark, "Targeted Nutritional Support for Bone Health," *Nutritional Pearls,* Vol. 33, February 1996.

Perez, C.B., and P.L. Tomsko, "Homeopathy and the Treatment of Mental

Illness in the 19th Century," *Hospital Community Psychiatry*, Vol. 45, No. 10, October 1994.

Peterson, Nicola, *Culpeper Guides to Herbs and Health*, London: Bloomsbury Books, 1989.

Powell, Cherith, and Greg Forde, "It's All in Your Head," *Natural Health*, August 1996.

Prendiville, J.S., and L.N. Manfredi, "Skin Signs of Nutritional Disorders," *Seminars in Dermatology*, Vol. 11, No. 1, March 1992.

Puhn, Adele, *The 5-Day Miracle Diet: Conquer Food Cravings, Lose Weight, and Feel Better Than You Ever Have in Your Life!*, New York: Ballantine Books, 1996.

Rackett, Scott C., Marti Jill Rothe, and Jane M. Grant-Kels, "Diet and Dermatology: The Role of Dietary Manipulation in the Prevention and Treatment of Cutaneous Disorders," *Journal of the American Academy of Dermatology*, Vol. 29, No. 3, September 1993.

Ramirez, Anthony, "You Were Right in Saying Some People Make You Sick," *New York Times*, December 15, 1996.

Reynolds, Robert D., "Vitamin Supplements: Current Controversies," *Journal of the American College of Nutrition*, Vol. 13, No. 2, 1994.

Riggs, Karen M., et al., "Relation of Vitamin B-12, Vitamin B-6, Folate and Homocysteine to Cognitive Performance in the Normative Aging Study," *American Journal of Clinical Nutrition*, Vol. 63, 1996.

Riley, David J., and Smita Thakker-Varia, "Effect of Diet on Lung Structure, Connective Tissue Metabolism and Gene Expression," *American Institute of Nutrition*, Vol. 22, No. 3166, 1995.

Rippe, James M., and Ann Ward, with Karla Dougherty, *The Rockport Walking Program*, New York: Fireside Press, 1986.

Robbins, Jim, "Trouble in Fly Fishermen's Paradise," *New York Times*, August 23, 1996.

Robinson, Killian, et al., "Hyperhomocysteinemia and Low Pyridoxal Phosphate: Common and Independent Reversible Risk Factors for Coronary Artery Disease," *Circulation*, Vol. 92, No. 10, 1995.

Romero, Y., J.M. Evans, K.C. Fleming, and S.F. Phillips, "Constipation and Fecal Incontinence in the Elderly Population," *Mayo Clinic Proceedings*, Vol. 71, No. 1, January 1996.

Rooney, P.J., R.T. Jenkins, and W.W. Buchanan, "A Short Review of the Relationship Between Intestinal Permeability and Inflammatory Joint Disease," *Clinical and Experimental Rheumatology*, No. 8, 1990.

Rosenberg, Mel, "Clinical Assessment of Bad Breath: Current Concepts," *Journal of the American Dental Association*, Vol. 127, No. 4, April 1996.

Rosenfeld, Isadore, *Dr. Rosenfeld's Guide to Alternative Medicine,* New York: Random House, 1996.

Rubin, R.T., J.J. Phillips, T.F. Sadow, and J.T. McCracken, "Adrenal Gland Volume in Major Depression: Increase During the Depressive Episode and Decrease with Successful Treatment," *Archives of General Psychiatry,* Vol. 52, No. 3, March 1995.

Sacks, F.M., P. Hebert, L.J. Appel, N.O. Borhani, W.B. Applegate, J.D. Cohen, J.A. Cutler, K.A. Kirchner, L.H. Kuller, K.J. Roth, et al., "The Effect of Fish Oil on Blood Pressure and High-Density-Lipoprotein Cholesterol Levels in Phase I of the Trials of Hypertension Prevention: Trials of Hypertension Prevention Collaborative Research Group," *Journal of Hypertension Supplement,* Vol. 12, No. 7, 1994.

Salachas, Anastasios, et al., "Effects of a Low-Dose Fish Oil Concentrate on Angina, Exercise Tolerance Time, Serum Triglycerides and Platelet Function," *Angiology: The Journal of Vascular Diseases,* Vol. 45, No. 12, December 1994.

Salmi, H.A., and S. Sarna, "Effect of Silymarin on Chemical Functional, and Morphological Alterations of the Liver," *Scandinavian Journal of Gastroenterology,* Vol. 17, 1982.

Santos, M.J., M. Jourado-Lopez, J. Llopis, G. Urbano, and F.J. Mataix, "Influence of Dietary Supplementation with Fish on Plasma Fatty Acid Composition in Coronary Heart Disease Patients," *Annals of Nutritional Metabolism,* Vol. 39, No. 1, 1995.

Scala, James, *Eating Right for a Bad Gut,* New York: Plume Books, 1990.

Scarpignato, C., and P. Rampal, "Prevention and Treatment of Traveler's Diarrhea: A Clinical Pharmacological Approach," *Chemotherapy,* Vol. 41, No. 1, 1995.

Schindler, Martha, "25 Natural Beauty Solutions," *Natural Health,* March–April 1996.

Schuppan, D., J. Atkinson, M. Ruehl, and E.O. Riecken, "Alcohol and Liver Fibrosis—Pathobiochemistry and Treatment," *Journal of Gastroenterology,* Vol. 33, No. 9, September 1995.

Scott, Phil, "Is This Herb Nature's Prozac?" *Self,* November 1996.

Seelig, Mildred S., "Consequences of Magnesium Deficiency on the Enhancement of Stress Reactions: Preventive and Therapeutic Implications (A Review)," *Journal of the American College of Nutrition,* Vol. 13, No. 5, 1994.

Senelick, Richard C., and Peter W. Rossi, with Karla Dougherty, *Living with Stroke: A Guide for Families,* Chicago: Contemporary Books, Inc., 1994.

Senelick, Richard C., and Caty E. Ryan, *Living with Head Injury: A Guide for Families,* New York: Bantam Books, 1991.

Shapiro, S., A. Meier, and B. Guggenheim, "The Antimicrobial Activity of Essential Oils and Essential Oil Components Towards Oral Bacteria," *Oral Microbiology Immunology,* Vol. 9, No. 4, August 1994.

Sharma, S., W.E. Longo, B. Baniadam, and A.M. Vernava III, "Colorectal Manifestations of Endocrine Disease," *Diseases of the Colon and Rectum,* Vol. 38, No. 3, March 1995.

Siguel, E.N., and R.H. Lerman, "Prevalence of Essential Fatty Acid Deficiency in Patients with Chronic Gastrointestinal Disorders," *Metabolism,* Vol. 45, No. 1, January 1996.

Siscovick, D.S., T.E. Raghunathan, I. King, S. Weinmann, K.G. Wicklund, J. Albright, V. Bovbjerg, P. Arbogast, H. Smith, L.H. Kushi, et al., "Dietary Intake and Cell Membrane Levels of Long-Chain N-3 Polyunsaturated Fatty Acids and the Risk of Primary Cardiac Arrest," *Journal of the American Medical Association,* Vol. 274, No. 1, November 1, 1995.

Smilkstein, Martin J., Daniel R. Douglas, and Mohamud R. Daya, "Acetaminophen Poisoning and Liver Function," *New England Journal of Medicine,* November 19, 1994.

Smith, Susan Male, "Super Foods That Fight Disease," *Family Circle,* July 16, 1996.

Soucie, J.M., R.J. Coates, W. McClellan, H. Austin, and M. Thun, "Relation Between Geographic Variability in Kidney Stones Prevalence and Risk Factors for Stones," *American Journal of Epidemiology,* Vol. 143, No. 5, March 1, 1996.

Soyland, E., J. Funk, G. Rajka, M. Sandberg, P. Thune, L. Rustad, S. Helland, K. Middelfart, S. Odu, E.S. Falk, et al., "Effect of Dietary Supplementation with Very-Long-Chain n-3 Fatty Acids in Patients with Psoriasis," *New England Journal of Medicine,* Vol. 328, No. 25, June 24, 1993.

Soyland, E., J. Funk, G. Rajka, M. Sandberg, P. Thune, L. Rustad, S. Helland, K. Middelfart, S. Odu, E.S. Falk, et al., "Dietary Supplementation with Very Long-Chain n-3 Fatty Acids in Patients with Atopic Dermatitis: A Double-Blind, Multicentre Study," *British Journal of Dermatology,* Vol. 130, No. 6, June 1994.

Spangler, Tina, and Laurel Vukovic, eds., "Natural Health's Guide to Natural Remedies for 25 Common Ailments," *Natural Health,* April 1996.

Specker, S.M., G.A. Carlson, G.A. Christenson, and M. Marcotte, "Impulse Control Disorders and Attention Deficit Disorder in Pathological Gamblers," *Annals of Clinical Psychiatry,* Vol. 7, No. 4, December 1995.

Spirt, B.A., L.W. Graves, R. Weinstock, S.J. Bartlett, and T.A. Wadden, "Gallstone Formation in Obese Women Treated by a Low-Calorie Diet," *International Journal of Obesity-Related Metabolic Disorders,* Vol. 19, No. 8, August 1995.

Stacey, Michelle, "The Fall and Rise of Kilmer McCully," *New York Times Magazine*, August 10, 1997.

Stansfield, S.K., M. Pierre-Louis, G. Lerebours, A. Augstin, "Vitamin A Supplementation and Increased Prevalence of Childhood Diarrhea and Acute Respiratory Infections," *Lancet*, Vol. 342, No. 8871, September 4, 1993.

Stedman, Thomas Lathrop, *Stedman's Medical Dictionary, 25th Edition,* Baltimore, Md.: Williams & Wilkins, 1990.

Stephensen, C.B., S.R. Blount, T.R. Schoeb, and J.Y. Park, "Vitamin A Deficiency Impairs Some Aspects of the Host Response to Influenza: A Virus Infection in BALB/c Mice," *Journal of Nutrition*, Vol. 123, No. 5, May 1993.

Stevens, Laura J., Sydney S. Zentall, Marcey L. Abate, Thomas Kuczek, and John R. Burgess, "Omega-3 Fatty Acids in Boys With Behavior, Learning, and Health Problems," *Physiology and Behavior,* Vol. 59, No. 4/5, 1996.

Stockley, Corinne, *The Usborne Illustrated Dictionary of Biology,* London: Usborne Publishing House, Ltd., 1986.

Stoyanovsky, D., A. Osipov, P. Quinn, et al., "Ubiquinone-Dependent Recycling of Vitamin E Radicals by Superoxide," *Archives of Biochemistry,* Vol. 323, No. 2, 1995.

Surh, Y.J., and S.S. Lee, "Capsaicin in Hot Chili Pepper: Carcinogen, Co-Carcinogen or Anticarcinogen?" *Food and Chemical Toxicology,* Vol. 34, No. 3, March 1996.

Sutorius, D., "The Transforming Force of Laughter, with the Focus on the Laughing Meditation," *Patient Education Couns.,* No. 26, Vol. 1–3, September 1995.

Suzukamo, Leslie Brooks, "Homeopathy," *Sunday New Jersey Star Ledger,* March 3, 1996.

Tariq, S.M., M. Stevens, S. Matthews, S. Ridout, R. Twiselton, and D.W. Hide, "Cohort Study of Peanut and Tree Nut Sensitisation by Age of Four Years," *British Medical Journal,* Vol. 313, No. 7056, August 31, 1996.

Ter-Kuile, N.M., P. Spinhoven, A.C. Linssen, F.G. Zitman, R. Van Dyck, and H.G. Rooijmans, "Autogenic Training and Cognitive Self-Hypnosis for the Treatment of Recurrent Headaches in Three Different Subject Groups," *Pain,* Vol. 58, No. 3, September 1994.

Ter-Kuile, N.M., P. Spinhoven, and A.C. Linssen, "Responders and Nonresponders to Autogenic Training and Cognitive Self-Hypnosis: Prediction of Short- and Long-Term Success in Tension-Type Headache Patients," *Headache,* Vol. 35, No. 10, November/December 1995.

Thomas, Lewis, *The Lives of a Cell: Notes of a Biology Watcher,* New York: Viking Press, 1974.

Tosi, A., C. Misciali, B.M. Piraccini, A.M. Peluso, F. Bardazzi, "Drug-Induced

Hair Loss and Hair Growth: Incidence, Management, and Avoidance," *Drug Safety*, Vol. 10, No. 4, 1994.

Tyler, Varro, E., "Herbal Medicine 101," *Prevention*, March 1997.

Vaananen, M.K., H.A. Markkanen, V.J. Tuovinen, A.M. Kullaa, A.M. Karinpaa, E.A. Kumpusalo, "Periodontal Health Related to Plasma Ascorbic Acid," *Proceedings of the Finnish Dental Society*, Vol. 89, No. 1–2, 1993.

Van Leeuwen, P.A.M., M.A. Boermeester, A.P.J. Houdijk, Ch. C. Ferwerda, M.A. Cuesta, S. Meyer, R.I.C. Wesdorp, "Clinical Significance of Translocation," *Gut*, Vol. 35, Supplement 1, January 1994.

Van Ree, R., L. Antonicelli, J.H. Akkerdaas, M.S. Garritani, R.C. Aalberse, and F. Bonifazi, "Possible Induction of Food Allergy During Mite Immunotherapy," *Allergy*, Vol. 51, No. 2, February 1996.

Veldman, A., "Probiotics," *Tijdschrift voor Diergeneeskunde*, Vol. 117, No. 12, June 15, 1992.

Vogelsang, H., et al., "Dietary Vitamin D Intake in Patients with Crohn's Disease," Vol. 107, No. 19, *Wiener Klinische Wochenschrift*, 1995.

Wade, Carlson, *Healing and Revitalizing Your Vital Organs*, West Nyack, N.Y.: Parker Publishing Company, Inc., 1978.

Wang, B.G., E.Z. Wang, and X.Z. Chen, "A Study on Combined Acupuncture and Enflurane Anesthesia for Craniotomy," *Chung-Kuo-Chung-Hsi-I-Chieh-Ho-Tsa-Chih*, Vol. 14, No. 1, January 1994.

Wang, Z.L., "Experimental Study of Preventing Liver Cirrhosis by Using Four Kinds of Chinese Herbs," *Chung-Kuo-Chung-Hsi-I-Chieh-Ho-Tsa-Chih*, Vol. 12, No. 6, June 1992.

Wantke, F., M. Gotz, and R. Jarisch, "The Histamine-Free Diet," Vol. 44, No. 8, *Hautarzt*, August 1993.

Wantke, F., W. Hemmer, T. Haglmuller, M. Gotz, and R. Jarisch, "Histamine in Wine: Bronchoconstriction After a Double-Blind Placebo-Controlled Red Wine Provocation Test," *International Archives of Allergy and Immunology*, Vol. 110, No. 4, August 1996.

Weil, Andrew, *Spontaneous Healing*, New York: Fawcett Columbine, 1995.

Werbach, Melvyn R., *Nutritional Influences on Illness: A Sourcebook of Clinical Research*, New Canaan, Ct: Keats Publishing, Inc. 1988.

Whitaker, Julian, *Dr. Whitaker's Guide to Natural Healing*, Rocklin, Ca.: Prima Publishing, 1996.

Whitaker, Julian, "How to Prevent Macular Degeneration," *Health & Healing: Tomorrow's Medicine Today*, Vol. 6, No. 10, October 1996.

Whitaker, Julian, "The Smoking Gun in Heart Disease and Stroke," *Health & Healing: Tomorrow's Medicine Today*, Vol. 7, No. 8, August 1997.

Witsell, D.L., C.G. Garrett, W.G. Yarbrough, S.P. Dorrestein, A.F. Drake, and M.C. Weissler, "Effect of Lactobacillus Acidophilus on Antibiotic-Associated Gastrointestinal Morbidity: A Prospective Randomized Trial," *Journal of Otolaryngology,* Vol. 24, No. 4, August 1995.

Wolfe, S.P., "Prevention Programmes: A Dietetic Minefield," *European Journal of Clinical Nutrition,* Vol. 49, Supplement 1, September 1995.

Wyshak, Grace, and Rose E. Frisch, "Carbonated Beverages, Dietary Calcium, The Dietary Calcium/Phosphorus Ratio, and Bone Fractures in Girls and Boys," *Journal of Adolescent Health,* Vol. 15, 1994.

Yu, Y.H., H.C. Wang, and Z.J. Wang, "The Effect of Acupuncture on Spinal Motor Neuron Excitability in Stroke Patients," *Chung-Hua-I-Hsueh-Tsa-Chih-Taipei,* Vol. 56, No. 4, October 1995.

Yu, S.Y., Y.J. Zhu, W.G. Li, Q.S. Huang, C.Z. Huang, Q.N. Zhang, and C. Hou, "A Preliminary Report on the Intervention Trials of Primary Liver Cancer in High-Risk Populations with Nutritional Supplementation of Selenium in China," *Biological Trace Element Research,* Vol. 29, No. 3, June 1991.

Zeman, Francis J., and Robert J. Hansen, "Chapter 11: Diabetes Mellitus, Hypoglycemia, and Other Endocrine Disorders," *Clinical Nutrition and Dietetics, 2nd Edition,* ed. by Francis J. Zeman, New York: Macmillan Publishing Co., 1991.

Zoler, Mitchel L., "Folic Acid Cuts Homocysteine Levels in CV Disease," *Family Practice News,* Vol. 29, January 15, 1997.

Anonymous, "Soy in A.M. May Relieve Sweats in P.M.," *Environmental Nutrition,* February 1997.

Anonymous, "Latex Gloves and Fruit: Unexpected Link," *Environmental Nutrition,* February 1997.

Anonymous, "Dietary Fibers: Insoluble and Soluble," *Educational/Technical Focus,* HealthComm International, Inc., 1995.

Anonymous, "Do I Dare Eat a Strawberry?" *New York Times,* November 22, 1995.

Anonymous, "Environmental Toxicants: How Do They Affect Our Health?" *LPI Newsletter,* Spring/Summer 1995.

Anonymous, "The '4R' Gastrointestinal Support Plan: Remove, Replace, Reinoculate, Repair," *Educational/Technical Focus,* HealthComm International, Inc., 1995.

Anonymous, "Detoxification," *Educational/Technical Focus,* HealthComm International, Inc., 1995.

Anonymous, "Health and Longevity: The Probiotic Revolution," *Health/Science Newsletter,* 1997.

Anonymous, "Kitchen Notes," *Health,* October 1994.

Anonymous, "Potential Cancer Fighters in Foods," *New York Times,* April 13, 1993.

Anonymous, "What's So Hot About Chili Peppers? Studies Provide Cultural Clues to Cancer Risk," *American Institute for Cancer Research Newsletter,* No. 53, Fall 1996.

Anonymous, "Antioxidants and Anti-Aging: The Fight Against Free Radicals," *American Council on Collaborative Medicine,* Vol. 1, No. 8, December 1995.

Anonymous, "Comprehensive Digestive Stool Analysis," *Assessing Physiological Function,* Asheville, N.C.: Great Smokies Diagnostic Laboratory, 1996.

Anonymous, "Science Questions and Answers," *New York Times,* January 14, 1997.

Anonymous, "Heartburn: How to Quench the Flames," *Consumer Reports on Health,* October 1996.

Anonymous, "Diet for Diverticulosis," *Consumer Reports on Health,* November 1996.

Anonymous, "Diet Therapy/Obesity Update," Supplement to *Nutrition & the M.D.,* May 1988.

Anonymous, "30 Foods That Fight Disease," *Health Magazine,* Supplement, 1995.

Anonymous, "Intestinal Permeability," *Assessing Physiological Function,* Asheville, N.C.: Great Smokies Diagnostic Laboratory, 1996.

Anonymous, "Functional Liver Detoxification Profile," Great Smokies Diagnostic Laboratory, 1995.

Anonymous, "Elderly and Can't Sleep? Try Scent of Lavender," *New York Times,* September 13, 1995.

Anonymous, "Modern Dilemma: Unloading Toxic Overload," *American Council on Collaborative Medicine,* Vol. 11, No. 6, July 1996.

INDEX

Adele Puhn would like to hear from you.
Please share your experiences with
Healing from the Inside by writing to:

Adele Puhn, M.S., C.N.S.
c/o Nutritional Industries LLC
14 Bond Street
Suite 387
Great Neck, NY 11021

Adele Puhn is available for lectures,
seminars, and workshops based upon this book.
Details will be sent upon request, or call
516-487-8684.

George Kerrigan

ABOUT THE AUTHOR

ADELE PUHN, M.S., C.N.S., has been a nutritional consultant for twenty years with a thriving private practice both on the Upper East Side of New York and in Great Neck, Long Island. She is the *New York Times* bestselling author of *The 5-Day Miracle Diet.*

She holds an M.S. in Medical Biology and a Certificate in Clinical Nutrition, and she is a Certified Nutrition Specialist as conferred by the Certification Board for Nutrition Specialists. Recently appointed the nutritional adviser of Self-Help, an agency that helps the families of mothers with AIDS stay together, she is also a frequent lecturer at seminars and conferences, and has worked at various health centers and with school systems on Long Island. Her nutrition research, complementary therapies, and wellness and weight-loss programs have made her a popular source for magazines, and her thoughts and ideas have appeared in *Mirabella, Harper's Bazaar,* and *The Wall Street Journal.*

Ms. Puhn lives in Manhasset, Long Island, with her husband. Her grown children and her five grandchildren frequently visit—which is Ms. Puhn's own ingredient for continuous joy and healing.